ANTHONY WALTON

Mississippi

Anthony Walton studied at Notre Dame and Brown
University and currently lives in Brunswick, Maine.

Movie theater, Belzoni, Mississippi, 1939

Anthony Walton

Mississippi

AN AMERICAN JOURNEY

VINTAGE DEPARTURES

Vintage Books

A Division of Random House, Inc.

New York

FIRST VINTAGE DEPARTURES EDITION, FEBRUARY 1997

Copyright © 1996 by Anthony Walton

Grateful acknowledgment is made to the following for permission to reprint previously published material:

Dutton Signet and Sanford J. Greenburger Associates: Excerpt from *This Little Light of Mine* by Kay Mills, copyright © 1993 by Kay Mills. Reprinted by permission of Dutton Signet, a division of Penguin Books USA Inc., and Sanford J. Greenburger Associates.

HarperCollins Publishers, Inc.: "After Winter" from *The Collected Poems of Sterling A. Brown,* edited by Michael S. Harper, copyright © 1980 by Sterling A. Brown; "Southern Road" from *The Collected Poems of Sterling A. Brown,* edited by Michael S. Harper, copyright © 1932 by Harcourt Brace & Co., copyright renewed 1960 by Sterling Brown (originally appeared in *Southern Road*). Reprinted by permission of HarperCollins Publishers, Inc.

King of Spades Music: Excerpts from "Come On in My Kitchen," "Drunken Hearted Man," "Love in Vain Blues," "Me and the Devil Blues," "Stones in My Passway," "Terraplane Blues," and "Walkin' Blues," words and music by Robert L. Johnson, copyright © 1978, 1991 by King of Spades Music. All rights reserved. Reprinted by permission of King of Spades Music.

Random House, Inc.: Excerpt from "Mississippi" from *Requiem for a Nun* by William Faulkner, copyright © 1951 by William Faulkner. Reprinted by permission of Random House, Inc.

All photographs are by Marion Post Wolcott. Used by permission of the Library of Congress, except the photographs on pages 179 and 197, which are used by permission of the Estate of Marion Post Wolcott.

The Library of Congress has cataloged the Knopf edition as follows:

Walton, Anthony, [date]
Mississippi : an American journey / by Anthony Walton.—1st ed.
p.   cm.
ISBN 0-679-44600-1
1. Afro-Americans—Mississippi—History.
2. Mississippi—Race relations.
3. Walton, Anthony, [date].   I. Title.
F350.N4W35   1996
976.2'00496073—dc20   95-32031
CIP

Vintage ISBN: 0-679-77741-5

Random House Web address: http://www.randomhouse.com/

Book design by Cassandra J. Pappas

Printed in the United States of America
10   9   8   7

for Claude, for Dorothy
for Claude and Dorothy

nobody knows the trouble I've seen

I sing,
only to weep again the pity of this house
—Aeschylus, *Oresteia*

Wellohwellohwellohwellohwell . . .
—Blues refrain

Contents

Prologue

I am walking down a side street toward the courthouse and town square of Holly Springs, Mississippi. It is a sweltering afternoon in June 1991. Eyeing the street's tired pastel and brick buildings, I can think of nothing more than air-conditioning and a cold drink. But my father, who is with me, is angry; he begins to recount the events of a Christmas Eve forty years ago.

"Right here." He stops and points at a battered gray door that is now the rear entrance of a shuttered restaurant. "Right here," he says again, "this used to be the colored waiting room at the bus station. James was in here, right here." His index finger hangs in the air, twitching in accusation. James Crump was a school and childhood friend of my father's, fifteen or sixteen years old at the time of which he speaks. "We'd been celebrating Christmas Eve, you know, blowing off some steam, and James was a little high, he was a little happy. We went into the bus station and James was singing and clapping his hands. He was just a boy, you know, having fun, but somebody called the sheriff and complained. I never found out who."

My father starts walking again, narrowing his eyes, oblivious to the heat. "The sheriff, his name was Holbrooks, came in the front door through the white folks' side, and somebody yelled, 'James, Holbrooks is coming!' James got scared and bolted out that door there." My father, fifty-six, massive and graying, his face a mask of weary experience, turns back and looks for a long moment.

"Then he run up this street here as fast as he could. Meantime, Holbrooks come back out the front door and saw James, James wasn't no farther than that blue van over there." He points to a truck a hundred feet away. "And Holbrooks pulled his .38 and shot the boy in the back. He didn't say 'Stop!'—nothing."

Mopping sweat from our eyes, we cross the street over to the courthouse, past cars circling the square, people taking care of Saturday business. My father points at a spot on the pavement. "Right there. That's where he fell, dead, on Christmas Eve."

ONE

Crossing the River

THE BRIDGE over the Mississippi River at Natchez is a matter-of-fact crossing, two massive steel spans cantilevered between Adams County, Mississippi, and Concordia County, Louisiana. The bridge is not much different from river crossings I've encountered elsewhere, as far north as Minnesota; here in the South, of course, the water is very wide, and has taken on a dull, gray-brown cast. The gray is from the muggy, slightly overcast sky, the brown from mud washed in by recent spring rains. I don't see any of the canoes, rafts, warships or steamboats of river lore, only a barge pushed by a tug off in the distance to the south.

Eastbound on U.S. 84 from Vidalia, Louisiana, just over the bridge, it's a quick left onto Business 84, two lanes that wind up a steep incline and through two weathered imitation Greek columns. The columns I take as an unofficial welcome to and boundary of the city of Natchez. From where I stand, on a splash of gravel alongside the road, the river reflects like quicksilver. The bridge presents an unremarkable Friday afternoon scene, an early summer coming and going of commuters, commercial vehicles and people arriving or leaving for the weekend; a day like most others in a small town in

North America. For me, though, the just-completed crossing is of tremendous consequence: I have gone over a river from familiar places and into the state of Mississippi.

If you look on a globe, or a good world map, between North and South America and between the Atlantic and the Pacific, you will see the Gulf of Mexico. Then, locating the city of New Orleans at the northern edge of this body of water, you can trace the ninetieth meridian north toward Memphis. The line you trace, between the thirtieth and thirty-fifth parallels, will roughly bisect the twentieth state in the Union, the poorest by most measures, a jurisdiction of eighty-two counties and 47,716 square miles, home to something over two million citizens.

As your finger slides you'll pass place-names like McComb, Poplarville and Natchez, Philadelphia, Clarksdale and Vicksburg, each name searing a scream in the minds and memories of people like me, black Americans. Mississippi can be considered one of the most prominent scars on the map of this country. When you trace the ninetieth meridian from New Orleans to Memphis you're fingering a scar, and that is why I arrive in Natchez with some trepidation. I intend to explore that scar.

There is something different about Mississippi, something almost unspeakably primal and vicious; something savage unleashed there that has yet to come to rest. Of the forty martyrs whose names are inscribed in the national Civil Rights Memorial in Montgomery, Alabama, nineteen were killed in Mississippi. How was it that half who died did so in one state?

I am a black person, a black male, a colored man, a Negro, and sometimes, certainly sometimes in Mississippi, a nigger. For the longest time, when I was young, the fact that I had been assigned those labels didn't much affect me. I grew up in working- and middle-class neighborhoods in midwestern suburbs, where people were, most of the time, polite and, most of the time, kept what prejudices they had to themselves. I was born in 1960, in Aurora, Illinois, and as I came to social awareness it seemed to me that large parts of America's tragic history were finally being overcome. Mississippi was, to me, something from which we blacks had freed ourselves, washed into the past.

I grew up on Rosewood, a street in Aurora that parallels the Fox River, which runs to the Illinois, which runs to the Mississippi. As a kid I often looked at maps of Illinois, of the Midwest, of the Mississippi Basin, or sat on the banks of the Fox watching the river run south. I'd think about Mississippi, the recent family trip down or the one soon to come, and wonder if I could canoe all the way there. I remember the first time I felt palpable fear, the night Martin Luther King was killed. I was seven years old and refused to take out the garbage or go to my room alone. I was terrified of the dark. I knew that Mississippi, and bad things I'd only vaguely heard about it, had something to do with my fear.

Rosewood, if not exactly a melting pot, was something of a pestle bowl of the lower-middle and working classes. In the late sixties virtually every ethnic subgroup in America lived on that street, one extremely long single block at the bottom of a hill hard by the river: African, Asian, Hispanic, European. They'd all come to Aurora, an industrial town on the edge of a prairie stretching virtually uninterrupted to Denver, to work in the factories or on the railroad that carried the bulldozers and tractors, the office and school equipment, produced there to the wider world. They all hoped for a better life, and many of their hopes came true, as factory workers in that time and place could often make more money than junior executives.

Even amid this prosperity, Rosewood's children regularly had occasion to discuss and imagine somewhere else. The Mexicans talked about Texas, the whites, Kentucky. Puerto Ricans bragged about their island in the sea, while we blacks talked of a place that seemed far more sinister and distant: Mississippi, six hundred miles away, out of sight, yet somehow always in mind. We had a nonsense song we blithely double-Dutched to: "Capital M-I-crooked letter-crooked letter-I-crooked letter-crooked letter-I-P-P-I!" And we had a silly trick riddle we didn't really know the meaning of: "What got four eyes and can't see?" "Mississippi!"

Sometimes it seemed as though every other time we piled into our old blue Chevy station wagon we were roaring off to Mississippi, sailing down Interstate 55 or 57, headed down south, as we called it, waving and smiling at the other cars with Illinois plates, cars laden with six or seven black folks and as much else as they could carry, all bouncing on the same seventy-mile-an-hour pilgrimage.

Going to Mississippi . . . where heavyset aunts waited to smother you with kisses and candy, where cryptic uncles would ignore you all day, muttering darkly about this and that, then suddenly surprise you with attention and a gift, a pocketknife or an invitation to go fishing. Where Big Mama, Mom's grandmother, lived several miles out in the country down an unmarked gravel road that wound past abandoned cemeteries and tin-roofed cabins deep in old-growth pines.

As I became a teenager I was allowed to choose not to go along on those trips, and Mississippi came to matter less and less. And in college my only real thought of Mississippi came when my school, Notre Dame, lost a bitterly fought football game to Ole Miss. I had thought, at my mother's urging, of attending the University of Mississippi; but seeing the Confederate hoopla surrounding the Rebels, I was glad I hadn't.

Then, in graduate school at Brown University, I met a young woman from Mississippi who contradicted some of my calcifying notions about the state and its relevance to me. Joan was kind, generous, imaginative and, most strangely of all, white. My friendship with her was a more natural fit than my relationships with most of my other classmates, black and white. The ease of her manner and her solicitous warmth reminded me of my mother and aunts, a connection that ran true right down to her verbal constructions and cadences. She'd smile slowly and wisecrack "Boy, you slow as Christmas" or "You right, I got here at night, but not last night." We'd argue about Chekhov and Sartre late into the night, and she gave me the first of what became an annual gift subscription to *The New York Review of Books*, a publication I had not been familiar with but that became one of my favorites. Mississippi didn't seem so far away, or so strange. And it had a human face I loved.

One night during this time my mother started asking me questions, out of the blue, about William Faulkner. She was taking a night-school course and wanted to write about the Nobel laureate from her hometown, New Albany. Why Faulkner, I asked, of all the writers in the world to care about? Why not Richard Wright, James

Baldwin or Zora Neale Hurston? "We're kin to some Faulkners," she said. I laughed out loud and informed her that *this* Faulkner was white. My mother smiled and said, "So?"

This growing awareness of the fine gradations of racial complexity in American life, an awareness that things weren't as simple as I had made them, nor the surface realities of situations what they seemed to be, was given a darker cast when I moved to New York City and learned some of the implications that racial history had for me, personally. In New York I experienced directly for the first time the petty, daily indignities that take such a toll on the psyches of American blacks. Ignored by cabbies, locked out of jewelry and electronics stores, rousted by security guards and doormen and, worst of all, routinely loathed by strangers fearful of young black men in public places, I found myself becoming at times physically ill.

My parents had moved in my teenage years from Aurora to Batavia, ten miles upriver. There we lived in an upper-middle-class neighborhood, increasingly oriented our lives toward the solidly respectable western Chicago suburbs and were, at least in my case, mindlessly assimilated. I went wherever I pleased whenever I pleased, dated white girls, had warm friendships with cops. I was dodging, I now realize, what younger African-Americans call the black tax, the tribute to white society that must be paid in self-effacement and swallowed pride. In New York I found myself wondering how I'd missed all this. Had I been dreaming, or too busy crossing over to notice?

My racial basic training wasn't quite complete. For a New York magazine, in the wake of the Yusuf Hawkins murder in 1989, I covered a protest march into the Brooklyn neighborhood of Bensonhurst. For the last two miles of that march, the sidewalks were lined with thousands of jeering whites throwing watermelons, rocks and dirt, spitting and shouting "Nigger! Nigger! Nigger!" while holding guns to their heads. Tens of thousands of Brooklynites were waving red-white-and-blue flags, screaming veterans were dressed in military uniforms, signs and banners proclaiming GO BACK TO AFRICA and LOVE IT OR LEAVE IT and AMERICA FOR AMERICANS were hung from buildings. I couldn't help feeling that I'd time-warped back to Montgomery or Selma, but there I was in contemporary New York.

I was beginning to know things about this country that I did not want to know. I was enmeshed, it seemed, because of who I was—or, more accurately, because of my skin color—in histories set into motion long before I was born. And I began doubting whether I was, or even wanted to be, an American. But what else, where else, could I possibly be? I certainly wasn't looking toward Africa: I was too contentedly bourgeois for that, and besides, which was my tribe? I didn't belong to anyone there either. Nor could I think of Mississippi as my home—the word itself calling up so many clashing memories that simultaneously combined and delineated public history and private experience, newsreels and home movies, sometimes with 35-millimeter black-and-white precision, sometimes Super 8 color fuzziness, all of it mixing with what I'd heard from my people and seen for myself. But the more I thought through the issues, the less I could deny it: I *was* from somewhere. Mississippi was my heritage and background, and if I wanted to decipher the tangle of contradictions and illusions around me, I would first have to learn to decipher myself.

AS I PREPARED to search for the past and present of Mississippi, something else was on my mind: guilt. I don't know how to describe or define it with precision, a kind of survivor's guilt, guilt at having won some sort of lottery, the simple guilt of one who has looked on from behind the lines and heard secondhand about a war while others struggled and died at the front. But nonetheless it nagged me, and I thought about it more and more.

There is a poem, Sterling A. Brown's "After Winter," that relates the hopes of a sharecropper:

> "Butter beans fo' Clara
> Sugar corn fo' Grace
> An fo' de little feller
> Runnin' space. . . ."

The poem also speaks of "Ten acres unplanted / To raise dreams on." As I've grown older, I have realized that I, along with the other privileged young blacks of my generation, was the "little feller," and that we were supposed to be the fulfillment of those dreams. Much had happened, good and bad, since Brown's words were written; some blacks had moved gloriously into the mainstream, while others had led or were leading almost absurdly tragic lives. But coming to grips with this inheritance, shouldering the hopeful burden of so many years, was proving to be a complex and, at times, crippling task for blacks of my generation, and for me.

My father's life, when I looked at it closely, seemed unreal. A better man than I, he'd come from degrading poverty in feudal Mississippi to property and accomplishment in the North. Having been granted few choices by life, he had worked to provide them for his children, to the point where some days it seemed as if *my* most pressing choice was whether to have espresso or cappuccino after dinner. In the larger, historical sense of Mississippi, this story had been writ large hundreds of thousands of times. Those blacks who'd come before me had wanted me to be free, and had paid the price. My luxuries of choice and freedom were a gift, freely given, and my current task was not to repay my forebears but to do something meaningful with those options. Perhaps the future could redeem the past. But part of what I had to do was educate myself about what, exactly, had gone before. Then I might know what my life meant, at what cost it had been purchased and just what I could accomplish. So much of American history is about greed and murder; it is also about ambition, hope and sacrifice, words that had created my "runnin' space." Could I find a place in that given space to live? Could I live *with* it, or up to it? Live simultaneously with and inside of history?

s o i f o u n d myself on a loess bluff—a cliff of loose, thin clay—high above the river in Natchez, watching the water flow south and cars cross the bridge. Maybe Mississippi could tell me something about all the things running through my mind, about my family, Faulkner, race. Certainly it would tell me something about myself. Since I had indeed lost my way, turned thirty years old and lost my old way of thinking about myself, Mississippi was suddenly my only road map. In Afro-American folklore there is a figure called the tar baby, the thing you grasp in need or greed and then can't get loose of. Mississippi had always been stuck to me; I just hadn't faced up to it. Now I was clasping it willingly, gladly, desperately, in the hope that the place I'd ignored and been ashamed of might tell me something about myself, my country and the life I was going to have to live therein. If I was going to have to live out the fate of being black and American, I felt I needed to know what that meant. And *that* meant Mississippi.

SEVERAL DAYS after arriving, I drove through thunderstorms exploring the stretch of the state from Jackson to Natchez. I went by way of the Natchez Trace Parkway, an immaculately maintained two-lane road, kept up by the United States Park Service, that roughly tracks the old Natchez Trace, the passage through the Old Southwest first broken by indigenous Americans. The Trace was gradually adopted in the eighteenth century by Europeans as the principal overland route from the frontier of the Mississippi River back to civilization, which commenced at Nashville.

In the heavy rain there were often several miles between cars coming from the opposite direction, headed north. More often I was passed by cars headed south and gaining from behind, blinking their lights and speeding off into the mist that was coming off the ground, hanging in the air and filtering into the dense growth of trees. The Trace possesses a transfixing beauty, with borders of thick green grass on either side of the asphalt spreading into dense forests of pine, oak and maple. Every so often, the forest breaks for a piece of farmland or pasture. As the highway dives deeper into Mississippi, the pastures give way to creeks and bayous, waterways gushing and overflowing that day in June, the time of year the Natchez Indians called the sixth moon, bringing mulberries. Except for the automobiles the Trace exists in an almost preternatural stillness, in an Edenic timelessness that must be quite close to the Mississippi the first Europeans and Africans, even the first aboriginals, saw.

As I stopped to get out of the car, I could imagine myself a disenfranchised white man of the eighteenth century, newly landed in the New World from Scotland, Ireland or England, stunned by the bounty of the lower Mississippi and incredulous it was all there for the taking. Or I could look through the eyes of the youngest son of a prosperous Tidewater planting family, who had no inheritance and needed some horizon on which to make his name, told by ethos, primogenitor and government to take as much land as he could keep.

I was going toward Natchez in search of that particular past, the antebellum South, the plantation era. Perhaps the town's remnants of Old Mississippi had something to reveal about the beliefs and terrors that spawned the Mississippi I carried in my mind, the impressions and images, many violent, that I now wished to unravel.

As I rolled down the blacktop at sixty miles an hour in air-conditioned comfort, the Trace couldn't have felt too much to me like the path by which Andrew Jackson and his volunteers straggled back to Tennessee in 1812, having been prevented by General James Wilkinson from invading British West Florida, or the road they marched up in glory a year later following the victory at New Orleans. It was the road thousands had taken, carrying civilization and slaves into the wilderness; but, because of the latter, I could not romanticize it.

The thick vegetation around the lower Trace had been the ancestral home of the Choctaw, Chickasaw and Natchez nations, removed to make room for the great wave of American expansion. This land, as well, had been the scene of several crucial engagements of the Civil War. Ulysses S. Grant had stalked these woods, probing for a way to take Vicksburg.

The mileposts of the Trace themselves are a short course in Mississippi history. At 78.3 was fought the Civil War battle of Raymond, in which twenty-five thousand Federals demolished a Confederate force in a first step toward taking and burning Jackson, amid the charred remains of which Sherman uttered his infamous "War is hell." At 73.5 is Dean's Stand, an eighteenth-century inn where a traveler, usually on foot and alone, could pass the night by a fire and out of the elements and enjoy some conversation. Milepost 61.1 marks the lower Choctaw Boundary, the border between the first white settlers and the aboriginals, past which whites could not move with any guarantee of safety. And at post 41.5 is a section of the original Trace that can be walked for about a quarter of a mile.

I got out of the car there and walked into the woods, under a canopy of vegetation so thick the heavy rain merely dripped onto the shiny brown pebbles at my feet. The afternoon was incredibly quiet and still, the only sound the falling drops of water all around. The

Mississippi wilderness seemed pregnant with life; even today the Trace appears an endless source of bounty. In his novel *Absalom, Absalom!* William Faulkner described what it once took to subdue that bounty: "So he and the twenty negroes worked together, plastered over with mud against the mosquitoes . . . working with quiet and unflagging fury. It took him two years, he and his crew of imported slaves which his adopted fellow citizens still looked at as being a good deal more deadly than any beast he could have started and slain in that country. They worked from sunup to sundown. . . ."

Such an outpost was built at milepost 15.5, Mount Locust, a very early cotton plantation on the Trace. Mount Locust today is an old white house set back among encroaching trees as wilderness reclaims the farm. Farther on, at milepost 10.3, is the Emerald Mound, built between A.D. 1300 and 1400 by precursors of the Natchez tribe. The earthen mound, which covers more than seven acres and is four or five stories tall, is, however, a relatively late development in the history of Native Americans in Mississippi. Human remains known as the Natchez Pelvis were found near the mound and carbon-dated to 8000 B.C., one of the oldest such findings in North America.

By the time I reached Emerald Mound, the afternoon storm had broken and a gorgeous sun was refracting off the wet grass. The moisture in the air combined with the rising heat in oppressive humidity, wisps of mist were still dissipating in the branches of trees. As I climbed to the top of the mound, I realized the paleontological depth of Mississippi, the ancient bones now like so many blades of grass beneath my feet. The Egyptians built the pyramids, the Mycenaeans a mound known as Agamemnon's Treasury, the Celts Newgrange; Mississippians five hundred years ago built Emerald Mound. In another five hundred or five thousand years, would the wilderness reclaim it and the soft wind carry it all away?

THE HISTORY of Europeans and Africans in Mississippi begins with escaped black slaves from the Caribbean, probably the first nonnatives to reach the American Gulf Coast and blend with North American tribes. Slaves had accompanied Columbus and had been dispersed from the beginning of the European arrival and settlement of such islands as Hispaniola and Cuba.

Hernando de Soto, conquistador, was the leader of the first group of white men to enter the territory now called Mississippi. De Soto, who had accompanied Don Francisco Pizarro on the sack of the Incas in present-day Peru and Chile in the early 1530s, landed in 1539 at Tampa Bay, Florida, as governor of the territory, representative of the Spanish Crown, commanding an army of six hundred men, including several priests and friars. They carried with them everything necessary for Catholic Mass, boatbuilding and metal forging, and for slave capture and maintenance.

De Soto hoped to gain wealth and fame beyond that of Cortés and Pizarro as he left Tampa Bay and marched up the Florida peninsula. He hoped to find El Dorado, the fabled City of Gold, Ponce de León's Fountain of Youth, or at the very least another Tenochtitlán or Cuzco. But de Soto and his men slogged for a year and a half through present-day Georgia, South Carolina, Tennessee and Alabama, and found every step wilderness. More than a hundred of his six hundred men died, and his forces faced battles with aboriginals more days than not. Just short of what is now Mississippi, north of today's Mobile, Alabama, de Soto and his men fought the Maubila in a bloody battle in which three thousand aboriginals died, succumbing to the Spaniards' superior firepower and technology, their metal swords, shields and spears. Eighteen Spaniards were killed, scores more injured.

This battle seemed to unhinge de Soto: his dream was slipping away. What he had expected to be a triumphant blitz of conquest was turning into a death march. Though relief ships had landed a mere six days' march down the coast, de Soto ordered his mutiny-minded men northward; perhaps he was ashamed of his grand expedition's failure and could not bear to return to Cuba or Spain empty-handed. A fellow conquistador, known as the Gentleman of Elvas, describes de Soto in the wake of the battle: "Instigated by disdain, he continued from there on until he died, wasting both time and life fruitlessly and travelling always from one place to another without order or harmony like a man who abhorred life and . . . desired to terminate it."

De Soto is thought to have entered Mississippi near present-day

Columbus, and he spent the winter of 1541 at Chicaca, near present-day Pontotoc. It was a brutal winter, very cold and with much snow, but de Soto's party was reasonably well supplied with food and initially had the friendship of the local tribes. De Soto decided to resume the expedition in late March and, as was his custom, demanded slaves from his Chickasaw hosts. This demand was perceived as following on several gratuitous Spanish insults. The Chickasaw attacked in the middle of a windy night and set fire to de Soto's camp. In two hours, amid raging flames and smoke, the Chickasaw killed forty Spaniards before retreating from a disorganized Spanish cavalry counterattack.

The conquistadors had lost most of their pigs and horses, many men were left without clothes, and their shelter lay smoldering in ashes. They moved the next day to another camp, where the survivors built a forge and rearmed themselves as best they could. On the twenty-fifth of April they resumed their march and, meeting a group of Alibamu, fought a pitched battle near present-day New Albany. They marched due west another two weeks, whereupon, in the words of Ranjel, de Soto's secretary, "they came to the first village of Quizquis, a league beyond this village they came upon another with an abundance of corn, and soon again after another league, upon another likewise amply provisioned. There they saw the great river."

That river was, of course, the Mississippi. According to historian Dunbar Rowland, this was probably in Tunica County, at Council Bend or Walnut Bend. To de Soto, the Mississippi was just another, yet another, obstacle. He and his men spent a month constructing boats for the crossing, while aboriginals across the river in what is now Arkansas rowed out daily to fire arrows at them. The conquistadors made it across the river in June without being engaged by the natives, and continued stumbling through the wilderness until de Soto's death the following year. De Soto was buried in the river, the Mississippi, and what was left of his band set out by land for Mexico. In Texas, realizing they were lost, they backtracked to the big river, again built ships, floated to the Gulf of Mexico and in 1543 reached Vera Cruz, where Cortés had started the saga of conquest twenty-five years before.

AFTER DE SOTO'S death, 140 years would pass before another European laid claim to Mississippi. This man was Robert Cavelier, the Sieur de La Salle, who in 1682 claimed the lower Mississippi River valley for France. La Salle was born in Rouen, France, in 1643, and had come to the New World in 1666, settling near Montreal. He became familiar with the aboriginals there, learning their customs and languages, and from them heard stories of the mighty rivers Ohio and Mississippi. These waterways, La Salle believed, might be the openings to a vast inland empire rich in land and spoils. In February of 1682, he and his lieutenant and closest friend, Henri de Tonty, emerged from the mouth of the Illinois River into the Mississippi, and by early March they had reached the mouth of the Arkansas across from today's Rosedale, Mississippi. A priest who accompanied them on the journey, Father Membre, wrote of their first encounter with the Mississippi: "The Sieur de la Salle immediately passed over to the other side with all his force, and in less than an hour threw up a retrenched redoubt on a point, with palisades, and felled trees, to prevent surprise and give the Indians time to recover confidence. He then made some of his party advance on the bank of the river and invite the Indians to come to us. . . . We offered them the calumet [pipe] of peace, and two Indians, advancing by signs, invited the French to come to them."

On March 14 La Salle and his men planted a cross and claimed the land for Louis XIV. They then continued down the river for several days, passing, among other aboriginal settlements, the site of present-day Vicksburg, and on March 23 came upon the town we know of as Natchez, the center of Mississippian Native American culture. According to Father Membre, the Natchez welcomed the voyagers warmly: "We slept there, and received as kindly a welcome as we could expect; the Sieur de la Salle, whose very air, engaging manners and skillful mind command alike love and respect, so impressed the heart of these Indians that they did not know how to treat us well enough." La Salle planted a cross in the Natchez village and received many presents from the tribe when he left.

La Salle reached the Gulf of Mexico in early April of 1682, and on the ninth of that month claimed for France, with shouts of "Vive le roi!" and musket blasts, the Mississippi River and all her tributaries, everything from today's Pittsburgh to Denver. His mission completed, La Salle headed back north.

Leaving de Tonty in Illinois at Fort St. Louis, La Salle returned to France for permission to build a great fort at the mouth of the Mississippi. The petition was granted in the summer of 1684, and La Salle sailed back to America, but somehow made a navigational error and missed the Mississippi, ending up in Texas, where he was delayed for several years. In 1687, short on supplies and lost on a desperate overland journey back to Illinois, Robert Cavelier, Sieur de La Salle, was murdered by his own men in a mutiny.

In 1686, de Tonty had come down the Mississippi from Illinois in search of his friend, sending search parties out in all directions from the mouth of the river. When these efforts failed, he left a letter for La Salle with a Natchez chief, who held it until the next group of white men passed through.

FOLLOWING THE failures of de Soto and La Salle, the third European attempt to claim dominion over the Mississippi territory was, after much struggle and death, successful. On October 24, 1698, a French force of four ships loaded with weapons, provisions and settlers set sail from the port of Brest, led by Pierre Le Moyne d'Iberville. In February of 1699, after a stop at Santo Domingo, Iberville and his men landed at Ship Island, off present-day Biloxi, located the uncharted southern mouth of the Mississippi River and received, from an aboriginal chief, the letter left by Henri de Tonty for La Salle thirteen years before.

Iberville then constructed Fort Maurepas on the mainland at today's Ocean Springs and left in May 1699 to return to France. Fort Maurepas encountered grave difficulties, as the colonists were plagued with malaria, dysentery and vermin and found growing crops extremely difficult. One settler described the beach at Biloxi in terms that are apt today: "The land is the most barren of any to be found hereabouts; being nothing but a fine sand, as white and shining as snow. . . ."

In 1701, the man Iberville had left in command, Sauvole de la Villantry, died of malarial fever and was succeeded by Jean-Baptiste Le Moyne, Sieur de Bienville, Iberville's younger brother. A year later the French forswore Biloxi as a settlement, leaving only a trading post. For the next few years they would concentrate their efforts at Mobile Bay and New Orleans.

In 1710, Antoine de La Mothe Cadillac was appointed governor of the territory. Among his other accomplishments Cadillac had, in 1701, founded the city of Detroit. He had also lost a power struggle with the governor of Canada and was subsequently "promoted" to Louisiana. Cadillac did not appear in the territory until 1713, and then fell into immediate conflict with Bienville, who had spent the intervening years mediating wars between the Choctaw and the Chickasaw, as the British were fomenting Indian trouble to undermine the French position. Bienville had also tried to aid the Spanish in their war against the British in Florida, and had been preoccupied with putting down a mutiny among his own subordinates.

The squabbling between Bienville and Cadillac became fateful, changing the course of Mississippi history, in 1715, when their inability to communicate led to a breakdown of communications with the natives. Contact with the Natchez, possessors of beautiful and strategic high bluffs above the Mississippi River, had been increasing, but Cadillac—whom Bienville had neglected to inform of the gesture's import—offended the tribe by refusing to smoke the calumet of peace. This inadvertent snub led to the murder of several Frenchmen by the Natchez, who took Cadillac's insult as an omen of ill intent. The French then felt impelled to avenge those deaths, and Bienville was dispatched on a police action in early 1716. In the First Natchez War, as it came to be known, Bienville constructed a trading post to attract the Natchez elders, then held them hostage for three weeks until the tribe executed the Frenchmen's murderers. The Natchez were also forced to build a fort for the French. Fort Rosalie, built in 1716, was the beginning of present-day Natchez, and the beginning of the end for the nation whose empire had begun more than a thousand years before.

ON A ROILING July day, I drove through Natchez on a wide boulevard lined with old mansions and moss-draped willow trees toward U.S. Highway 61, then south past the sandy brick of Jefferson Davis Hospital, one of the largest buildings in town. I turned left onto Jefferson Davis Boulevard and drove east several blocks through a precisely manicured subdivision of expensive contemporary homes. At the end of that street, in a complex of fields and woods along St. Catherine's Creek, sits the Grand Village of the Natchez, once home of the great aboriginal tribe.

As it stands today, the Grand Village consists of several football fields' worth of cultivated grass in and among clumps of sweet gum, magnolia, box elder, myrtle wax, acacia, ash, cotton tree and dogwood—punctuated by mounds where various temples and chieftains' huts were built. These mounds, smaller versions of the Emerald Mound I had climbed a few days before, were the ceremonial centers of Natchez life. When a war chief died, his body lay in state for three days in his house, then the corpse was paraded in a procession led by the tribe's oldest surviving war chief, circling the dead man's house three times. Next, as the procession headed for the temple, the litter bearers would turn around in a circle every ten paces and again proceed, followed by ten or more of the deceased's family and subordinates, voluntary suicides who were to go with him in death. Inside the temple, the war chief was buried, and his followers killed and buried. Then the war chief's house and all of his possessions were burned, making room for the hut and family of the next chief, who would live, literally, on the ashes.

The Natchez in their glory numbered more than forty-five hundred. Their culture was oral, profoundly religious and based on the observed rhythms of nature. The first moon after the vernal equinox was the moon of deer, followed by the moons of strawberries, little corn, watermelons, peaches, mulberries, great corn, turkeys, bison, bears, cold meal, chestnuts and nuts. The Natchez worshiped the sun, the great holy fire symbolized in their settlements by a sacred central fire guarded by priests and parceled out in coals to each household. The supreme chief, known as the Great Sun, was believed to be the incarnation of the holy fire. Upon his death, the hut in which he had lived on the Great Sun's mound was burned and, as with war chiefs, on its ashes was built the dwelling of the next Great Sun. Temple mounds were built with the bones of Suns and their relatives and entourage, while other mounds (including Emerald) served as burial sites for lesser nobles and commoners, their bones cleanly picked by burial dressers and piled high in the Mississippian culture. (The largest mound of all, Monk's, at Cahokia, Illinois, is one hundred feet tall, seven hundred feet wide, and one thousand feet long.)

The Natchez saw death as merely the passage to eternity, something to be embraced, a return to the lush earth that had made them. The wife of one chief, about to die in a ritual suicide, told a French observer that her husband was "in the country of the spirits, and in two days I will join him and will tell him that I have seen your hearts shake at the sight of his dead body. Do not grieve. We will be friends for a much longer time in the country of the spirits than in this, because one does not die there again. It is always fine weather, one is never hungry. . . . Men do not make war there, because they make only one nation. . . ."

Walking through the Grand Village, I could see why the Natchez came to worship the sun. Southwestern Mississippi provided, in abundance, everything necessary for human society; and the natural bounty of the land was such that little agriculture was needed for sustenance. The sun was steady and faithful, and so warm I was dripping sweat standing still. But much as I wanted to, I was unable to see the Natchez as they really were, to understand their ferocious balance with their surroundings. Would we ever know what had been lost, what wisdom had passed with them into history? All that remains 250 years after their demise is the mounds, which at this late date and in this bright light look like nothing so much as parts of a golf course in the middle of suburbia at the end of Jefferson Davis Boulevard, where it is so quiet you can hear only the droning whir of lawn mowers trimming the grass on graves in the distance.

THAT EVENING I wandered a more prosaic village, the Natchez Mall. Interactions in the mall seemed about on a par with what I'd seen so far in the relations of Mississippi blacks and whites: polite, even friendly exchanges in formal encounters involving members of the two groups, but otherwise social segregation. People wandered in groups drawn on racial lines, and neither group seemed to have much to do with the other. Northern social patterns were similar; but the color line in Mississippi seemed even more clearly and invariably drawn than it was in New York and Boston. There were two exceptions in those several hours I walked and sat in the mall. I saw a young white woman walking with a group of older black women and children in what looked like a family situation. And a young white woman teased and bantered about overdue birthday presents with a young black woman in a shoe store, an exchange that ended with a mock "Uh-huh, I'm gonna fix you" on both sides.

I drove back to my motel room and cranked up the air conditioner. Flipping on the TV news out of Jackson, I was startled to see that both anchors, a man and a woman, were black. Was this the new Mississippi, blacks having full and equal access to the best of jobs, or simply an aberration? (I later discovered that it was a black-owned station.) I had already begun thinking about Mississippi in terms of a science-fiction movie, *Alien Nation*, in which a secret population of aliens lives among humans in Los Angeles and moves about in a parallel society. Blacks and whites in Mississippi, to my initial observation, seemed to move around each other with the same blithe unawareness. But given what I knew about the state's racial history, I couldn't help wondering whether that surface indifference masked some deeper reality, bonds of hatred and, perhaps, dependence. I fell asleep listening to Jay Leno and thinking about aliens.

THE NEXT MORNING I stepped out of my room into the subdued light and overwhelming wet heat. That was something else I'd noticed: Natchez didn't have the blinding sunshine of a Los Angeles or Miami; rather, it carried an atmosphere of filtered, refracted daylight, almost like that of a jungle. There was so much vegetation for the light to work through that instead of glare it produced a strange, slightly veiled clarity—if you could see past the sweat clouding your eyes. At 8:30 in the morning it was ninety degrees, and the humidity factor was close to 100 percent. After the coolness of the air-conditioned motel room the heat felt all the more intense, like a furnace opening, and it kept coming, as it would all day, in waves. I got tired just walking to the car.

Arriving in the South, I had proceeded with great trepidation, not sure I knew enough about how people behaved, racially speaking, toward each other in public to blend in and avoid trouble. My memories were of the newsreels of the fifties and sixties, and of the stories—some folklore, some factual—of how blacks were expected to conduct themselves. And I remembered that when I was a child, trips south were circumscribed by a carefully drawn net of phrases spoken by both parents and family friends: "We don't go there," "Black folk don't do that," "That's not any fun anyway." Alone now, I was a bit nervous about trooping into strange establishments. But I'd come, in part, to investigate these barriers for myself. And I was startled to discover that, at least on one level, Mississippi was much like any other place in the United States. At breakfast in a diner near my motel, what I encountered made me much less apprehensive than I had been a few days earlier. The place was apparently run by five black women, and their unprepossessing black-and-white clientele was an everyday mix of truckers, local businessmen in ties and shirtsleeves, tourists and the same old men shooting the breeze and reading newspapers that you see in most any diner across America.

Sitting there, I felt a little foolish about some of my preoccupations. But was I really that wrong to question the state of race relations? As I had the night before at the mall, and during my explorations of the Trace and other stops, I saw blacks and whites sharing public space peacefully, moving among and around each other easily, without friction, and yet not seeming to talk to each other except in superficial transactions, passing sugar shakers good-naturedly from table to table, swapping sections of the newspaper, holding doors open and nodding "thank you." So if there was no apparent rancor, still this affability didn't extend far beyond the surface. Members of the two groups did not sit together and share meals.

However easily these groups accommodated each other, I was still in Mississippi, in *Natchez*, Mississippi. When I had told my

Memphis cousin Freddie Cummings of my plans, she had gasped and wisecracked, "Natchez! That's Confederate country! Why would you want to go down there?" According to her, there was Mississippi—meaning Oxford, Tupelo, New Albany and Holly Springs, the quiet, pretty towns our people were from—and then there was *Mississippi*, meaning Jackson, Vicksburg, Natchez and McComb, distant mythological nether regions where the Civil War was still being hotly fought. Beyond there were Philadelphia, Money and Ruleville, places too dark and terrible to be contemplated.

Along with Charleston, South Carolina, and Savannah, Georgia, Natchez is a living symbol of the Old South. When we think of slavery, we probably call to mind images and metaphors based on the physical reality of Natchez, where plantation life reached its zenith. For people concerned with such things—like the sponsors of the promenades, balls and cotillions still held in the city each spring— Natchez is a blank screen upon which can be projected the glories of the white empire, of days "gone with the wind." One can, though, with equal fervor and vehemence, project visions and memories of black subjugation, slave auctions and unremitting toil in hundred-degree heat. In the diner that morning, we all sat munching our muffins and eggs in equanimity, without irony; just another July morning, sitting on five hundred years of North American history.

After breakfast I drove into town, toward the river. Contemporary Natchez has at least two contrasting faces: a typical New South village of franchise strips and quiet neighborhoods, private and remote, and a time-warped collection of antebellum mansions. Natchez can present this wealth of physical history and beauty only because it was out of the line of Civil War conflagrations, and because after the war its landowners were too cash-poor to modernize. I was on my way to visit one of the town's mansions, and as I rode through sleepy streets I found myself enjoying the area's slow pace, its mannerliness—everything, in fact, but the heat.

I parked in a lot on a bluff above the river, not far from where I'd stopped when I first arrived. I was just south of the site of Fort Rosalie, the first permanent white settlement in the Old Southwest. Rosalie grew, with the addition of slaves in 1722, into a bustling settlement which thrived until November 28, 1729, when the Natchez attacked in a surprise raid, killing all white men at the fort save four: the tailor and the carpenter (whom the Natchez apparently thought might be useful) and two soldiers who happened to be delinquent in the woods when the Indians struck. All told, more than 200 were killed that day; 450 women, children and slaves were taken prisoner.

This massacre, planned as part of an intertribal effort to murder every white man in Mississippi, failed in the end because the Natchez had, for reasons obscure, struck several days earlier than the other tribes. This discrepancy gave the French, in the person of the two lucky soldiers, just enough time to spread the word, organize and send reinforcements up from New Orleans, troops which then embarked upon the series of reprisals that led to the extermination of the Natchez by 1740. Under Bienville, the French also made war against and destroyed all tribes that gave aid or shelter to remnants of the Natchez. But despite these actions, the French failed to reestablish any serious presence in Natchez or Mississippi (then called Louisiana), and the area gradually ceded to English, then Spanish and, again, English control. The French and the Natchez, both moved to slaughter in order to possess Mississippi, had canceled each other out.

I STOOD outside the gates of Rosalie, a mansion built in 1823 near the site of the old fort. The actual location of the fort, on a rise behind the mansion, is now a wide green lawn on which stands only a white gazebo overlooking the river. The mansion Rosalie is owned and preserved by the Mississippi Society of the Daughters of the American Revolution, which gives tours of the house most days on the hour and half hour.

The house is still and serene, without a trace of the strife that has marked its site. Designed by Baltimore master builder James Griffin, built of red brick fired on the premises by slaves of the owner, Peter Little, the house is, according to a brochure, "of the late Georgian type with a large gallery upheld by four massive Tuscan columns." To me it looked like the administrative centerpiece of some large and prosperous private college: ancient, solid and final, its bricks settled with the wide and flat authority of centuries.

As a tour group leisurely assembled on the mansion's broad steps and veranda, I opened a black iron gate in front of the house and went into the gardens. I was beginning to think that such glory was routine in Natchez. Wisteria, camellias, roses, azaleas and magnolias were just several of the blossoms surrounding me, those I thought I recognized, organized in rows along the sidewalks or in groups behind knee-high wire fences. Lush color spread everywhere, the flowers in their hundred shades, the varied greens of the grass and tree leaves, the clear and limitless blue of the sky. I looked past the flowers to the side yard, where two little girls were taking great pleasure in repeatedly ringing the war-memorial bell. Among the scores of staff and tourists the only black person I saw was a gardener, who smiled and nodded as he passed me going to turn on a hose.

Our tour guide—coiffed, plump and pleasant in a dark blue sailor dress—opened the door and smiled broadly, enthusiastically waving us in. After a split second's hesitation, doubt as to whether I belonged there, I hurried up the steps and joined the group. For thirty minutes we toured Rosalie, exclaiming over the fourteen-foot ceilings, the sparkling chandeliers, the silk-and-mahogany couches and Queen Anne chairs, the sumptuous, sunlit parlors, the dining room with table and service for forty. We went upstairs and saw the bedrooms, and I felt a mixture of pride and awe when I lingered after the group in the large but dark bedroom, complete with silver tea service, that Grant had used while directing the Vicksburg campaign.

The tour guide was sweet to me, as polite as virtually everyone else I'd met. She invited me to play the piano in the women's parlor, a heavy old Chickering thought to be the first concert grand brought to Mississippi, and I felt welcome, my presence reassuringly insignificant.

But I could not see, in the painstaking preservation of the house and grounds, an innocent love of history. If I felt welcome amid this splendor, I also felt angry: it is all of it enjoyed too much, and what it cost willfully ignored. Rosalie and houses like it are clenched symbols of a time that has passed and is mourned, when whites reigned unchallenged and supreme, and the world, to wealthy Mississippians, had beauty, order and symmetry. Is it possible, I wondered, to praise and cherish Rosalie without, by implication and association, praising and cherishing all that went with it, that built and maintained it? When does the history, or nostalgia, of one group slide into insult of another? And is the preservation, the glorification, of antebellum Natchez an indirect expression of a continued wish to oppress blacks? The town serves as a shrine to some of the darkest moments of American history, and in a Mississippi that needs to pass education initiatives and develop economic strategies for the next century, such worship seems insidious.

LATER THAT WEEK I visited Ellen Douglas, a descendant of one of the owners of those great Natchez mansions. A handsome woman of about seventy, full of curiosity and solicitude, she spoke in a rich honeyed drawl, the product of a life spent almost exclusively in Mississippi. With a warm, deeply tanned oval face framed by reading glasses and medium-length gray hair, she smiled often as we spoke and was prone to long, studied pauses in which to consider her thoughts. Ms. Douglas is the author of several novels and books of stories that detail the lives and concerns of Mississippians, black and white, and the ways in which those lives intertwine to nourish and sometimes strangle each other.

We sat and talked for several hours one afternoon in the living room of her home on a leafy street near Baptist Hospital in Jackson. We drank iced tea, and the sounds of children playing outside punctuated our conversation.

"I think, realistically, that all the pressures to conform and live in separate worlds still exist," she said in reply to my question about the current state of race relations. "Intermarriage is still a threat to most white people in the South. Socializing leads to romance, and romance leads to marriage, and marriage leads to children. People, white people, are still afraid of that. I suppose it comes from the threat to social position and prestige that intermarriage would bring. There's been two, three hundred years of violence because of that. It dies hard. My mother's generation of southern white people would not have perceived it as an objective threat; that is, that you would've lost your social position, your economic position. They saw their opposition as having a genuine moral basis. Superiority was the genuine perception for those people. They believed it from when they were little children. People of my generation also believed it, but I think they see intermarriage more as a social and economic threat.

"I think that in a state like Mississippi what enters into it is the whole business of control. That is, if black people got out and voted the way they should, according to their numbers, then the whole political scene would change. The reason that blacks are not completely in control of a lot of this state is that they won't get out and vote. I think, politically, white people are afraid of that. 'Afraid' might be the wrong word. I think white people don't want to lose their power. They don't want to admit the past, they want to say 'Everything's fine now,' they want to block off any recollection of how things were.

"I grew up in a strongly family-oriented, strongly religious Presbyterian world. I grew up with two grandmothers who lived until I was in my thirties; I knew them well, both as a child and as an adult. And that complex world of cousins and aunts and uncles was a joy! I loved it. We used to spend lots of time with my grandparents in Natchez, and Natchez is a romantic place to be from, all that glamour. Both of my grandmothers lived in those big old pre–Civil War houses. I'm a seventh-generation Mississippian. It's in the blood, so to speak.

"From adolescence I've had a strong interest in what was going on between black people and white people and why things didn't work very well. My cousin, who was also my best friend, had a black woman who lived in the house with them, who ran the household. Her mother was busy doing other things and she was the authority figure in that household. She was very powerful, very reserved. She very much had a sense of herself, a very strong character. I think my awe of her as a child, my recognition of the peculiarity of the situation—by that time not many people had a black housekeeper living in their house, and she didn't live in a servant's house in the back, she slept in a nice bed, lived in a bedroom in the house, had a desk, the finest rocking chair, a chest of drawers— it was a novel situation. I think the impression that made on me, and my effort to figure out who she was, was one of the major reasons why I began to look at black–white relationships so closely."

She paused and was pensive. "Another thing, a terrible thing, but it's true, is that when I was maybe in my early teens, I guess fourteen or fifteen, somebody from *Fortune* magazine—this was the depth of the Depression—came down to the South and looked at sharecroppers, rural blacks, rural whites, and did an article on them. This reporter went to Natchez, and one of the families that he took a picture of lived on the place my grandmother owned. There they were, lined up in their ragged clothes in front of their pitiful house. And I remember how—it seemed to me at the time—puzzled my parents were, particularly my mother. 'Why did they want those people's picture?' They just didn't know what was going on. That had a very strong effect on me. I knew why they were having that picture taken. In intellectual terms, the year I was a senior in college I read *The Mind of the South*. That really affected me, really started organizing my thinking. Of course I read William Faulkner, too. I read 'Spotted Horses' and 'Dry September.' If a seventeen- or eighteen-year-old southern white girl reads those stories and she's got any sense, they'll have an effect on her.

"The main problem in Mississippi was the press. The press was controlled by the Hederman family, and they were violently racist. They owned the Jackson *Daily News*, the *Clarion Ledger*, two television stations, four or five county weeklies, radio stations. In Greenville, where I lived, the climate was different. We had a newspaper where the editor was fairly liberal. They had reporters who, if somebody was in jail, they went out to see why. That was extraordinarily important at that time. I think that made a difference in Greenville. We were the first public-school system to integrate without a court case. I think the press contributed to the climate where people didn't feel so threatened, afraid that their businesses would be boycotted.

"People's houses were being bombed. In Indianola, when they started the private-school system, the Citizens Council went around and told the businesses how much they had to contribute. They told service station owners, for instance, that if they didn't contribute, no one would buy gas from them. So they put up the money. But a lot of people didn't want to put up the money, you know. There was a guy there who made bricks, he had a very thriving brick business, and he sold his bricks mostly away from Indianola. They weren't building

all that many great brick buildings in Indianola. They came by and
informed him that his share was twenty-five thousand dollars. He
said, 'You've got to be kidding! Why would I give twenty-five thousand dollars to the Council school?' And they said, 'Well, you're a
citizen, and we're trying to start this wonderful new school that's going to improve education.' That's what they always said, they were
'improving education.' He said, 'I believe I'm going to have to sweat
it out.' But there weren't many people in a position to be able to
do that.

"I don't think Mississippians are any more violent than southerners in general. They all carry guns, use weapons, settle things by
fights. I think that up until not very long ago, it was *such* a rural society the sheriff was often twenty miles away, and if you didn't settle
your fight it wasn't likely he was going to get there to help you out.
Mississippi was very patriarchal. The guy who ran the plantation
was in charge. And since it wasn't very far from a slaveholding society, I think there were people who regarded black people as not fully
human, and therefore killable."

AFTER THE TOUR of Rosalie, we were free to roam the mansion
at our leisure. From the second-floor balcony was the most majestic
view of the river I had yet seen, and I thought of a passage in Richard
Wright's *Black Boy* in which the author describes being mesmerized:
"There was the vague sense of the infinite as I looked down upon the
yellow, dreaming waters of the Mississippi River from the verdant
bluff of Natchez." Wright was watching the river from the West
Side, the sprawling black neighborhood north of Rosalie, and the
wretched childhood he described in *Black Boy* was, of course, a
residue of the grand life of places such as Rosalie. Here was the fault
line of Mississippi history: Rosalie, the Littles and people like them
were on one side of a chasm, Richard Wright on the other; and I began to think that understanding the strands of those two histories
and the ways in which they crossed would go a long way toward explaining Mississippi.

———

THERE HAD BEEN many published black writers before Richard Wright: Phillis Wheatley, William Wells Brown, Charles Chestnut, Paul Laurence Dunbar, Jean Toomer, Langston Hughes, James Weldon Johnson, W. E. B. Du Bois, Alain Locke, Countee Cullen, Arna Bontemps and Zora Neale Hurston, to name several. These artists were all accomplished, some more so than Wright, but none had entered the national and international psyche as profoundly as did Wright in the early 1940s, leaping with his first novel, *Native Son*, to worldwide prominence and fame, articulating the plight and consciousness of African-Americans with a fervor and ferocity not previously witnessed.

How did a self-described "black boy," born in 1908 on the Hoggatt family's Traveller's Rest Plantation northeast of Natchez, rise from poverty and ignorance to live at the center of twenty years of racial and economic change in Chicago and New York, and travel to Africa and Asia, to die in 1960 in Paris, lionized by the French public?

Drawing such a curve can be said to simplify and distort Richard Wright's life and achievements. Wright had gross failings as a man: he had great difficulty sustaining his closest relationships; and he was often a simple and shallow thinker with a weakness for the surface pieties of Marxist and Freudian theories. Despite his fame he died alone, virtually broke, under siege from American, British and French governments covertly and overtly hostile to his Marxist, anti-imperialist views. His was an accomplishment purchased at great cost.

I first encountered the work of Richard Wright as a boy of eleven or twelve. One of my uncles, having recently returned from the army and Vietnam, left a trunk in our basement for safekeeping, and I felt obliged to pry open the lock and see what was inside. There wasn't much, mostly shirts, army fatigues and a couple of blankets— but a few things did catch my interest. The trunk contained books by authors I had never heard of: Camus, Salinger, Baldwin and Wright. *Black Boy* was the first book I surreptitiously slipped from the trunk and into my room, where I read, for the first time, about Mississippi. I have never forgotten this passage, describing Wright's experience after he'd asked to learn a trade when he wasn't much older than I was as I read in Illinois:

"This is a *white* man's work around here," he said. Good morning no more. When I was just a bit slow in performing some duty, I was called a lazy black. I kept silent, striving to offer no excuse for the worsening of relations. But one day Reynolds called me to his machine.

"Nigger, you think you'll ever amount to anything?" he asked in a slow, sadistic voice.

"I don't know, sir," I said, turning my head away.

I read on as the narrator's psychological terror turned to fear for his physical safety:

"Richard, Reynolds here tells me that you called me Pease," he said.

I stiffened. A void opened up in me. I knew that this was the showdown. He meant that I had failed to call him Mr. Pease. I looked at Reynolds; he was gripping a steel bar in his hand.

This was the Mississippi I'd heard whispered about, the place my father had only just begun to describe to me. I read on, and never stopped.

The journey of Richard Wright's life in some ways mirrors that of African-Americans as a group in the twentieth century. Born to sharecroppers "too far back in the woods to hear the trainwhistle," as he put it, in fifty-two years Wright went the distance normally traveled by four or five generations, a feat that would have been astounding even for one born into more favorable conditions. To achieve this from rural Mississippi early in this century—all the while fighting the strictures of Jim Crow, that collection of laws and customs that dictated racial separation and white superiority—verges on the incredible.

As a Mississippi black, Wright was supposed, according to both black and white expectations, to live out his life as an uncomplaining sharecropper, field hand or store clerk. If he got very lucky by the standards of that society, he might have become a schoolteacher in the black system or a preacher at a black church large enough to support him. Had he attained only competent literacy and a comfortable life in the black bourgeoisie, he'd have gone much further than his mother could have hoped on the day he was born.

By the age of six, Wright was shuttling between Natchez, Jackson and Elaine, Arkansas, with side trips to Memphis and Greenwood, Mississippi, as his mother searched for work and struggled to support him and his brother, Leon. Often ill, she had been abandoned by her husband, Richard's father, and worked as a cook and maid before returning to her mother's home when Richard was around ten.

In Natchez, Wright's family lived on Woodlawn Street on the West Side, which cannot look much different now than it did in 1918: frame houses, many of them rickety, crowded on narrow streets, some streets still gravel on red clay, lined with kudzu and willow trees draped with Spanish moss. Some homes are immaculately kept; many more are in various stages of disrepair. In Jackson, Wright's family "stayed" on quiet Lynch Street, which is now a four-lane thoroughfare leading to Jackson State University. Like the homes in Natchez, most of these appear to have been merely held together, tenuously balanced, for the past seventy-five years: railroad shacks propped on bricks and lumber, oil drums and gasoline cans.

Ralph Ellison described three ways in which black youths from such neighborhoods could survive the society of the early 1900s: "They could accept the role created for them by the whites and perpetually resolve the conflicts through the hope and catharsis of Negro religion; they could repress their dislike of Jim Crow social relations while striving for a middle way of respectability, becoming—consciously or unconsciously—the accomplices of whites in oppressing their brothers; or they could reject the situation, adopt a criminal attitude, and carry on an unceasing psychological scrimmage with the whites that often flared forth into physical violence."

Wright survived the Mississippi crucible by staking out and defending personal psychic geography in an unconscious rejection of the prevailing system. He never gave in to what was expected, to Jim Crow, to self-hatred, to violence against fellow blacks. This was, as Ellison notes, a statement of individuality. It also represented a kind of moral insight, as Wright refused to cooperate with what he knew to be evil. This surprisingly sophisticated worldview developed within him as a young man, leading him to entertain fantasies of escape to a life that promised adventure, perhaps to one of the distant places he'd learned of in his incessant reading. He was vaguely aware of the journeys black Mississippians were making in search of greater freedom, and was hardening in his resolve to create what would one day be seen as an American epic in both his work and life. To do this he had to become aware of both himself and the cultures surrounding him:

> Whenever I thought of the essential bleakness of black life in America, I knew that Negroes had never been allowed to catch the full spirit of Western Civilization, that they lived somehow in it but not of it.

Whatever tension, pain or desire entered Wright's heart as a child, he nurtured and fanned until it fueled his escape from the South, and he carried it with him to Chicago and beyond. He learned how to describe what he was feeling in his heart, the heart of a black man, in new ways, and his truthfulness and ferocity cleared the way for many black authors who followed. It is hard to imagine Ralph Ellison, James Baldwin, Malcolm X, Toni Morrison or Alice Walker without Wright's example. His work also bridges the political achievements of Douglass, Washington and Du Bois and the later efforts of King, the Black Panthers and thousands of black elected officials. Wright brought stories of modern black America into the mainstream society (*Native Son* was a selection of the Book-of-the-Month Club) simply by narrating, forcefully and accurately, his experience in the world, and his stories became a window to something never before seen by millions of whites and blacks. He opened for blacks a mode of honest expression that would eventually become predominant in African-American discourse, and he exposed the white mainstream to truths it had not known existed. He challenged whites rather than cajoled them; he did not dissemble about his pain and rage. Born into a sharecropping family on a Mississippi cotton plantation, Wright freed his mind from the shackles of fear and social inferiority, proving, in his words, "that if men were lucky in their living on earth they might win some redeeming meaning for their having struggled and suffered here beneath the stars."

COTTON IS a member of the Malvaceae family, genus *Gossypium*, and is found in most subtropical countries. The portion of the plant most commercially important is the seed-hair fiber in its maturity. This fiber grows from the skin of seeds that push out of pods packed tightly upon the shrub, which is generally pruned and kept under five feet. Before the seedpods, or bolls, burst—in midautumn in the state of Mississippi—the plants blaze with beautiful white flowers, which eventually turn pink, falling away to make room for the swelling bolls fat with the fibers, or fruit, of the endeavor.

The fibers are generally white and grow to a length of roughly one to two inches. They are 87 to 90 percent cellulose, the polymeric carbohydrate that is the principal constituent of the cell walls of all plant tissue, represented by the chemical formula $(C_6H_{10}O_5)_x$. Cellulose is useful in the manufacture of paper, explosives and, especially, textiles. In addition to cellulose, cotton fiber contains 5 to 8 percent water and 4 to 6 percent impurities. Cotton fibers are classified as falling into one of three groups based on the average length of a fiber sample from a bale, ranging from the longest and highest-quality fibers, those of at least one to two and a half inches, known by such names as pima, Egyptian and Sea Island, through the medium grade known as American Upland, one-half to just over one inch long, to fibers of less than an inch, used in carpets, blankets and canvas and in blends with other fibers and synthetic fabrics.

After they ate the fruit of the Tree of Knowledge, Adam and Eve's eyes were opened, and "they knew that they were naked; and sewed fig leaves together, and made themselves aprons." Thus began, in one account, the textile industry and its quest for ever more resilient fabrics with which to clothe, shield and shroud humans. After fig leaves, skins and furs of animals were used, then such natural fibers as linen, wool, cotton and silk. Fabrics woven of these fibers followed the rise of agriculture and domestic life. Linen textiles dating from 5000 B.C. have been found in Egypt, woolens from 3500 B.C. in Scandinavia and Switzerland, cotton scraps from 3000 B.C. in India and 2000 B.C. in Peru, and silk is known to have been woven in China no later than 1000 B.C.

The ancient Greeks wore woolens, and Herodotus speaks of cotton in the fifth century B.C. According to legend, Alexander the Great brought cotton, "vegetable wool," back to Greece from India, and its use spread from Greece to Egypt and eventually, nine hundred years later, to Spain, where it was incorporated in the cloth of sails used by Columbus, among others, to explore the globe. Cotton had been cultivated in the Caribbean for three thousand years before Columbus's arrival, and was introduced to the North American colony of Florida by the Spanish in 1556 and by the English to Virginia in 1608.

In 1605, the English had begun trading at Surat, India, for pepper and fine cloths such as madras. These goods, and an increasing supply of raw cotton from the American colonies, fueled demand for the previously rare fabric. There were, however, limitations on the cotton trade: in India, monetary exchange posed problems, while in the colonies growing vast amounts of cotton was found to be untenable, since processing the fiber was brutally labor-intensive. After bolls were gathered from the fields, seeds had to be separated from the white fibers by hand, a task that took countless hours per pound.

In 1793 a young American, Eli Whitney, invented a machine with which, in his words, "one man will clean ten times as much cotton as he can in any other way before known." The cotton gin suddenly made the cultivation of cotton and, in America, the institution of slavery immensely profitable. Before the invention of the gin, slaves had cost more in food than they could produce in market-ready cotton. Americans stepped up the slave trade, which had been slowing, to feed the growing cotton culture of the Deep South. Planters flocked to Alabama, Louisiana and Mississippi, which then constituted the American frontier, to claim land and make their fortunes; and they needed workers, slaves, for labor. In Mississippi alone, the slave population grew from 498 in 1784 to 196,577 in 1840. Across the ocean in England, Whitney's gin also helped speed the Industrial Revolution as men like Richard Arkwright, Samuel Crompton and Edmund Cartwright rationalized and mechanized the milling process, enabling British textile mills to produce ever-growing stacks of finished cotton. In 1790 British mills handled 189,500 pounds of cotton from the American South; in 1808, more than 10 *million* pounds; and by 1846, some 535 million pounds.

The cause of all this change, Whitney's gin, was a stunningly simple machine, designed to pull cotton fibers through a mesh screen too fine for seed to pass through. First a small tube with a crank on its side, the machine evolved through continuous refinement to the massive ginning contraptions that can be seen throughout the Mississippi Delta today. Without the gin, slavery might have died down or even ended, with subsequent alterations in American and world history; instead, a chain of events was set in motion that led, ultimately, to the Civil War and to much of the domestic conflict that has marked this country since.

EIGHTEENTH-CENTURY Mississippi historian J. F. H. Claiborne described the official arrival of Africans in Mississippi dryly: "In July [1720] the first cargo of negroes arrived." Other events noted for that year were a Chickasaw massacre of Frenchmen, the arrival of thirty Frenchwomen as wives for colonists and the return of Chateaugue, a brother of Bienville and Iberville. The next year, 1721, however, merited this report from Claiborne:

> The slave trade, with all its horrors, was under full headway. A ship of war arrived with one hundred and twenty, having lost one hundred and eight on the voyage. Three other vessels followed. They were half starved on the passage and put on short allowance after their arrival, there being a great scarcity of provisions in the colony. The ship St. Charles, with a cargo of slaves, took fire sixty leagues from the coast. The crew took to the boats, leaving most of the negroes to burn with the vessel.

The slave trade in the colonies had been in full swing prior to this time; but with the emergence of the Mississippi region as a viable agricultural concern, the demand for large numbers of Africans became insatiable. Some were brought directly from Africa, via the dread Middle Passage. Others were marched from the Atlantic coast overland through the Allegheny and Appalachian Mountains (a journey of a month), and down the Natchez Trace to the cotton plantations of the Old Southwest.

For those who survived the Middle Passage, the "horrors" noted by Claiborne started long before the ship put to sea, with their capture and subjugation in their homelands. Gustavus Vassa, born in

Guinea in 1745 as Olaudah Equiano, gives this account from his boyhood:

> One day, when all our people were gone out to their works as usual, and only I and my dear sister were left to mind the house, two men and a woman got over our walls and in a moment seized us both, and, without giving us time to cry out or make resistance, they stopped our mouths and ran off with us into the nearest wood. Here they tied our hands and continued to carry us as far as they could till night came on, when we reached a small house. . . . I discovered some people at a distance on which I began to cry out for their assistance. But my cries had no other effect than to make them tie me faster and stop my mouth, and then they put me in a large sack. . . . The next day proved a day of greater sorrow than I had yet experienced, for my sister and I were then separated, while we lay clasped in each other's arms. It was in vain we besought them not to part us; she was torn from me and immediately carried away, while I was left in a state of distraction not to be described. I cried and grieved continually, and for several days did not eat anything but what was forced into my mouth.

They were later to have an unusual and tragic reunion in Africa, when Vassa was held overnight in the house to which his sister had been sold. The two again were parted, this time forever, as Vassa was shipped to the New World on a slave ship:

> The first object which saluted my eyes when I arrived on the coast was the sea and a slave ship, which was then riding at anchor and waiting for its cargo. These filled me with astonishment, which was converted into terror when I was carried on board. I was immediately handled and tossed up to see if I was sound by some of the crew. I was now persuaded that I had gotten into a world of bad spirits, and that they were going to kill me. . . . When I looked round the ship too and saw a large furnace or copper boiling and a multitude of black people of every countenance expressing dejection and sorrow, I no longer doubted my fate. . . . I fell motionless on the deck and fainted. When I recovered a little I found some black people about me, who I believed were some of those who brought me on board and had been receiving their pay. . . . I asked them if we were not to be eaten by those white men with horrible looks, red faces and long hair. . . .

Vassa was whipped for not eating, and daily longed to commit suicide:

> The stench of the hold while we were on the coast was so intolerably loathsome that it was dangerous to remain there for any time, and some of us had been permitted to stay on the deck for the fresh air; but now that the whole ship's cargo were confined together, it became absolutely pestilential. The closeness of the place, and the heat of the climate, added to the number in the ship, which was so crowded that each had scarcely room to turn himself, almost suffocated us. . . . This wretched situation was again aggravated by the galling of the chains, now become insupportable, and the filth of the necessary tubs, into which the children often fell and were almost suffocated. The shrieks of the women and groans of the dying rendered the whole a scene of horror almost inconceivable. . . .

Vassa was relatively lucky: he was purchased by a benign master, a British sea captain whom he accompanied on expeditions around the world, and was eventually able to buy his freedom. He became a British citizen, a prominent abolitionist who petitioned Parliament to outlaw the slave trade, and later returned to Africa as a Christian missionary. His *Interesting Narrative* was published in London in 1789.

Most were not so fortunate, ending up in slave markets in Virginia, South Carolina and Louisiana. Historian Charles Sydnor describes the instructions given by Natchez planter William Dunbar to slave traders Thomas Tunno and John Price of Charleston: "They were directed to procure for him slaves from Africa to the amount of 3,000 pounds sterling under the following specifications: The negroes should be between twelve and twenty-one years old; well-formed and robust; three or four times as many men as women; and from the Niger River region. He stated that negroes of the 'Iboa' nation were disliked in the Mississippi region and should, therefore, be excluded from the order. Preference was expressed for Africans of the Bornon, Houssa, Zanfara, Zegzeg, Kapina, and Tombootoo tribes."

Plantation owners such as those in Mississippi required slaves from organized, agricultural societies accustomed to sustained field work and the systematic organization of tasks. As had been found to be true of Native Americans, hunting and warrior tribes made poor slaves, and planters developed sophisticated mechanisms for procuring workers suited to their conditions, a global network of trade, transport and distribution that was a thoroughly rationalized business.

Some Mississippi planters, like Leonard Covington, brought their slaves with them from plantations elsewhere. Covington came to Mississippi from Maryland to serve as an officer in the army; other planters came once they had exhausted their land growing tobacco in Virginia and Maryland and needed a fresh start; still others were the children of wealthy families in the original colonies who sought to possess places of their own. Covington wrote his brother, who had gone to Mississippi ahead of him, "Do the negroes in that country generally look as happy as and contented as with us . . . ?"

There exists a brief record of a slave who refused to accompany Covington. His brother had left behind a slave, Sam, in Maryland, and Covington was to determine what should be done with him. According to Covington, "Sam himself maintains a sullen silence on the subject and neither yields consent to accompany my people, or to be sold or exchanged." Apparently Sam had a deeply personal reason for wishing to remain in Maryland, and it is to the Covingtons' credit that he was allowed to stay, traded for another slave.

William Wells Brown, in his *Narrative*, describes an incident which occurred when he worked on a slave trader's boat delivering fellow slaves along the Mississippi River:

> On our way down, and before we reached Rodney, the place where we made our first stop, I had to prepare the old slaves for market. I was ordered to have the old men's whiskers shaved off, and the grey hairs plucked out, where they were not too numerous, in which case he had a preparation of blacking to color it, and with a blacking brush we would put it on. This was a new business to me, and was performed in a room where the passengers could not see us. These slaves were also taught how old they were by Mr. Walker, and after going through the blacking process, they looked ten years younger; and I am sure that some of those who purchased slaves of Mr. Walker, were dreadfully cheated, especially in the ages of the slaves they bought.

We landed at Rodney, and the slaves were driven to the pen in the back part of the village. Several were sold in this place, during our stay of four or five days, when we proceeded to Natchez. There we landed at night, and the gangs were put in the warehouse until morning, when they were driven to the pen. As soon as the slaves are put in the pens, swarms of planters may be seen in and about them. They knew when Walker was expected, as he always had advertised beforehand when he would be in Rodney, Natchez, and New Orleans. These were the principal places where he offered his slaves for sale.

The slave market was conducted in a clinical, businesslike fashion. A typical advertisement, quoted by historian Charles Sydnor, reads:

NEGROES FOR SALE. The subscriber has on hand seventy-five likely young Virginia born negroes, of various descriptions, which he offers to sell low for cash, or good acceptance; any person wishing to purchase would do well to call and suit themselves. —I will have a constant supply through the season. —I can be found at Purnell's Tavern.

Natchez, December 1st 1826. "Austin Woolfolk"

Revenues from the trade became an integral part of the state's tax income. The following is a list of traders working the Natchez market and the amount of a 1 percent tax on gross sales paid for half a year. (The actual number of traders in Natchez was greater, as those who had permanent headquarters in the district were not subject to the tax.)

Amount rec'd by Robert Bradley late Tax Collector of Adams County from Vendors of Slaves:

Paul Pascal	$157.26
Thomas McCargo	79.43
Benjamin Hansford	43.88
Grigsby & Oldham	168.15
John W. Anderson	113.75
Samuel Wakefield	200.00
Levin D. Collier	40.50
Warren Offutt	65.00
John Clark	2.00

Harris Williams & Co	80.93
Isaac Franklin	200.00
Stephen R. Chinworth	41.75
Michael Hughes	54.92
Prince Griffen	67.47
Robert & Nelson Tindal	18.00
Landon Harrison	13.00
Woolfolk and McDaniel	52.41
William Lee	2.90
William G. Clay	43.74
Obediah Gordon	45.85
William G. Skillman	57.70
William W. Eldridge	70.00
Merrit Williams	66.00
Joel White	96.25
R. A. Puryer	93.80
Moses Singleton	40.50
A. R. Wynn	60.80
Thomas Henningway	10.50
Samuel Wakefield	182.70
George Redman	47.75
O. G. Cates and G. Taylor	35.70
James Polk	135.27
	$2,388.11

The first man on the list, Paul Pascal, stated in his tax return of the same year that he had "sold slave [sic] to the amount of fifteen thousand seven hundred and twenty six dollars up to this date May 30th 1833," and swore that "the above is a trew and perfect account of all sales of merchandise or sales of slaves made by me since the preceding Return or collection of Taxes so help me God."

Slaves who made it to the plantations faced a life of toil, sunup to sundown and often beyond. On Mississippi plantations, slaves were required to cook their own meals, care for livestock and start labor in whatever field was being worked before daylight. If they refused, they could be whipped. According to Yale historian John Blassingame, "Depending upon the season or the crop, the laborer would grub and hoe the field, pick worms off the plants, build fences, cut down trees, construct dikes, pull fodder, clear new land, plant rice, sugar, tobacco, cotton and corn, and then harvest the crop. . . . Cotton planting started the last of March or first of April, cotton-picking lasted from August to Christmas and frequently until January or February. The corn was harvested after cotton-picking ended." By Mississippi law, all slaves had to labor at all times under the supervision of a white man.

Here is an early-eighteenth-century description of cotton picking:

> There begins another push, which continues until the whole crop is gathered and housed. During "picking time" . . . the hands are regularly roused, by a large bell or horn, about the first dawn of day, or earlier so that they are ready to enter the field as soon as there is sufficient light to distinguish the bolls. As the dews are extremely heavy and cool, each hand is provided with a blanket coat or wrapper, which is kept close around him until the dew is partially evaporated by the sun. . . . The hands remain in the field until it is too dark to distinguish the cotton, having brought their meals with them. For the purpose of collecting the cotton, each hand is furnished with a large basket, and two coarse bags about the size of a pillow case, with a strong strap to suspend them from the neck or shoulders. The basket is left at the end of the row, and both bags taken along; when one bag is as full as it can well be crammed, it is laid down in the row, and the hand begins to fill the second the same way. As soon as the second is full, he returns to the basket, taking the other bag as he passes it, and empties both into the basket, treading it down well, to make it contain his whole day's work. The same process is repeated until night, when the basket is taken upon his head and carried to the scaffold-yard, to be weighed. There the overseer meets all hands at the scales, with the lamp, slate, and whip.

In search of a true plantation (lamp, slate, whip), I drove thirty minutes through dense, almost tropical kudzu, willow and live oak trees, hanging vines, swamps, cotton, bean fields and pine forests. Sometimes the lush vegetation came right to the edge of the road. I drove north of Natchez to the large white door of Springfield, a working plantation that has been maintained in historically accurate eighteenth-century detail since its establishment in 1786 by Thomas Marston Green. I knocked, and the door was opened by Arthur La Salle, an intense, kind, white-haired preservationist in charge of the maintenance of Springfield's historical artifacts.

The plantation of one thousand acres (once several thousand

more) is located in Fayette, roughly fifteen miles outside Natchez. I walked through the great house, a modified Greek Revival structure which, with its original interior, is not nearly as sumptuous as the restored and modernized house at Rosalie. "Most folks don't realize they're not looking at the house as the residents actually lived when they're in Natchez," Mr. La Salle explained with a wry smile. He showed me the yellowed parlor where, in 1791, Thomas Green hosted the notorious wedding of Andrew Jackson and Rachel Robards, who later was found to have been married to another man at the time.

Springfield, like Rosalie, had a second-floor gallery that afforded a tremendous view. This view was quite different, if equally majestic: a stretch of fields of cotton, hay and beans that claimed miles in all directions—the Mississippi's true legacy. In the yard below me were oak and pear trees and, close to the porch, forsythia in bloom. I felt the breeze, stronger here in the country, and heard it skim through the trees.

I went back downstairs and out to the empty barnyard, through a pass gate, then walked a quarter of a mile down a shaded clay road to the last surviving "quarter house"—denoting "slave quarter"—on Springfield. Restored by Mr. La Salle, the house is a ten-foot-square box of boards on bricks and timbers, covered by a tin roof; though the structure is solidly put together, at the same time it seems as though a strong wind would knock it all down. Standing there by the edge of the woods, looking out over the fields back toward the big house, I wondered how much different the physical landscape could have been two hundred years ago. I stepped into the cabin, which had no windows, only doors, and noted how close and cramped it was—and dark, even in bright daylight—and stood for a time in the silence. I had come across this description of slave life by Charles Sydnor:

> The last and lowest link in the chain of the human species . . . was the class of negroes who labored on the great plantations and small farms of the state. . . . Agriculture in Mississippi was built upon the hoe gang and the plow gang. Both of these, together with all other slaves who could be put into the field, were converted into a great

army of cotton pickers . . . slaves in the old Southwest, of which Mississippi was the heart, were forced to work harder than slaves to the east and north of this region. They are constantly and steadily driven up to their work, and the stupid, plodding machine-like manner in which they labor, is painful to witness.

Planters expected each slave to produce on the average from five to seven bales of cotton a season, each bale weighing four hundred pounds.

The slavery of Mississippi differed from that of early Greece or Rome in that it was based on skin color and economic motives, rather than following directly from war and conquest. Greek slaves worked alongside their masters and were hard to distinguish from them. Roman slaves could become teachers and philosophers, as did Epictetus. American slaves, by contrast, were robbed of much of their personal and psychic dignity, and the residue of that deprivation marks American society still, as millions of African-Americans have yet to recover the ground their ancestors lost in slavery times. Slavery led to sharecropping, another form of race-based peonage, in which blacks received seeds and supplies on loan from the plantation owner and repaid him out of crop profits that never quite materialized—a system my father experienced as a child and young man. The end of sharecropping led to the migration of millions of blacks to the urban North, where many were, and are, caught in the snags of social disarray. A direct line can be drawn from slave ships and quarter houses to housing projects and killing streets.

Standing in the shadows of the quarter house, I found myself wondering if they, the slaves, might have speculated that life would be better for some of their descendants. If my presence didn't redeem what they had lost, I hoped it at least gave some meaning to that loss. I was what came after, and my present perhaps gave further shape to what had gone before.

I walked around to the back of the shed, along a shallow ridge where traces of the rest of the quarter houses remained, bricks and boards littered with rusty Budweiser cans, plastic bags and empty antifreeze jugs. On my way back to the big house I stopped in the Green family cemetery, a small patch of ground behind the mansion.

After several minutes I located the gravestone of Thomas Green, the founder of Springfield. His stone had nearly sunk into the ground. I'd seen a copy of Green's will, recorded in the office of the chancery clerk of Jefferson County, in the room that had been Green's office and which now served as the same for Arthur La Salle. On the fifth of December 1812, Green wrote, "I consign my body to the dust from whence it came to be buried in decent Christian burial and my soul into the hands of Almighty God who gave it. And touching such Goods, and worldly effects as it has pleased heaven to bless me with I dispose of them in the manner following. . . ."

Among those "Goods, and worldly effects" to which Green conveys title are "negro slaves." To his son, Joseph, Green bequeathed "Tallton, Emmanuel, Andrew, together with Peter, Lucy, John and Esther also their increase forever. . . . Also five cows and calves, one yoke of oxen, four head of horses, five head of sheep, one feather bed." To his daughter Eliza, "Quamany, Martin, Rose, Milly and Joe, with their increase." Eliza was also given two feather beds. To son-in-law John Hopkins, "Jack, Charlotte and Jude also three hundred and ninety-seven dollars fifty cents to be paid out and applied to the purchase of a young negro for my Grand Daughter Mary Jane Hopkins. . . ." And so on. "To daughter Mary, four slaves, Charles, Antoine, Harriet and Rachel, to daughter Jane, four slaves, Jacob, Lewis, Amy and Harry." To daughter Rebecca, "Phil, Cooper, Aley and their infant child and Hager." To daughter Augusta, "Anaka, *Anaka* [separate person], Damon, Sophey, Patti, Little Moses and Tom the son of Harriet also a saddle horse the value of one hundred dollars." And this, to wife, Priscilla: "my mansion house and Springfield Estate, together with all the negroes, stock of horses, cattle &c. belonging to the same except such property as has been hereinbefore disposed of."

Green also requested that his "old faithful and trusty servants" Tom, Amaritta and Philes "be not compelled to labor unless they choose so to do and that they be not suffered to want."

By 1850, Natchez and surrounding Adams County had a population of 18,343: 3,949 white, 14,395 black. The blacks had been, with the exception of those few who were free, captured and hauled halfway across the world to subdue a wilderness.

ON MY WAY back to town I stopped at Windsor Ruins, twenty-three Corinthian columns standing mute and worn by the wind. Windsor overlooked what had once been the Smith Coffee Daniel plantation. The Ruins—a weighty name indicative of the southern myth's grasping for grandeur—are the remains of a burned-out building located a short distance from Alcorn State University, an all-black agricultural school whose most famous graduate is Medgar Evers. The land immediately surrounding the building appears to be reverting to wilderness, and this helps the romantic pillars transcend simple vanity, the ruined but noble beauty of the South. It's easy to think of Windsor as the burned-out shell of Faulkner's Sutpen house. And in a certain light, the pillars in fact look like nothing so much as the Acropolis, inexplicably stranded here in southwest Mississippi.

Smith Daniel built this temple to ambition and failure in 1858, intending it to be the South's most majestic house. During the Civil War, the Confederates used it as an observation tower and the Federals as a hospital. So grand was the house that Mississippi riverboat captains, including Mark Twain, used the crown on its roof as a point of orientation from half a mile away; and, in the fifties, Elizabeth Taylor and the crew of *Raintree County* filmed a scene amid its abandoned pillars.

It is a peculiarly American fever that leads a man to clear 100,000 acres out of the great wilderness, a landscape overrun with buffalo, panthers, snakes and parrots, purchase hundreds of African slaves and build a five-story Greek mansion from which to rule. Smith Daniel claimed Windsor and built a palace to loom over it, but his dreams, in the end, exceeded his grasp. When Windsor burned in 1890, "except for a few pieces of jewelry, nothing was saved."

Sitting there before the Ruins on the roof of my car, the sun just beginning to set, I thought of something Octavio Paz had written:

> Past epochs never vanish completely, and blood still drips from all their wounds. . . . Sometimes the most remote or hostile beliefs are found together in one city or soul. . . . Man is not simply the result of history and the forces that activate it, as is now claimed, nor is

history simply the result of human will, a belief on which the North American way of life is implicitly predicated. Man, it seems to me, is not *in* history: he *is* history.

Mississippi was, I was realizing, a baffling place, a dedicated consumer of human dreams. I would return, again and again, by myself, with my parents, with close friends, with total strangers, and each time the state would show another dazzling or deceptive face. For the moment, gazing at Windsor Ruins in the gathering dark and encroaching wind, I could only mull over the questions I had brought with me, listening for answers in the evening songs of grackles and a mockingbird and nothing else.

Natchez

Humid beautiful city, theme park
of slavery and the old ways

sitting pretty upon the unsifted
sediment of history, cycles of pain

working their way down
through layered labyrinths,

the intestines of the French,
Spanish and British.

Americans claim innocence
and necessity, the ghosts

of slaves and aboriginals
weigh down the drooping willows

like Spanish moss
around manicured mansions

that wait as expectantly as
wedding cakes, trying not

to melt in this wet heat,
the reflexive sweat of history,

the waking dream from which
I cannot wake, walking

and falling through the history's blind
untroubled sleep.

Cotton

The loom of history
will not spin them into pattern,
the millions ground to floss

in Lowell,
Manchester
and Natchez, debris
from milling souls, cotton
and money
to fabric

fit for the laundered
shirts and sheets,
the napkins and sailcloths
of London, Amsterdam
and New York.

Embroidered for retail,
the weave remembers
nothing more
than utility; little room for color
in these tapestries, smooth
as dreams in sunlight,
white, flawless,
clean.

Slave Labor

The sense of beauty
we assume was beyond
them, though in their hands
they held the execution
of beautiful things.

Colorblind in iridescent gardens
perpetual novices in each and every trade,
unworthy of any trust
save the cultivation
of the crucial crops.

Invisible, silent,
they linger in the shadows
and crannies of their work,
material residue
what was lost,
souls, names, wages,
unpaid, unsaid, unsung.

TWO

Dorothy

H AVING BEEN through, once, what was for me the abstract Mississippi of history, imagination and legend, I thought it was time to approach the state from another direction. Mississippi wasn't only a place; it was also a way of being that had defined and circumscribed the lives of millions of black Americans, my antecedents and relatives. Inside the grander themes I'd been exploring were the threads of common lives whose experiences told the story. The proper noun "Mississippi" carries in the American language an incredible amount of weight, a complex of emotion and belief, and I hoped to get closer to its meaning through the stories of my family.

My mother, Dorothy, and I were southbound on Interstate Highway 55, traveling through the shallow rolling fields of central Illinois, when we saw an exit sign for U.S. Highway 24 and the small town of Chenoa. Interstate 55 is one of the two main automobile routes—lifelines, really—between Chicagoland's 1.5 million blacks and the "ancestral" home of the vast majority of them, Mississippi. Highway 55 traces the route coursed by old U.S. 66, southwest over the black loam of central Illinois, skirting the farm towns of Wilmington, Dwight, Pontiac, Bloomington and Lincoln on its way to the state capital (and Abraham Lincoln's hometown) of Springfield, continuing on past Litchfield and Edwardsville south and west to East St. Louis, where its four lanes of asphalt cross the Mississippi River and bear a hard left, paralleling the river due south to Arkansas and Memphis, Tennessee.

On a trip to Mississippi, choosing between 55 and the alternative, Interstate 57, is a matter of taste and circumstance: 55 is a winding scenic route; 57 is straighter and thus more boring, but its lack of curves can save two or more hours of travel.

The October day my mother and I chose to set out on the twelve-hour trek "home" was a day of beautiful clear fall weather, Indian summer. We'd decided on Interstate 55 because we were in no special hurry; we thought the ride would be pleasant, and it was. We passed by hundreds of miles of harvested corn and soybean fields standing beige-brown against green prairie grass; regular intervals of deciduous woods with trees just starting to turn; inevitable tributaries winding to the big river every few miles; and overhead a big, clear and cloudless sky made the horizon seem limitless. On either route you can see a mileage sign—ST. LOUIS, 263 or CAIRO, 312— and, looking at that horizon, feel that you'll never arrive. In that landscape, distance becomes a function of time, not landmarks, and the question is how to fill the time: in my childhood, we whiled away the hours playing games, singing, making up stories about the people in other cars, sleeping. Today my mother and I were talking, and, about two and a half hours into the trip, the large green sign for Chenoa called up memories.

In 1972, several members of a family from Aurora, our home-town, were killed here at a railroad crossing on old 66. Their station wagon had stalled and was hit broadside by a freight train; the mother and a daughter, one of five children, survived. They were coming back to Illinois the Sunday after Thanksgiving, returning from holidays with relatives in Mississippi, and I remember my seventh-grade friends and I were alarmed and upset because that accident could have happened to any of us. I'd passed through that crossing many times myself (it couldn't be avoided in the pre–I-55 years). When I reminded my mother of this story, she sighed and said, "A lot of things have happened on these roads. There's been a lot of traveling back and forth, most of it in tragedy."

Dorothy spoke of a trip she remembered more than any other. "I'm remembering when I went back with Papa in 1959, the year before you were born. We were carrying Mama home to be buried."

"Grandma died in Illinois?" I'd always thought that my mother's mother, Annie, had lived all her life down south.

"She came north for surgery—we thought the doctors might be better—but it was too late. She died a month after getting to Illinois. We buried her in New Albany, at Beaver Dam [the home church of Dorothy's family], that's what she wanted. Papa and I rode the Illinois Central, trying to cheer each other up. We talked to the other people, too. You know, it's funny how you see people going places, flying, driving, on the train, and you think it's a pleasure trip. But many times they're traveling in tragedy. On that train when we took Mama home, there was a young man on his way to Arkansas to bury his grandmother, another lady going to Memphis to look after her mother who was dying, another going to Mississippi to bury an aunt. And this was just on one car." She hesitated and caught her breath. "When we got to New Albany it was dark, but the streets were crowded. People had come out, lined up at the depot to meet us. Everybody had come out to meet Annie Modena."

This sense of community was the other half of the black experience in Mississippi, the palliative to the difficulties of Jim Crow, and the unifying glue—the larger, self-contained and self-sustaining bond—that some felt had been lost with the advances of the civil rights age. The trip we were on was itself touched with a sense of both community and tragedy. Our cousin Mary Dilworth was riding along with us because her daughter Debbie, who'd returned to live in Mississippi after growing up on the South Side of Chicago during the sixties and seventies, had taken ill and entered the hospital in Tupelo. Mary heard through the family grapevine that Dorothy and I were headed out that morning, and literally caught us as we were walking out the door.

Later, well into central Illinois, over a lunch of chicken wings and soda, Mary reminisced about simpler times. "Dorothy, remember being on the train, *everybody* eating chicken?"

"Oh yes." Dorothy smiled. "I remember how the porter would walk around and just automatically pass out these garbage bags to everyone, saying, 'Put them bones in here.' "

"Them was some good old days," Mary said. "You'd get on the train, get settled, and them brown bags would come out—in those days people wanted to share. Sometimes the train wouldn't even be out of the station and people would be saying, 'You want some chicken, a piece of this cake?'"

DOROTHY WAS BORN on July 10, 1936, in New Albany, widely known as the birthplace of William Faulkner and the site of de Soto's battle with the Alibamu during his last expedition. Dorothy Cannon Visor was born at home in a black neighborhood called the Flats, near what is now the center of town. She was delivered by the midwife Ludie Cooper, who presided over the parturition of most of the town's black children. Dorothy was the first and, as it turned out, the only child of Annie Modena Edwards, who was young, just twenty years old, and single, two grave liabilities for a black mother at that time. Annie, who was then working as a cook in a New Albany hotel, has been described to me as fiery and headstrong, traits that mellowed into vigilance, determination and faith as she grew older.

Dorothy and I had driven through New Albany so that she could introduce me to the quiet, dusty town. I had, of course, been there many times before, but hadn't then cared about its history or present. An uneventful collection of half-empty two-story buildings and low-slung, leaning houses, New Albany stands at the junction of Highways 15, 30 and 78. Every structure seems tired and half covered with clay, the washed-out pinks and greens and yellows sprinkled with ocher. The population, according to the town sign, is 7,072.

Our first stop was the cemetery at Beaver Dam Baptist Church, several miles north of New Albany proper. As a crossroads town, New Albany has several communities of blacks within its larger population, and I am direct kin to at least two of them: Little Zion, south of town on the road to Oxford, and Beaver Dam to the north. In the latter is the church to which Annie Modena was required to bring the infant Dorothy, to stand in front of the congregation and ask forgiveness for breaching, egregiously at that time, the mores of the community. She had insisted on being buried there.

The current brick church at Beaver Dam sits on a slight rise, in a clearing of standard north Mississippi forest of maple, live oak and pine. The church is a nerve center for Union County blacks, and for clans that spill north into Tippah, east into Lee, and south into Lafayette. The cemetery is a short walk from the church, on a gently sloped hillside of clay falling into woods. This red clay is perhaps my strongest childhood memory, its color a deep, rich red with a tint of orange, its texture thick, clumpy, unlike the even, fine black dust of northern Illinois. The clay seemed to get all over everything—shoes, pants, bicycle gears and, especially in my memory, cars. Bouncing around northern Mississippi as a kid, I could easily tell social rank—that is, who lived in town, who in the country—by the amount of red dust on the lower half of vehicles.

We found my grandmother's grave without any trouble, marked by a large, contemporary stone: OCT. 27, 1913–MAR. 20, 1959. Many of the graves in the cemetery had crude, homemade markers, sparse information scratched in home-mixed concrete; some of the markers, years old, were the plastic kind placed there by the undertaker immediately after burial. Other graves had no markers at all; people knew who was where from memory, aided by general family groupings.

"She was born up in Tippah County, just north of here," Dorothy said. "I believe there was a Beaver Dam up there, too. But this is where Annie considered herself as being from, and when she grew up she moved to town—New Albany—and she worked at different jobs, in various people's homes. She worked in particular for this doctor and his family, then at the hotel as cook." Dorothy smiled happily. "My uncle used to bring me down to the hotel and my mother'd let me sit in the kitchen with her while she worked. She couldn't keep me with her at that time, so I stayed with my grandmother until she got married."

"What happened after Annie Modena and Mr. Visor married?"

Dorothy smiled again, remembering. "I'll never forget it. They pulled up in this big, black car, one of those old cars with a trunk on the back of it. My mother got out and said, 'I come to get my baby.' She and Grandma talked about it for a while and then they carried me out to that car and we went out to Little Zion. It was another world out there."

She turned and pointed northeast, into the forest. "Grandma stayed out at what we called Connersville, about three miles over there."

I looked out over the trees and into the high pale sky. The only things moving around us were crows, cawing and walking along the ground, and insects that revealed their presence with buzzes and shrills.

"I was proud of my mother," Dorothy continued, "because she taught herself so much. She had to go out on her own quite early in life and get a job. It was a big family and she was the eldest girl. The oldest boy was already gone, and Grandma needed her help to take care of the other children. So my mother had to work and do what she could."

"Did she finish school?"

"No. She didn't get to go. I think she finished eighth grade, she was what we call a good eighth-grade scholar, because whenever they needed a substitute in the little country school out at Little Zion they'd come get her. She wanted to be a schoolteacher, and that was special to her when she got to help out a little bit at the school."

"You could teach with only eighth grade?"

She chuckled. "Most of the teachers had only eighth grade in the grammar school. They knew enough to teach reading and writing. I think they were better than some of these you got today."

The thought of my grandmother standing firm in front of a classroom brought something else to mind. "Everybody says she was so proud, how could she be like that in Mississippi back then?"

Dorothy laughed out loud, then quieted. "Even in Mississippi I was never raised to think I was second class, even when I was walking behind the white folks' bus. They used to ride past us every morning while we walked, but it didn't occur to us that we weren't as good as those kids riding. It was just a myth of white folks. They were mean and they wouldn't let us ride, but we were taught we were as good as them, and so, to me, that meant that I could have gone to Ole Miss if I'd wanted to, which was the ultimate achievement.

"My mother would not allow people to put her down. Most white people would call older black people 'auntie' and 'uncle' and names like that; Annie Modena never allowed it. She would say, 'I ain't your aunt.' The white people would look at her like 'This woman's crazy.' But she was forty-six years old when she died and certainly wasn't old enough to be called anyone's 'auntie.'" Dorothy's face was stern. "We had this thing called a rolling store, a truck that came up through the country with all the different things that you would need to buy: yarn, material, various dry goods. We needed it because we didn't often get to town. It would have candy, baked goods, it seemed like everything. The rolling store came by one day and we went out to get some stuff, and the man came around the side, smiled and said, 'What can I do for you today, Auntie?' Annie Modena said, 'I ain't your aunt,' turned around and walked back into the house. He wasn't going to make no sale that day. What I'm trying to say is, that's how we were brought up.

"I remember when I started to realize that black people were considered to be different from white people. White people would say to your parents, 'Why you sending them any farther in school? They can be working here on the farm or they can help Miss So-and-So clean up the house.' Gradually you realized that they didn't intend for you to do anything in life. We were living on these people's place when I was in high school and the lady said, 'Why is she'— 'she' meaning me—'still going to school? She could be here helping you help me keep house.' Annie Modena, being who she was, looked at her and said, 'My daughter isn't going to be cleaning your house. She's not going to school for that.' It kind of broke up a little friendship between them, but I did finish high school."

We walked farther into the cemetery, looking at names on gravestones: Bryson, Crayton, Simpson, Foster, Stone and Berry, names I'd known in Illinois as well. Many of the graves, I was surprised to see, were marked by government-issue stones commemorating service in foreign conflict: World War II, Korea, even a few from World War I. I couldn't help but think of the irony surrounding these men who had gone, willingly, to defend the United States and its interests thousands of miles away, only to return to a state that considered them at best three-fifths human. I mentioned this to Dorothy, who only pointed down the hill, just below the section that held Annie Modena's grave. Down there lay veterans of a more recent conflict, and one stone in particular stood out for me:

CHARLES M SHUMPERT
MISSISSIPPI
SGT CO B 506 INF ABN DIV
VIETNAM BSM-PH
OCT 28 1948 FEB 11 1970

I had never met Charles, by his last name a distant cousin of mine. I couldn't imagine his death in a jungle half a world away, a twenty-one-year-old fighting for neighbors who had yet to fully acknowledge his worth as a citizen. Was he sorry to be fighting for a racist America, or glad to be out of Mississippi? What was he thinking in his last moments? Perhaps in those moments he was just a soldier trying to hang on to life and didn't have time to reflect upon the philosophical implications of his predicament. That, I realized, was left to me.

CHARLES SHUMPERT'S gravestone in the Beaver Dam cemetery made me think of another grave marker I'd seen recently, at Arlington National Cemetery outside Washington, D.C. You can find that grave, Lot 1431, Grid BB-40, in Section 36, just inside the main gate, by taking a right turn off Memorial Drive onto Schley, proceeding about half a block, then going down a set of steps on the right. At the bottom of those steps, turn right, and there, amid Lot 1431's identical graves, bone white in the green grass and under a grove of trees, is Medgar Evers's resting place. The marker is a simple rectangular white marble stone, thirteen inches wide, four inches thick, twenty-four inches tall, crowned by an engraved Latin cross.

MEDGAR W EVERS:
MISSISSIPPI
TEC 5
WORLD WAR II
JUL 2 1925
JUN 12 1963

Just south and slightly west of this spot are the graves of John F. Kennedy, who gave an epochal national address on civil rights the night Evers was slain, and was himself assassinated six months later, and his brother Robert, also a martyr, five years later, to the turmoil then ripping the nation. Just beyond their graves is Arlington House, built to honor George Washington and his family, and once inhabited by Confederate general Robert E. Lee, who had married into Martha Washington's family. To the north and east, across the Potomac River, are the Kennedy Center, the Lincoln Memorial and the Washington Monument.

I had become interested in Medgar Evers because of a story I'd heard his older brother and fellow soldier Charles Evers tell an interviewer about his days in the army in World War II. While serving in France, Evers had altercations with white soldiers from Mississippi; verbal taunts and threats escalated into actual fisticuffs and wrestling. The whites did not take well to the attitudes of autonomy and assurance with which Medgar and other black soldiers were learning to carry themselves in Europe, away from the strictures of Jim Crow.

When Evers got very friendly with a local French girl, the whites felt compelled to enforce the American code of fear, submission and silence—determined to extend the fundamental threat to "avoid white females or die" onto the fields of France. Many black soldiers abroad, including Evers, chose to ignore the implications of behavior which at home would have meant death. The showdown came; Evers duked it out with three or four of the southerners, fighting them to a draw. After they were separated by military police, Evers dusted himself off and looked at his older brother Charles. "When we get out of the army," he reportedly said, "we're gonna straighten this out."

Medgar Wiley Evers was born in Newton County, in east-central Mississippi. His hometown, Decatur, is west of Meridian and south of Philadelphia, a town that would later become legendary as the site of the Schwerner, Chaney and Goodman murders. His parents were known for their intense individualism and for owning their land, something of a rarity in that place and time. James Evers worked at a sawmill; Jesse, his wife, worked for several local white families. Medgar Evers's forebears on both sides were also known for their refusal to fear whites. James often got into fistfights over "sidewalk privileges"—over who, white or black, would get off the sidewalk when both met—and Jesse's father is reputed to have shot and wounded two white men in a dispute, an act which resulted in his having to leave town. When Evers was fourteen, a close friend of his family's was lynched, and he described the event as follows: "He was supposed to have insulted a white woman. We would see his bloody clothing still on the field months later. Some of the blood spots looked like rust on the grass." It was this episode that fueled his initial desire to work for racial justice.

Two years later, after his sophomore year, Evers dropped out of high school to join the U.S. Army. He was sent as an infantryman to the European theater, serving in England, then France, and eventually participated in the D-Day landing at Omaha Beach. Later, during the Occupation, the incident with the white soldiers occurred. Discharged in 1946, Evers returned to Mississippi, along with other experienced young veterans who would play crucial roles in the civil rights struggle, and began agitating.

At the time of his return, no blacks were registered to vote in Newton County. Evers, his brother Charles (who later was elected mayor of Philadelphia, Mississippi) and several other friends registered to vote, but on Election Day were forcibly ejected from the polls and chased from town by an armed white mob. "We were whipped, I guess," Evers recounted, "but I made up my mind then that it would not be like that again—at least not for me."

That same fall, Evers began working to complete his high school diploma, and in 1948 entered Alcorn A & M in Lorman, Mississippi, majoring in business. He played football, ran track, edited the newspaper and the yearbook and was a member of the debating team. In the summers he worked construction in Chicago.

I sometimes wonder why Evers didn't simply stay in Chicago. Or he could have, as many black soldiers did, remained in France after the war. Later, my father escaped Mississippi in the aftermath of the Korean War, and returned only for family duties; Mississippi, he said, was a zoo of thieving white cowards, no place for a black man to live. As I write, Medgar could be sixty-five years old, fat and prosperous, selling insurance in Denver, owning a car lot in Milwaukee or a grocery store in Pasadena. He could have kept his mouth shut and done something similar in Mississippi, joined the Prince Hall Masons and become a black czar, living a long, secure life in the glow of war glory and economic boom. But he turned away from each opportunity, and kept coming back.

That decision to return and agitate was the turning point in his life. He graduated from Alcorn in 1952, having recently married Myrlie Beasley, a fellow student seven years his junior, and moved with her to Mound Bayou, an all-black Delta town between Clarksdale and Cleveland. His first job out of Alcorn was as an insurance agent for Magnolia Mutual, a black-owned firm; but in the back of his mind was an admonition the president of Alcorn had given his black students, asking them *not* to register to vote. This kind of "leadership" disgusted Evers, and, at the behest of Dr. T. R. M. Howard, the founder of Magnolia Mutual, he became active in a new organization called the Regional Council for Negro Leadership. Through his business travels and his work with the council, Evers began to develop a nuanced understanding of the difficulties faced by blacks in Mississippi, especially the poor, and of the sorts of strategies and tactics it would take to dislodge the white monolith.

Medgar also began working with the NAACP, and in 1954 he became field secretary, a full-time position and, in effect, the organization's most important job in Mississippi. At the time, city black families in Mississippi had to survive on less than a thousand dollars a year, and rural families on less than five hundred dollars. The state was changing rapidly, due to the mechanization of cotton farming and the end of its traditionally large usage of human labor: many blacks were following what appeared to be economic and social opportunity north, while many others remained, destitute. And whites who felt extremely threatened by such events as the Supreme Court's 1954 *Brown* decision, outlawing school segregation, were digging in for massive resistance to social and economic reform.

In late 1953 Evers had applied for admission to the law school at Ole Miss, the first black person known to do so. He filed the necessary papers and had an admissions interview, but was rejected less than twenty-four hours later. Per stated Ole Miss regulations, Evers had filed letters of recommendation from Mississippi citizens in Newton County, where he grew up, including one from a white person. In reviewing his application, the Ole Miss board decided (overnight, apparently) that letters of recommendation should instead be from the county of current residence; in Evers's case, Bolivar. After denying his application, the board then stipulated that all future applicants submit five letters of recommendation from white citizens who had known them for at least five years.

In the aftermath of the Emmett Till murder in 1955, Evers's activities became widely known throughout the state and country. As field secretary for the NAACP, he was the most prominent black spokesman on the case; he also played an important investigatory role, going undercover in overalls and boots to visit sharecroppers' fields and Delta towns to gather information about Till's murderers.

Over the next several years, Evers crisscrossed the state, documenting racial incidents and voting-rights discrimination, laying the groundwork for the coming Mississippi movement. In 1959 he helped focus national attention on the Mack Charles Parker lynching, in which a possibly innocent young black man who'd been accused of raping a white woman was removed from his cell and killed with the complicity of Poplarville law enforcement. In 1961, along with Justice Department officials John Doar and Bob Owen, he investigated voter complaints throughout the state. In 1962 he orchestrated James Meredith's attempt to enter Ole Miss, and in 1963 he implemented the first large-scale civil rights initiative in Mississippi history.

On May 19 of that year, in an FCC-ordered televised response to a speech by Jackson mayor Allen Thompson, Evers set forth a challenge:

> I speak as a native Mississippian. I was educated in Mississippi schools and served overseas in our nation's armed forces in the war against Hitlerism and fascism. . . . Now the mayor says that if the so-called outside agitators would leave us alone everything would be alright. This has always been the position of those who would deny Negro citizens their constitutional rights . . . [a black person] sees a city where Negro citizens are refused admittance to the city auditorium and the coliseum, his children refused service at a lunch counter in a downtown store where they trade. . . . He sees a city of over 150,000 of which forty percent is Negro, in which there is not

a single Negro—in which not a single Negro policeman or police-woman, school crossing guard, fireman, clerk, stenographer. . . . He sees hospitals which segregate Negro patients. . . . The mayor spoke of the twenty-four-hour police protection we have. There are questions in the minds of many Negroes whether we have twenty-four hours of protection or twenty-four of harassment. . . .

Evers's 1963 campaign started with a boycott of white businesses in downtown Jackson. When negotiations between the mayor and the NAACP collapsed, white citizens took direct action against Evers's group. During a sit-in downtown, black students and a white profes-sor from Tougaloo College were splattered with ketchup, mustard and sugar, then spray-painted and beaten. A former Jackson police officer kicked one student repeatedly in the face. As the professor lay bleeding on the floor, other whites poured salt on his wounds.

The city of Jackson was soon in open conflict. The White Citi-zens Council rejected one potential settlement negotiated by black ministers and the mayor; Evers's home was bombed; and high school students singing freedom songs at lunchtime were attacked by police with clubs and dogs. On June 7, at a fund-raiser, Evers told a crowd of 3,500: "Freedom has never been free. I love my children and I love my wife with all my heart. And I would die, and die gladly, if that would make a better life for them."

Five days later, on June 12, President Kennedy made a nationally televised speech:

We preach freedom around the world, and we mean it. And we cherish our freedom here at home. But are we to say to the world—and much more importantly, to each other—that this is the land of the free, except for Negroes, that we have no second-class citizens, except for Negroes, that we have no class or caste system, no ghet-tos, no master race, except with respect to Negroes? . . . We owe them, and we owe ourselves, a better country.

That same night, Evers was assassinated in his driveway, within earshot of his wife and children. The children screamed "Please, Daddy, please get up!" as he lay in a pile of sweatshirts inscribed JIM CROW MUST GO, which he'd been carrying into the house. An hour later he was dead.

Byron de la Beckwith, a vocal member of the White Citizens Council, was arrested, tried and acquitted twice by all-white juries for the murder of Medgar Evers. In both trials, hung juries led to mistrials. The weapon used in the attack was registered to Beckwith; Beckwith's fingerprints were found on it; and several Jacksonians testified that he had sought out directions to Evers's home. No one else was tried for the crime, which remained open for thirty years. The administration of Governor Ray Mabus made several attempts, in 1989 and 1990, to extradite the seventy-year-old Beckwith from Tennessee to Mississippi for a third trial. He was finally remanded to Mississippi custody in 1993 and, after much defense maneuvering to exclude black jurors, was convicted of murder. In Jackson in February 1994, Byron de la Beckwith was sentenced to life in prison by a jury of eight blacks and six whites.

AFTER LEAVING the cemetery, Dorothy and I drove farther up into the woods north of New Albany, following gravel county roads marked only by small blue signs where the roads forked. We were looking for the cabin Dorothy's grandmother, Annie Edwards, had lived in until her death in 1968. Family had lived in the cabin after that, but it had been empty for the past several years, and we wanted to see if it still stood. I used to visit the log cabin with the rusty tin roof during my summers in Mississippi as a child. I hated going there and took it as punishment, being exiled to the woods without electricity or plumbing, but with all kinds of threats from nature, real and imagined. The long, slow evenings there were lit by kerosene, and my great-grandmother sewed in her rocking chair and sang to herself. Then we, my siblings and cousins, were forced to turn in hours earlier than we were accustomed to in the North, and we'd lie awake in bed, three or four of us, afraid that every twig snapping in the distance was caused by some strange creature coming to do us in.

At my great-grandmother's we had to walk to an artesian well, pump ice-cold water out of the ground and carry it sloshing back to the cabin, where it would sit in bowls and buckets awaiting its various uses. If we needed to bathe, we had to heat the water on the woodstove and pour it steaming into the same tub used for washing clothes and hauling vegetables. And we weren't allowed any of the drama that came at bath time in Illinois, arguing and fighting, then luxuriating with toys in an endless supply of warm water. At Big Mama's cabin, both the water and its warmth were finite; any lolly-gagging decreased your own comfort as well as that of those waiting for their turns. This, and all the various chores, such as feeding hogs I only half believed would end up as meat on the table, made Mississippi seem like a series of endless deprivations. Why didn't these folks just move on up to Chicago?

Dorothy and I drove past trailers and cotton fields ready for picking, and occasionally a splendid home hidden in isolation. We turned down a fork and ended up in a small black sharecropper settlement which shares the name of its church, Jemison's Corner. Orienting ourselves by the church, we were able to find the correct red-clay-and-gravel road which led us, about six miles in, to Big Mama's clearing, where we found the cabin intact. For as large a space as it occupied in my memory, it wasn't much to see, some boards propped up on bricks in the middle of a woods of pines and deciduous trees, whose leaves were just beginning to change.

The outhouse I remembered was still there, and the chicken coop, which, like the house, had seemed much bigger in recollection. The barnyard was overgrown, and I had trouble placing the hogs I so explicitly remembered within it. The place seemed diminished, and I turned to my mother. "Where's the well?"

She walked down a slight slope away from the cabin, kicking dead leaves and acorns from the ground. "It was over in here somewhere." We were standing about fifty yards from the cabin, and the hog pen, another fifty yards away, formed the third point of a triangle. Eventually we found the well, now just a hole in the ground covered by a few planks. As we looked at it, Dorothy said, "We also would put out barrels to catch rainwater. We didn't want to overuse the well."

We walked to the side of the cabin and sat on the porch ledge next to a flowerless but thriving rosebush, one of the few luxuries Annie Edwards had allowed herself. "I was such a cherished child here," Dorothy said. "Still, Grandma's house was organized around Grandma. She was the leader of the family, she gave the orders."

"How many of you were there?"

"Eight. Those of us who didn't have our fathers with us, and Uncle Wesley and Uncle Clyde. My aunts were there, too, the younger ones. We were just one big family. We were kids, we didn't know anything else. We didn't have anything to do but play. That was our job."

Annie Edwards was born in Lafayette County in 1891 and never ventured, in her long life, farther than the towns of New Albany and Oxford. As a very young woman she married Tom Edwards, a sharecropper, farmed with him until his death, then raised their children and several of their grandchildren in the cabin north and east of Beaver Dam.

ON A LATER DAY, driving back to New Albany from an afternoon in the woods north of Oxford, we talked to my aunt Jesse about her life—which was very different from Annie Edwards's. Jesse is the oldest daughter of my mother's stepfather, Arthur Visor, and his first wife. She'd gone north in 1950, following her brothers Freddie and John, and married there, settling in Aurora, Illinois, to raise four sons and a daughter. After the death of her first husband, Jesse moved back to Mississippi in 1976, where she remarried, and has lived since in New Albany. She is one of many African-Americans who have returned, in a sort of reverse migration, to the South. Some return for the weather, the lower cost of living, the slower way of life. Others are fleeing the inferno of northern cities, hoping that some of the peacefulness they remember from their youth remains, perhaps enhanced by improved race relations.

Jesse loves to talk; when I asked her about the differences between the Mississippi of the forties and that of today, she took a moment to savor her answer. "Well, there's a lot of differences. White people, some of them are nicer, and some of them are about the same as when I left."

Dorothy interrupted. "Do you think the niceness is real?"

Jesse laughed bitterly. "Oh, I guess so. But if I had it to do over again, I'd stay in the North. I ain't gonna say it's that much different in the living, though you do get more for your work in the North.

It's because my people are all in the North now, so I'd rather be there. I see *that* as home, almost. I'd rather be up there."

"But what about the kids?" I asked, thinking of the tragic snare the northern ghettos had become for many young blacks. "Don't you think it would have been better, safer, for the next generation if you all had stayed down here?"

Jesse pondered my question and then said, "I don't know that any of those children would have turned out any different down here. I have a friend down here, both her boys are in jail. She said to me, 'Jesse, I don't see how I could have raised boys like that.' And her girls are bad, too. All her children turned out to be something she never thought they'd be." Jesse shook her head forcefully. "A lot of times a woman didn't have any help with her family. Then the kids, they went—I want to say—haywire. They just didn't seem to know which end of the rope to take. They didn't care about what they did, they just went and did it. There was a time when if the man was gone, the bigger ones would pick up and help raise the younger ones. Maybe it was better then. But I still don't think it's any better here in the South *now*. Not now."

Jesse halted for a second and then continued, "In the nineteen-forties, the fifties, the sixties, the South might have been safer. But now it's the same. If you were to go to the park in New Albany to-morrow evening, you'd see something just like in Chicago, or Aurora. There'll be any number of young people there, girls and boys and women and men, doing everything and doing nothing. They're drinking. New Albany's a dry town, but they go over to Tupelo and they get their drinks and their drugs and they bring it back. It's right there in that park, *right there*. Is this what people tried to be free for?"

SEVERAL NIGHTS later we sat down to a dinner prepared for us by Lessie Belle McKenzie at the house she shares with her husband, Floyd, in New Albany. Dorothy and Lessie Belle are first cousins and, in the manner of Mississippians, more like siblings; because of their closeness, I've always thought of Lessie Belle and Floyd as my aunt and uncle. After a dinner of fried chicken, pork chops, stewed beef, cream corn, green beans, okra, baked potatoes, yellow squash and cornbread, with ice cream and cake for dessert, we sat around the table and talked.

Lessie Belle, a young-looking woman in the neighborhood of fifty, resembles Dorothy, her pleasant and unlined round face regularly breaking into grins. The two of them were discussing how they usually got clothing as children. "Many times your mother would be working for someone, and instead of giving her money they'd just reach over in the closet and hand her that."

Dorothy laughed and looked at me. "Mama'd cut it down and take it in and make us a dress out of it. She wouldn't get money for her work, but she would make us something." This complaint of labor without cash compensation was something I heard over and over again from blacks in Mississippi.

"You remember," Lessie Belle said, "how we used to go out and pick grass to put in those mattresses?"

Floyd broke in. "Crabgrass."

"You mean the straw," Dorothy said. "A tick. A straw tick."

Floyd was insistent. "Crabgrass!"

Lessie Belle laughed. "Whatever it was, it slept good. You'd wake up in the morning and wouldn't want to go nowhere. Of course it wasn't like Grandma's feather bed. We used to love climbing in that bed."

"Once you got built up in it," Dorothy said, "you just kept sinking down. And when you got out, you'd have to smooth it down just right. I remember Grandma would come in and say, 'Somebody didn't make that bed up right.' She'd know we'd been in it."

They laughed; life hadn't been only cotton and Jim Crow. After a moment of silence, Dorothy spoke. "It's something, how resourceful people were then. They had to be to survive. You didn't have no money. Nowadays it seems like we have money and here we are, we can't make it. Those were some good times."

I didn't know quite how to take the last statement. "I thought you couldn't wait to leave."

"To us at that time," she said, "it was good. We didn't know any better. We thought 'up' was sneaking into Grandma's feather bed. If somebody put two rabbits and some biscuits on the table with gravy, that was a big dinner—we thought the Lord had put everything we needed right here on this earth."

This prodded Floyd. "They got to play for higher stakes nowadays. When we was coming along, it seemed like that was all there was out there—rabbits, squirrels, possums. You might kill you a wild turkey or goose every once in a great while, but now it's got to be deer meat, you know? We liked getting a little goat now and then, but now, now it's got to be *deer*."

"You all hunting deer now?" This from Dorothy.

Floyd frowned. "I don't want no deer."

Lessie Belle picked up the strand. "We used to have what we called pullets. Chicken. They'd tell us, 'Now you go out and catch that chicken over there. If you catch him'—they'd be meaning a certain chicken—'if you catch him, we'll have us a chicken dinner.' Now that chicken was going to be *caught*. You'd grab it, boy, and you'd have him with some gravy and biscuits. That was special."

They started talking about school and lunches, and Lessie Belle was suddenly subdued. "There were a lot of children who didn't have a lunch. I always did, and I remember them. And I remember having my little old molasses bucket and my little food in it."

"I," Floyd said gruffly, "never toted no lunch."

"You were too mannish," Dorothy said. "You didn't want anybody to see that you only had a biscuit and a piece of meat."

"No, I just never did. They had a little old store round the corner from the school where I was always buying something. Whatever was a dime. I was going to spend my little money."

Lessie Belle laughed. "Oh Lord. I remember we used to go out and pick cotton and get us a dime, or a nickel, so we could go buy soda or cheese and crackers. We were going to pick cotton and get to that store and spend that little money." Lessie Belle stopped to reflect. "But, you know, those were some good days."

"Fun days," Dorothy said.

"There was something better about them, too," Floyd added quietly.

"Is that," I asked Floyd, "why you stayed?"

He seemed startled by my question, and repeated it. "Why did I stay? Why *did* I stay?" He smiled broadly, then sobered. "Well, I've had a couple of pretty good jobs, it might be as simple as that. I had a good job up in Racine, Wisconsin, but I'm peculiar about my insides. I was working in a foundry, and that black sand there at J. J. Case was blacker than—they'd have you go in there to the furnace and in literally two hours you couldn't tell who was who until you pulled off your glasses. I can't stand that. But that's where everybody I knew was working. The work wasn't that hard. I just couldn't stand the sand. I told them I'd had enough dust when I was plowing a mule. Everybody said, 'You're leaving this good job?' I told 'em I planned on being here on earth a good long time, and that dust wasn't going to help it. Then it seemed like a bunch of 'em was going to Evanston, Illinois, to do concrete work, but I'd done that in Nashville and I didn't care for that either."

"You stayed in the South because you didn't like northern jobs?"

"I didn't like the jobs I could get up there. I'm telling you, I wasn't about to think about toting that concrete around. And in Racine, all they had was them foundries. All that dust. The guys that came out of those places, you know how long most of them last? How long most of 'em got to retire? Not long."

I'd heard relatives say that people who went north in the fifties and sixties often "gave up" because they couldn't adjust to the different realities of urban life, but until Floyd I hadn't talked to anyone who'd ventured north, tried it, didn't like it and came back.

"What did you think of the way of life in the North?" I asked. "You know, the pace, the activity, the nightlife?"

"I wasn't into that stuff. I didn't like it, and what they were doing seemed stupid to me."

"So you just prefer the South?"

"I just want to live *here*. I went one time to a club in Chicago, I think it was called the Chicken Shack, everybody used to say, 'Oooooh, we're going to the Chicken Shack tonight.' Well, I went, and I couldn't believe it. We wasn't there thirty minutes and here comes this fellah sitting down with us and playing with this gun, spinning it around in his hand. I said, 'Well, y'all, I think I'm gonna go on home.' Them bullets ain't got no eyes." He stopped to think for a beat, then looked directly at me. "You ever been to Evanston, Illinois?"

I nodded yes.

"Then you know it's bad. There's nothing there. Nothing for a man to like."

I laughed. "I like it. If I were living in Chicago, that's where I'd want to live."

Floyd vigorously shook his head. "No way. It's all closed up, close, brick walls, that strange light from the lampposts all on the wall. Why would a young fella want to be in a place like that?"

I found his distaste mystifying. My father, Claude, a bosom buddy of Floyd's, had spent his youth actively scheming to leave Mississippi—as had my mother, if in a less urgent manner. Yet here was Floyd, as anti-Illinois as they were anti-Mississippi, at least in terms of a place to live. "Floyd," I asked, "did you think things were going to change the way they did? Did that encourage you to stay?"

"Every year made a difference. Every year made a difference. From the time I was a kid to about the time I was fifteen, things loosened up, and as I got older it was even more change. It took a while for the jobs to come along, but at that time there wasn't nobody working, black or white. There wasn't but two factories here. With the change in farming there wasn't enough to do. Everybody was getting tractors, and that killed the three or four people the man had living on his place. He didn't want 'em anymore. So they had to give 'em a little work. That's when the factories came in, and that's how it started to change."

"Do you think a black man will ever be governor of Mississippi?"

Floyd nodded gravely. "Absolutely. You know if Virginia got one, we gonna finally get it, just like everything else. It just takes time. But we'll finally make it. Only we move slow. We don't move that fast, we move slower."

"What do you mean?"

"Up there in Memphis, there was a guy, a politician, if he hadn't debated the white candidate, he would've won the primary and been on the Democratic ticket. He could have been sheriff. But you see, don't no black man want to go debate with no white man because the white man got more people sitting down and writing him things that people gonna ask him. A black man don't have that kind of help. He's on his own. I think he knew he was gonna get beat, but maybe he thought he could wait and get in later. It looks like he might do just that." Floyd tapped his temple with his index finger. "Black men are smart. Nobody gives it to them, but they're walking around, they're moving. The problem with this guy in Memphis, see, he come too fast. He saw he could lick that white man, and he should, but just not yet. But we're getting some pretty good places now, and there's gonna be more."

"Do you think that the black people who stayed in the South are better off than those who went north?"

Floyd thought for several seconds. "I think so. Black people in the North could be better off, but the average one, the first thing he do is get a good job, then go out and buy everything, get him a lot of credit, a car, a house, a stereo, then he's stuck. They should just get a little bit here and a little bit there until he establishes himself. The first thing he want to do is get him a new car. You got to get a little at a time. See, when the whites started giving us jobs around here, the first thing they did was wait and watch for people buying too much. Then they made it harder, because you couldn't quit. But I'm telling you, you can make it. And you ain't got to be no stool pigeon. You got to take it slow."

"Can you tell me what it was like here when you were a little boy?"

"After I got up to about eight years old, I started working, plowing mules all day. Weren't any such thing as a tractor then. When the morning come, we had to get up and go to the barn to milk the cow, feed the hogs. At night we went over the same thing again. That was our routine. In between we worked the field."

"What about school?"

"School was the same length it is now, except that we used to go two months in the summer, we'd start in July and go most of August if the cotton didn't open up. We'd go those two months, then everybody'd come out at the end of August and start picking cotton. They'd cut off school because the cotton had opened. You'd pick cotton and make your sorghum and pull your corn, then you'd get ready to go back to school."

"That being about the end of October?"

"Yes. We'd go to school the rest of the winter. And we walked, wasn't no bus coming for us."

"Do you think this area—New Albany, Oxford, Tupelo—was an easier part of Mississippi for black people?"

"I've traveled lots of Mississippi, and right around here—Tippah and Union and Marshall—those are the best areas. People are much more friendly than in the rest of the state. Now you take my hometown, Grenada, they aren't friendly, period. White or black."

I had been in Grenada earlier that year. "They're still having trouble with the Klan there. Somebody tried to burn out a black family. Why are they so mean down there? Does the Klan have more of a hold?"

Floyd grimaced. "Actually, I never heard nothing about the Klan until I was grown. When this thing started, there were a whole lot of things going on, but that wasn't the Klan—it was just plain old people doing all that burning and trying to keep us off the bus and such. But I'm going to tell you something, I'm going to tell you why all of this around here and in Mississippi was going on. *They didn't want the black man going with the white woman.* That was the whole size of it. And they didn't want him to have a job because my wife, if I got me a good job, she didn't have to go work for him and his wife. I could let her stay home, and they knew that. They used to use them words 'cut off your nose to spite your face.' Well, they weren't gonna cut off their noses to where their wives couldn't sit up and manicure her fingernails all day, so they figured they'd keep us back as long as they could. They wanted us just scraping by. They knew if we had factory jobs, when we got home we was gonna want our suppers done, too. We was gonna want our cold water. We gon' want our houses clean. We was gonna have a little extra here, a little extra there, and our wives wasn't gonna have time to spend eight hours out yonder taking care of their babies. She'd take care of her own babies. They tried to keep us out of the factory, one would tell the other, 'Don't hire him, he was my hand.' But that didn't work. They had to hire us and keep hiring us and now ain't none of us hardly working in houses and those that do are making a good little sum. They have to pay 'em well to work or else they'll just go on food stamps."

THE NEXT DAY Dorothy and I were in our car riding through the Delta, marveling at the endless expanse of flat, open fields—comparable in sweep and physical beauty to the ocean—and talking about the armies of black people that once worked those fields, generations made obsolete by machines. Before the cotton picker, the second great machine after the gin to alter the lives of Mississippi blacks, those workers had been essential to the state's economy.

"What," I asked, "is your first memory of white people?"

"When I lived up in Connersville, where we were the other day. White people lived all up through there."

"You had whites in the neighborhood?"

"It was their land or whatever, their place. That's why you described yourself as living on So-and-So's place. One of the families had a daughter—a teenager—and she always wanted to come over to my grandmother's house or my Aunt Pearl's. Aunt Pearl rolled her hair for her and she was constantly coming to get her hair done. I don't remember much about the rest of them."

This kind of easy, private interracial exchange was more common than might be expected, according to Dorothy. Could people, in their personal lives, be in and out of each other's homes so easily, yet be at each other's throats in all other matters? I asked her when she remembered becoming conscious of the effect white people had on her life.

"I believe it was about the time I first went to live with my mother. It wasn't really a problem when I first started school, though you were aware something was a little bit different about them—white people seemed to have things that we didn't—but as a child you didn't know why. You're little and you don't understand that stuff. I remember when we lived on the Gregory farm for a long time. They had a son who was about my age, and he used to play with me and my brother R.V. I remember when it came time to go to school it became clear that he was going to one school and we were going to another. And as he got older, it seemed he would act differently toward us when he had company. Or when other white kids came around. I could never understand why sometimes he'd be so friendly and other times not."

"What about school?"

"You'd get a little feeling like there's something not quite right, and you don't understand it. But you grow up and it's just there. When I went to my second elementary school, it was a pretty good walk to school and we would be walking behind the school bus; we didn't have a bus but the white kids did. It wasn't actually a bus, it was like a man driving a covered wagon with car tires on it, and he would pick up the white kids. We would walk behind it. They'd be calling us names and so on. We'd retaliate if we could, calling them names, kid stuff. We never really took it that serious. We felt we were going to grow up and get out of there."

"So you were looking to get out as a child?"

"It was always on your mind. After you get old enough to realize that there *was* someplace else, you want to go."

"How did you know?"

"I didn't know exactly where, but we had a radio and I heard different shows and I knew there was another world out there and that was what I was thinking about." Dorothy fell silent and then said, "I also had this little friend, little white friend, who changed the way I felt about certain things. Her name was Hilda, Hilda Juanita. We were really pretty good friends, as far as it could go, for quite some time. But she was the same as that Gregory boy. Sometimes she could be so good to me, we talked like little girls do, but then she would be mean, or different, and I didn't quite understand that. As I came to understand it, I would get mean with her as well. There were times when I'd say, 'The heck with you.' The thing is, Hilda's father was a drunkard and a lot of times when he got out of control, her mother and sisters and she would run up to our house to get away from him, to keep him from beating them all up. They'd stay with us until he settled down. But they still felt like they were a little better than we were. No matter how poor or corrupt their families were, it seemed they felt they were better than any black person. It didn't matter how hard you worked. They had been taught by the generation before them that white ways and white skin were better than anything that was black. *And* we'd always been their servants. They didn't know anything about black people historically, we were brought here in chains, and they thought we were just supposed to be on the bottom. I think they were taught not to question it. It—it was also social. They didn't want any *real* socializing to go on. It was okay to spend a bit of time together. As long as it didn't get too close, they were happy to say 'Ole So-and-So's a good nigger.'

"But somehow there was still a genuine feeling between people sometimes. I remember after me and Hilda grew up and went to high school, we would still have conversations from time to time. And in later years she moved to Illinois, I remember somebody asking me about her, they said that she was up north and asking after me. I never followed up on it. It was one of those things. We could probably have been really good friends. But it was just the southern way. You don't mix."

I had never heard Dorothy talk like this. "But *why* were they like that? Everybody tells me *what* happened, but nobody says why."

"I don't know, except for the fact that maybe the whites thought that there would be mixing between blacks and whites as far as falling in love and affection between the sexes and there'd be more mulatto children, etcetera. They just thought it was wrong. Maybe they thought that people would get married, or that things might get a little better for black folks or something. They always wanted somebody underfoot. If you became true friends, then they couldn't step on you. We'd have to be equals. And that kind of socializing would lead to children, and they just did not want white women having children by black men. They wouldn't care if that Gregory boy and me had a sexual relationship, but they wouldn't want his sister going with one of my brothers.

"They were even suspicious of strange white men. I remember when one of the older Gregory girls went away to Ole Miss for a year, she was kind of on the wild side and after she was gone she went to New York and met this Jewish man and got married. When she brought him home, R.V. and me thought, 'Now we got to get us a good look at this Yankee.' We'd heard she had married a 'Yankee' and we didn't know what they were talking about. A Yankee? When we saw him, we saw that he was just a white man like the rest of them. So we wondered, 'Why they calling this man a Yankee? What's so special about him?' He did talk different, I believe he gave us a nickel or a dime, at that time you could buy a bar of candy or a bottle of pop with it. But the family, they were not happy. She was supposed to marry one of the good old boys from *here*."

Dorothy gazed out the window into the bright sunshine and the fields that stretched endlessly away from us. Then she approached my earlier question from another angle. "The thing with white people didn't jump out at you as a child. It's subtle. The realization that this is serious sneaks up on you. It sneaks up on you that you are considered different. All of the sudden you're not Arthur and Modena's little girl anymore. All of the sudden your friends, your white friends, are being mean to you, and you're less in their eyes. In your family you are a cherished child, but then all of the sudden somebody calls you black nigger and the kids that you've been playing with start to turn and point their behinds at you.

"You don't remember any specific event where it was announced what the deal was."

ONE AFTERNOON in New Albany, I had a cup of tea with Perna Simmons Robertson Wallace, "Aunt Pernie" to me, though I'd never quite figured out how, or even if, we were related. Born in 1906, she was one of the last survivors in our family of pre–World War I days, the dark ages of black experience. At that time whites were hardening the political tyranny they had imposed during Reconstruction and entrenching the sharecropper system, erasing the slight gains blacks had made after emancipation.

A healthy-looking elderly woman whose chief concession to age seemed to be a conscious deliberation in thought and speech, Aunt Pernie laughed and smiled during our conversation, happy to talk. "Oh, I remember lots of things that I seen and that happened," she said, "only I may remember some of them this week and some of them next week or way on over yonder. I'm eighty-four years old, and you don't think of it all in a row."

"What are you remembering today? Your school days?"

"I never went much to school."

"You never went to school?"

"No. I was the second child and there was four more under me and by the time I got big enough to go to school, why then, with them others, I had to help my mother. I had to stay with them little ones while my mother worked. And, like children do sometimes even now, I had bad legs [rickets] and I couldn't walk and our school, it was only three or four months right in the hard wintertime and sometimes we didn't have any way to get there. When I got around ten or twelve years old I went to working like folks worked then. You see, we didn't have no jobs like they have now, 'cause then you worked over to Miss Ann's [generic term for white women] house and clean up the house and whatever else they wanted cleaned up and that's about the only job you had until I was around thirty-five or forty years old, washing and ironing and all them things like that."

"Around World War II it started to change a little bit?"

"Yeah, it changed a little." She shrugged. "World War II changed it a little better than it was from World War I. World War I, it changed a *little* bit then. By World War II, I was married and keeping my house."

The entire modern civil rights movement, from Booker T. Washington and W. E. B. Du Bois to Martin Luther King and Malcolm X, had transpired in Perna's lifetime. How much had it affected her daily life; of how much had she been aware? "Aunt Pernie, do you remember a white man named Bilbo?"

"I don't remember him. Mostly I remember Roosevelt, when he came in we heard a lot about him, and he helped us. I could tell you more about him, but it might be over into next week before I think about it."

"Well, are you surprised by how much has changed here?"

She tilted her head to the side and shrugged. "I ain't exactly surprised, but I know how much it has changed. When my momma come on and raised all them kids, she didn't get *nothing*, all she got in pay was hand-me-downs. She'd go work for folks, but all they would give her would be something from their house that they didn't want. No money. We didn't get no money, hardly ever. When they did get a little money and buy us children something, it didn't cost more than a nickel. We'd get as much then for a nickel as you can get now for a dollar. Why, you could go up to the store and get a quarter's worth of sugar and it would last you a week. When I was coming up as a child, you could get ten or fifteen pounds for two dollars. It's so much different than it used to be, just about as much difference in times now as night and day."

"And that difference is for the better?"

"The better is now, because then we didn't have much. We lived on whatever we had, but it weren't nothing, weren't no improvements like there is now."

"Do you think the real difference came with Martin Luther King?"

She shook her head. "The change up to what it is now came along then, but when Roosevelt came along it was a bigger change than it was with any of them other presidents. You got more for your crops, you got more for your work, everything."

"Did your parents ever talk about slavery times? Did they remember?"

"My grandmother was born a slave. She was five years old when they freed them. I heard her say a whole lot about that, but she wasn't big enough to do nothing, except know that hard times were coming. I don't know too much about the slavery times because when I had gotten big enough to understand it, it used to be [it was in the past], but still a lot of folks can't realize how much it's something new. Every time it changes from one thing to another, something goes up different. You get more pay now, but you got to pay more for what you get. Whatever they put in to help you, something else over there gets a little more to take one way or another. They may not keep it as close as it used to be, but still, if you don't stay close to what you got, you can get as bad off as the fellow who don't got nothing. I used to hear my grandma and my momma say, 'Come day, go day.' "

"What does that mean?"

"Come day, go day. It be like folks work and get something for the work that day and use it that day and don't have nothing the next day. Come day, go day."

"But it's a lot different now?"

She shrugged again. "For some of the folks it's come day, go day. They get more than we ever got and still they ain't getting nothing. You understand? They don't have nothing."

MY COUSIN Deborah Dilworth was in the house and eventually sat and joined us. Debbie is thirty-four years old, and her life story mirrors much of Afro-American experience since World War II. My cousin Mary's daughter, Debbie was born in Chicago, growing up in the Robert Taylor Homes on the South Side, later moving farther out to the mid–South Side. She and her older siblings grew up in the urban maelstrom of Chicago in the sixties, seventies and eighties— drugs, teen pregnancy, street gangs. One of my stronger childhood memories is of being told that Debbie's brother Thomas had been shot on their front porch because he refused to join the local branch of the Blackstone Rangers, the only neighborhood organization that could guarantee a young man's safe passage to and from school. But Thomas survived, the gangs miraculously giving up on him and his brothers, and Mary's children struggled along to average American lives.

Debbie had a child, Quanniec, at age seventeen. Her health steadily declined from diabetes and kidney disease throughout her twenties, and it was thought that she and her children would be safer in New Albany with "the kin folks" and the slower pace of life. She moved back to Mississippi in the early eighties. I reminded her of our childhood summers at Grandma Edwards's farm.

"I didn't like to go up to Grandma Annie's house," she said, "because when you'd go up there it'd be *so* dark you couldn't see your feet, you couldn't see your hands. And they wouldn't let you use the outhouse at night, they thought you might get lost. So they made you use that little white pot with the red rim around it."

"That damned slop jar." I groaned. "I remember it."

"And it seemed like every part of the house was warm except for the one spot or maybe it was just the bed that was warm, because Grandma always had them doors open, she'd have everything wide open. Anything could have flown in there. But it wasn't like you were gonna tell Grandma, 'Close them windows!' Uh-uh, not way up there. You were on your own. I remember she got up real early and killed this hog and she came back and made me breakfast. I was eating these eggs and I thought they were about the best thing in the world, and I said, 'Grandma, these are some good old eggs,' and she said, 'Girl, them ain't no eggs, them's brains.' "

"Do you remember the rides down?" I asked.

"Mama would send me as soon as school was out. Oh, that Illinois Central was hot. That train would really be loaded. But I had to keep out of trouble. I always loved it, really. That's why I brought my own son back." Her son was now an A student and the star halfback for New Albany High School.

"What's the difference between Chicago and Mississippi?"

"Down here, it's slow. A slower lifestyle and that's why I brought my son down here, because I didn't want him to come up in that environment that I come up in. The gangs and drugs. It was as bad when I was growing up as it is now, but if I'd stayed up there I might have lost my boy."

"Do you think it's better here for black folks? Do you think we're better off down here than in the city?"

She sat up. "No, no. There's too much prejudice. People here in Mississippi, they show their prejudice. At home in Chicago they'll grin in your face. They'll grin in your face here, too, but they'll let you know where they're coming from."

"Wouldn't you rather have that?"

"I don't care what they think. I just want them to be polite. We ain't friends anyway."

Debbie had been one of the first blacks I had known to make the contemporary return migration. Older people have always retired south, but increasingly young people are making efforts to return and stay. I said, "In the thirties the majority of blacks was in the South, then in the sixties it was in the North, and now it's back to being in the South. I almost think they should have stayed in the first place."

Debbie called her mother into the room. "Mama, Anthony thinks we should have stayed in Mississippi all along. Why did you leave?"

Mary sat on the arm of a chair. "I left because I saw my mother going down on her knees scrubbing floors, out picking cotton and all of that, cleaning white people's houses, down doing their dirty work. I wasn't going to do that. As soon as I got out of school, I was leaving. I wasn't going to have none of that."

"But was life in the projects any better?" I asked her.

Mary held her ground. "At that time, yes, it was. It was a lot different than it is now. And for me it was better. It was better than what I was remembering. And we weren't always in the projects."

"But when you look at what's happened to black men my age, between, like, Thomas and me, half of them are dead or in prison. All that happened in the North."

She was subdued. "There were a lot of them that came up with my children that are dead or in jail, that's true, but a lot has to do with how you raise children. I don't care where you are, when it starts getting dark, you have to know where your children are. I didn't let mine run the streets. I didn't go to the movies, but I dropped them off at the movies and waited and picked them up at the movies. They got up and went to school and when it was over they came home from school. A lot of parents let their kids rip and run."

"She found it better for her up there," Debbie interjected, "like I found it better for *me* here. I could have stayed there, she could have stayed here. We would have dealt with it."

"Black folks were being held back in Mississippi," I said, "but at least they weren't suffering the way they seem to be now in Chicago."

"If you put it that way," Debbie answered, "then down here is better. The Klan isn't like it was when Mom and them was coming up. Now if the Klan come out, they liable to get crucified. Dead." Her mood changed, and darkened. "I'm going to tell you a little story. There was a boy here, his name was Robert Patterson. He was going with this girl, she was a white girl, on the rich side. She wasn't one of them poor white gals. There was this other boy, his name was Chris Ross. Robert and Chris were together this particular night, and they were going to meet their girls, both the girls were white, and they checked into that motel out there, the Southland. But when they checked in, somebody must have made a phone call. Robert had a Trans Am, Chris had a Grand Prix. Somebody called them and Robert had to leave, but he took Chris's car, supposedly to get these girls, but he never came back. They found him the next morning in the motel swimming pool, and the boy didn't swim. You see, Chris fell asleep, but when he woke up Robert was in the pool, Chris's car had disappeared and Robert's car was in the lot. It was a setup."

"Then what happened?"

"It brought the blacks together. I don't like to see blacks only come together like that, in tragedy. I'd rather see us together in normal times. These people around here, black people, they wanted to just murder, kill up white folks."

"Shouldn't they?"

"Why should you?" Debbie was incredulous. "Why should you kill a lot of people you don't know and you don't know who did what and when? You see, Robert was dealing with a rich white girl, not middle class, not one of these ones on welfare and food stamps, they don't care about that anymore. They say, 'Go on, take her.' But when you dealing with somebody's daughter that got a lot of money, you got a problem. They got to find some way to get rid of you. That's what they did, just a few years ago, right here in New Albany."

LYNCHING WAS on my mind the next day as Dorothy and I drove on. We were headed toward Oxford and Ole Miss on Highway 30, a perfectly maintained asphalt ribbon that snakes through the tall pines of the Holly Springs National Forest and the hamlet of Enterprise, where, in the late 1920s, a cousin of Arthur Visor's, L. Q. Ivy, had been lynched.

Ivy had been working on a five-man timber crew in the forest one Sunday afternoon—blacks frequently worked off-days to earn extra money—and had taken a water break. While walking to a well, he encountered a young white woman who later accused him of rape. Ivy maintained that he never so much as spoke to her, but the whole crew was arrested and jailed. After several hours of questioning, the other men were released; Ivy was seized from the county jail and murdered by a white mob.

Our destination, Ole Miss, had made Dorothy think of L. Q. Ivy. When I was deciding on colleges as a senior in high school, there was talk in our family that I might, in a triumphant return of sorts, go south and attend the University of Mississippi, where it had been Dorothy's unattainable dream to matriculate. Due to pressure from the murdered man's family, however, the never-solved Ivy lynching had resurfaced in the local news around that time; and it soured my mother on the idea of my heading south. (While no white man was ever charged in the murder of L. Q. Ivy, local black lore had it that every white man involved died "mysteriously before his time," from house fires, tractor accidents, well drownings and the like.)

My mother had been afraid that I wouldn't perceive or obey the codes of Mississippi life, the unstated norms of daily existence of which lynching was the ultimate enforcement. Extrajudicial vigilantism in the service of taboo has probably existed for as long as humans have lived in society—witness stonings of women to enforce monogamy, or tarring and feathering to enforce endogamy—and the American South has proven no exception.

Blacks were not the only southerners to have been "lynched," a term derived from the activities of one Colonel Charles Lynch of Virginia, whose kangaroo court flogged Crown sympathizers during the Revolutionary War. Lynching became a punishment of outlaws (see *The Ox-Bow Incident*) and rebellious slaves in the mid-nineteenth century, and during Reconstruction became the preferred mode of intimidating newly freed blacks. As Professor William Hair states, "the free blacks, no longer valued as property, were seen as threatening the existence of white civilization. The specter of Haiti, and its bloody slave rebellion of the 1790s, white fear, and predictions of race war helped multiply acts of terrorism."

The lynching fever reached its peak in the 1880s and 1890s, with 230 lynchings in 1892, the highest national number recorded. (These numbers reflect only those reported to the federal government and the urban press.) Mississippi accounted for 581 lynchings since 1882 (all but 42 of them black), the highest number in any state. These murders, often carried out with the complicity of legal authorities, were intended to punish several real or imagined offenses by black males: being "uppity," running afoul of a white man in business dealings, stealing, murder and, most certainly and most commonly, raping or fraternizing with white women, or merely making them uncomfortable. The last redoubt of southern white male ideology was "the sanctity of the white female," and any black man who broached this divide could expect to pay with his life.

The last man known to have been lynched in Mississippi for "despoiling" a white woman was Mack Charles Parker. As author Howard Smead relates, the lynching of Parker "carried many of the notorious elements of past Southern lynchings: charges of interracial rape, a mob storming the jail, widespread and detailed knowledge of the lynching conspiracy before and after, and no punishment for the mob." The Parker lynching occurred in 1959, before the eyes of the FBI and the nation.

Mack Charles Parker was born in Walthall County in 1936 and grew up in Lumberton. He was a dark and slight young man, who left Mississippi to join the army in 1954. In 1956, after being court-martialed twice for petty thievery and spending some time in the brig, he was separated from the military. Parker then returned to Mississippi, began driving a lumber truck for a living and, by all reports, was considered an average hardworking young man. He did not get into any trouble with the law.

Late on the night of February 23, 1959, while driving down dark Highway 11, Parker and several friends came upon the stalled automobile of the Walters family of Petal, Mississippi. The car's engine had seized from a thrown bearing, and Jimmy Walters had gone on foot for help, leaving in the car his pregnant wife, June, and young daughter, Debbie. Walters's departure is the last event of the evening that is universally agreed upon. A few minutes afterward, Parker and friends stopped, looked in the Walterses' car and drove off. Parker's friends claimed that he spoke then of raping the woman, and, after dropping them off in Lumberton, he allegedly returned to the stranded car, broke the window, opened the door and said, "You white trash bitch, I'm going to fuck you," then proceeded to rape June Walters in front of her child.

After a dragnet in Mississippi and Louisiana, thirty black men were brought in that night to Lumberton. Following a tip by the father of one of Parker's companions, the police arrested Parker the next morning, savagely beat him, then placed him in a lineup with the other blacks. Each man was forced to say "You white trash bitch, I'm going to fuck you" for June Walters to hear, and she dismissed each one until she got to Parker, who was last. June Walters identified Parker at that moment, but later said she couldn't be sure. The evidence against Parker was otherwise circumstantial, and he denied even having passed the car; but on the victim's identification and the other evidence he was indicted for rape and kidnapping. He was temporarily moved for safekeeping to Jackson, where he passed several lie-detector tests. Later moved back to Poplarville in preparation for the trial, Parker was held in the Pearl River County Jail, known for the statue of racist hero Theodore Bilbo on its front lawn.

On the night of April 24 a mob gathered, apparently motivated by the fear that Parker, like Robert Goldsby, a contemporary black Mississippian charged with murder, might be acquitted. Those in the mob also wanted to "redeem" the honor of June Walters, to prevent her from being questioned by Parker's attorneys on the stand and, concomitantly, to send a message to all "black fiends" in Pearl River and Lamar Counties.

Using keys provided by a deputy sheriff, a gang of men wearing masks entered Parker's cell, grabbed him, beat him with clubs and a garbage can, dragged him down three flights of stairs and down the jail's front steps to the town square, beat him further there as he screamed and threw him into the backseat of a car. The gang drove to Bogalusa, Louisiana, planning to dump him there, then changed their minds and drove back into Mississippi, where they parked, walked him out to the middle of the Bogalusa Bridge and shot him twice in the heart. His body was wrapped in chains and dumped into the Pearl River.

With Parker's disappearance, the FBI entered the case, charging the Mississippi State Highway Patrol with combing the fields and rivers of Pearl River County while federal agents staged one of the most intense door-to-door investigations in the bureau's history. The lynching had greatly embarrassed President Eisenhower in Europe and the Soviet Union, and the government, if only for purposes of propaganda, wanted the crime solved quickly and cleanly. The Parker case also caused much upset among moderates and conservatives in the South, as it gave impetus to northern liberals like Wayne Morse and Jacob Javits to pass new civil rights legislation in Congress.

Parker's body surfaced a week and a half later on May 4, amid a jam of drifting logs, two and a half miles downriver from the bridge. His body was identified by fingerprints and buried immediately after the autopsy. The coroner attributed the cause of death to "the hand of a person or persons unknown."

The white people of Poplarville, however, did know and closed ranks against the FBI, first blaming June Walters's relatives from Hattiesburg (who had publicly requested that Parker be left alone and brought to trial), then simply constructing an impenetrable wall of silence. Within the white community, the names of the perpetrators were common knowledge. Men had been solicited to join in the lynching, most refusing; later, the murderers bragged openly of what they had done. When questioned by the FBI, ringleader and Baptist minister James "Preacher" Lee proclaimed: "God's word set forth that the Negro is a servant." The FBI, concerned about the damage to its reputation the unsolved case would cause, heightened its pressure on a group of suspects.

The case took a tremendous toll on the whites of Poplarville. A female witness to the kidnapping attempted suicide to avoid questioning, then left town; mob member Houston Amacker attempted suicide and nearly succeeded; after FBI grilling, mob member Arthur Smith collapsed from what was thought to be a cerebral hemorrhage; Preacher Lee was hospitalized for internal injuries inflicted by Parker during the lynching; mob member Crip Reyer was institutionalized, along with his wife, for mental illness.

White Poplarville fought as long and as hard as it could. "It is strange," said state auditor Boyd Golding, "that the FBI wasn't invited to help catch the Negro Parker when he raped a young pregnant white mother while her little daughter was forced to look on." Suspect J. P. Walker complained of the FBI's talking to him "like I was a nigger or a dog or something," and of the bureau's wasting "$100,000 because of that nigger who was worth two cents."

As the townspeople and white supremacists around the state tried to discredit the FBI in order to derail the investigation, the case was also exploited by ambitious local politicians, in particular one Ross Barnett, who attempted to duplicate the regular historical trick of riding racial conflict into the statehouse. A Barnett supporter charged that the current governor, J. P. Coleman, and his attorney general, Joe Patterson, had failed to uphold "the rights of Mississippi citizens against the arrogant 'gestapo tactics' . . . of the FBI. White citizens of Pearl River County have been subjected to such harassment by the FBI that a number of them are hospitalized . . . perhaps the fact that our governor begged the FBI agents to come to Poplarville explains this. It is painfully obvious that our governor is overreacting in his toothsome role as Mississippi's goodwill ambassador to the integrated hinterlands."

The town's stonewalling and antifederal insurgency worked. On Monday, May 25, 1959, the Justice Department announced that the FBI was unable to prove any violation of federal law in the lynching of Mack Charles Parker. Though it was known that the murderers had crossed from Mississippi into Louisiana, making the crime a federal offense, this could not be proved; and federal civil rights violations were much more narrowly construed than they would be a mere three years later. The bureau turned over its extensive files to the state, where the perpetrators could be charged with capital crimes. But the failure of the federal effort was tantamount to exoneration, as whites were not convicted of killing blacks in Mississippi state courts in the 1950s. As Howard Smead states, "Without pressure from the federal government, the mob would remain free, and everyone in Poplarville, Pearl River County, Mississippi and the South knew it."

Parker's guilt has never been proved, nor has his innocence. There are strong arguments on both sides, and the victim and sole legally competent eyewitness, June Walters, never stated unequivocally that she thought her attacker was the accused. Ross Barnett was elected governor later that year and led what would become the last stand of massive resistance to racial change, including the now-legendary showdown with twenty-three thousand federal troops at Ole Miss. Mack Charles Parker was lynched and his murderers went unpunished; but the old ways were losing their inevitability.

DOROTHY AND I walked onto the Ole Miss campus in the middle of a bustling Thursday afternoon. It was homecoming week, but otherwise this seemed a typical day on a college campus, students either rushing back and forth across the green and in and out of buildings or else loitering peacefully, sitting at tables and under trees, enjoying the warmth of the late-fall day. This was Dorothy's first visit to the campus in fifteen years, since she had accompanied me when I came as a high school junior; and she was frankly amazed by the ease with which visible numbers of black students now traversed the campus. We sat down on a bench across from the Lyceum administration building—the very place where Governor Ross Barnett stood in 1962, promising white Mississippians that blacks would never enter and setting events in motion that would culminate in riot.

Dorothy started talking about the black students she saw. "A lot of them don't really identify with the cause of Mississippi or with blackness, or with what it took to get here. They don't care what it took as long as they can get in on some of the benefits. I mean, they probably don't even know who James Meredith is."

This lamentation about the historical amnesia of young blacks was never far from the surface of any conversation I had with their elders. I'd even heard statistics on that trend cited by an Ole Miss professor: "I heard that somebody took a poll here, and nine out of ten black kids didn't know who Medgar Evers was."

"That's what I'm saying." Dorothy looked pained. "All that stuff happened right here." She pointed at the steps of the Lyceum. "I used to dream about Ole Miss. We were taught that if we went to school and tried to take care of ourselves and not get into trouble, we could get our education and be whatever we wanted to be. That's what I tried to teach *you*. Now for *us* that was a lie, but we didn't know it and we kept trying for it. We had to keep going. It seemed like it was such a special place. We wanted to come to Ole Miss because it had such special significance for the white folks. But these kids today, it doesn't mean as much to them. They probably think that I could've gone here if I'd wanted to. All they know is that they can go, and that it's going to be something special for them on their résumé. Look at them, they don't even acknowledge other black folks." Very few of the Ole Miss blacks greeted us, an omission unthinkable for Dorothy's generation. "They're walking past us and pretending we aren't sitting here. Do they know what happened at this spot? I'm not saying you have to go around slapping everybody on the back, but we weren't always just strolling around this great symbol of the South. These kids need to remember what it cost."

The cost of which Dorothy spoke was, of course, the 250-year battle of black Mississippians for recognition and civil rights; and she was, more specifically, referring to the battle for Ole Miss. In 1962, James Meredith, Medgar Evers, John and Robert Kennedy, John Doar, the Justice Department, the Mississippi NAACP and federal troops, National Guardsmen and U.S. marshals fought Ross Barnett and a mob of thousands over whether Meredith would be the first black to register and attend classes at Ole Miss. Medgar Evers had tried in 1953, and failed. Clyde Kennard, another unsung hero of the civil rights movement, had applied to Mississippi Southern College (now the University of Southern Mississippi) in 1960, and had suffered grievously.

Kennard, a scholarly veteran of World War II, had finished his junior year at the University of Chicago when both of his parents became ill. A native of the Hattiesburg area, Kennard returned to Mississippi to care for his parents and attempted to enroll at Southern, the best local school. His application was denied; and in a campaign of terror that illustrated the malignant dedication of Mississippi whites to segregation, he was in the next three years arrested for possessing alcohol in dry Lamar County, a charge which didn't stick because he was a known teetotaler, then framed for the theft of five bags of chicken feed found in his garage. Kennard was convicted of this felony, though someone else confessed to the crime and admitted to having placed the bags there. Kennard was sentenced to seven years of hard labor at Parchman penitentiary. He could never again apply to a Mississippi college, as this privilege was denied felons, but his travails did not end there: Kennard became gravely ill with cancer while in Parchman, and the prison authorities denied him medical attention for more than a year. They relented in 1963 and released Kennard, who, broken at last, returned to Chicago and died shortly thereafter.

Medgar Evers had organized Kennard's various legal defenses, and the stakes must have weighed on him heavily as he strategized with James Meredith on what would prove to be the final assault on segregated higher education in the state. Meredith, an air force veteran, was born in 1933 to property-owning blacks near Kosciusko, Mississippi. His air force experience exposed him to whites as social equals, which emboldened him to challenge the entrenched system. The federal legal precedents for integration, like *McLaurin* and

Gaines, had been in place for almost ten years, but Mississippi schools were no closer to actual open enrollment when Meredith applied than they had been in 1950.

By Labor Day 1962, the legal obstacles designed to delay Meredith's registration and matriculation had been removed by an order of the federal district court in New Orleans, which had jurisdiction. Governor Barnett immediately responded by promising, in a televised speech, that the ruling would not stand. He then personally prevented Meredith from entering the university by standing in the door of the registrar's office. Meredith responded by getting a further court order, along with a threat of federal contempt charges against Barnett and Ole Miss officials.

On September 25, John Doar, an assistant to President Kennedy, and U.S. marshal James McShane escorted Meredith into the federal building in Jackson, where he was to register as per a newly wrought agreement with Barnett. Historian Taylor Branch describes, though, what happened next, in a Mississippi state government building:

> Barnett, bathed in television lights, blocked the threshold of room 1007. Legislators inside climbed atop chairs for a better view. As Doar moved forward to explain the Fifth Circuit's orders to Barnett, television and radio stations transmitted the confrontation to Mississippians across the state. Barnett "interposed" Mississippi's sovereignty, as embodied in his own person, between Meredith and the university officials, who maintained an outward willingness to obey the orders.
>
> "Which one is Meredith?" Barnett inquired, sparking titters of laughter, as the familiar and well-known Meredith, standing in front of Barnett, was the only Negro in sight. Barnett read to Meredith his second proclamation of interposition, ending that he did "hereby finally deny you admission to the University of Mississippi." A Rebel Yell went up from the crowds gathered around transistor radios ten floors below. . . . One state senator hailed Barnett's stand as "the most brilliant piece of statesmanship ever displayed in Mississippi." Another vowed to persevere "regardless of the cost to time, effort, money and in human lives."

U.S. attorney general Robert Kennedy, however, was determined that the federal government's authority not be mocked or undermined, and the next day a series of political maneuvers was started on both sides. Ross Barnett continued to breathe fire in public. His peroration at that Saturday's Ole Miss football game featured such statements as "I love Mississippi, I love her people, her customs! And I love and respect her heritage!" uttered while forty thousand partisans chanted "Never, never, never, never, never, no-o-o, never!" and waved the Confederate battle flag. Secretly, however, Barnett tried to negotiate with the Kennedys, but his subterfuge in the end led to one of the worst conflagrations between U.S. troops and civilians in history, a battle that can be considered one of the last of the Civil War.

The day after Barnett's speech, Meredith returned to the campus escorted by a civilian force of five hundred U.S. marshals, border patrolmen and deputized prison guards. The Mississippi National Guard was mobilized and pledged to obey federal authority, and several airborne units of the U.S. Army were on alert as far away as New Jersey, poised to converge and deploy at Oxford in four hours if needed. On the other side, a mob of two thousand stood outside the Lyceum building, chanting and throwing rocks and bottles and produce, goaded on by Barnett, Senator George Yarbrough and other officials.

At 7:25 p.m., Mississippi highway patrolmen were ordered to pull out of the increasingly violent situation by their commanders, and their departure precipitated the full-fledged uprising. Rioters with high-powered weapons fired on U.S. marshals and border patrolmen. The siege continued all night, as the mob tried to smash into the marshals' sanctuary in the administration building with a car and then a bulldozer. One hundred sixty marshals were wounded, and a French journalist was killed.

The next morning, after the direct intervention of three thousand regular army troops with twenty thousand more in the immediate area, eleven days after his first attempt, James Meredith registered and attended his first class at the University of Mississippi.

ALL OF THIS had happened within my short lifetime, twenty-eight years ago, in the same place where I now sat with Dorothy. "It seems like," she said, "most of us black folks have become so shallow that we're not interested in how we came to be here, whether in the United States or in Mississippi. Or Ole Miss. You kids aren't interested in the forefathers fighting and sitting in the square and trying to vote so you could vote. We went to little country schools and learned what we could from a teacher who probably had not been past the eighth grade and we kept fighting to make it better for our kids, but they don't seem to be interested in that. They don't understand what it took to get them here. As a child I would never have thought I'd be walking the Ole Miss grounds like this, let alone seeing all these black children here. I remember I thought this must be someplace very special. I used to think that if I could get a chance to go here, that would make everything all right—you wouldn't be second class or anything anymore. It seemed like Ole Miss was where it was at. Even for white folks. I used to think that even after I was grown, when I got enough money I would come here, just to say I had. It doesn't hold quite that significance for me any longer. Not being able to come here, that was kind of a slap in the face, but now I kind of feel like, 'Hey, look at me now,' because we did get black kids here. We did it."

But something about contemporary Ole Miss angered me. "What about all this Johnny Reb stuff. All this Confederate nonsense." The campus remains a museum, if not a temple, of Confederate memorabilia, flags, statues and names of buildings and streets. "Why should blacks have to be around all this praise of holding them down?"

"I don't pay that any attention. It's just a way white people have of hanging on and bragging about their accomplishments. It's not like *they* have actually done anything themselves. They like to brag on the lie, the myth. They have the money and they own everything and they can do whatever they want. I don't let it bother me. The most important thing is that we are here. Just because somebody calls you a nigger doesn't mean that you are. You know that you are not. Johnny Reb don't mean a hill of beans to me. I never knew who he was, anyway. If Johnny Reb came and knocked on my door, then I might think about him. A little. But he's just a figment of these white folks' imagination."

"Do you think it was worth it?"

"What?"

"What it cost."

"Definitely."

"Even if younger blacks, as you say, are forgetting what it took to advance? If they've forgotten those who died?"

Strangely, she smiled. "It was. It was. It was worth it. Yes. We have a right to have what everybody else has and we played our part and paid our dues in this society, even if it was just pulling cotton sacks or chopping the row. We paid our dues. My forefathers were brought here and they paid a price and I feel that these children have a right. Somebody had to pay that price for our freedom, just like you have to pay the price for anything else you might want. It was worth it. We want to be able to say, 'Yes, I went to Ole Miss,' we want to be part of the Old South. We were here, weren't we?

"These white folks ain't gonna get rid of us. We had our share in building this country and we were not allowed to express ourselves and have freedoms." Then she shifted, and addressed me directly. "Look where you came from, how hard your forefathers had to work for what we have. If we'd had a chance to go to school and live in the real society, think of what we could have accomplished! It was worth it. Martin Luther King would say it was worth it. Medgar Evers would say it was worth it. He'd say, 'I didn't get to go there, but, hey, you all still got somebody there.' I think he's looking down from somewhere in glory, he's laughing and shaking his head and saying 'We did it!' He might have had to give his life, but that's the way it goes. Somebody has to pay. If you give your life to something worthwhile and it goes on after you, then what more can be said?"

"And the pain?"

"It was worth it. Somebody here at Ole Miss appreciates it. Maybe even somebody white. Somebody here will be glad that all of us made a new path for them."

Elegy for the Memories of My Mother

I see her stare into the distance and imagine
she sees the same yield of cotton,

then her mother, who did not live to see
today, to stand across this future field and harvest

and wave her home. It is October, creeping
toward frost, the leaves are turning

from dreams to grief, and I wish I knew a song
to sing to my mother, a song that would stop

me from thinking that she is my mother
and should be singing to me. We are under the sky

of her childhood, distant blue memories.
Geese float lazily south, today and in her

memory, their white wings swing lazily
like the pages of a book no one reads

left open in the breeze. She wants to read
to me, and remember, but the words fade

to a mercury gray, and slip away,
by blindness and time betrayed.

Medgar Evers

There is a road
into the sunset
that does not begin
and has no
destination,
a country road
in the Delta,
gravel, blacktop,
dirt; a black ribbon
binds the world.

There you are,
past where you
were going,
where we
cannot arrive.
The darkness nods
and spills
dark blood
from the bottle of night.

Migrations

Over water, through long empty space
great flocks of birds

Through jungles and forest, over
land, over
            mountain ranges

Wind, wing, diesel, wind-driven
ships, large combustion machines
Large flocks of birds follow trains
tracing rivers and valleys,
the high ways, the fly ways
                        of north and south

From here to there surviving gin
and thresher, years, defibrillating spinners
spinning
                        black wings
                        black birds
                        black angels

THREE

Rebels

DURING MY early travels in Mississippi I had come to understand something of the mythology and the reality of the state, and had come to a closer understanding of my mother's experience there, of what it had meant to her and, by extension, me. The more I learned, the more I became aware of white society in a way I'd never before been. Though much of the public history of Mississippi seemed to revolve around African-Americans, I was beginning to see that at least half the real story lay in places other than those commonly considered.

With the conclusion of the War of 1812, the United States became truly a nation, unthreatened anywhere on the continent, ready to seize what would come to be known as its manifest destiny, God's supposed intent that whites possess, exploit and rule North America. Erasing from the Old Southwest and the frontier both British and native influence, settlers began pouring into the Mississippi Territory, of which only the western half (the southern portion of the state today) was organized. The territory consisted of thirteen counties gained in the 1805 Choctaw Cession: Jackson, Hancock, Greene, Wayne, Lawrence, Marion, Pike, Amite, Wilkinson, Franklin, Claiborne, Jefferson and Adams, the seat of which was Natchez. (These constitute the present-day counties bearing the same names, plus Lincoln, Jefferson Davis, Covington, Jones, Walthall, Lamar, Forrest, Perry, George, Stone, Harrison and Pearl River.) The remainder of the state was Indian Country, "wilderness" traversable only by the Natchez Trace, the Jackson Military Road and riverboat; but that would soon change.

On March 1, 1817, the Mississippi Territory was divided in two, roughly the areas that form present-day Mississippi and Alabama. In July of that year, delegates from every county met in the town of Washington to write a constitution in preparation for petitioning to become a state. The constitution of 1817, as it is called, held that representation in the lower house would be determined by the white taxable population, a measure chosen to protect the interests of landowners (the largest taxpayers). Voters were limited to white male taxpayers and those serving in the state militia, and elective office was proscribed to all except those meeting the following restrictions: representatives had to own 150 acres or five hundred dollars of real estate; senators, 300 acres or one thousand dollars of real estate; and the governor, 600 acres or two thousand dollars. Free slaves were prohibited from the legislature without their former owners' personal consent. And the constitution forbade the importation of new slaves into Mississippi as merchandise. This last provision, however, was not a sign of progressivism: local slaveholders felt that slave traders and holders from out of state were dumping inferior and troublesome workers on them and wished to stop this practice. The ban of 1817 and several others—in 1819, 1832 and 1837—did little to prevent actual trading in state, and in 1846 all prohibitions were lifted and the trade flourished. The constitution of 1817 also stated that slave owners should treat slaves humanely, and provide all essentials, and that the state could seize and sell any slaves who were mistreated.

The Mississippi state constitution was accepted by President James Madison on December 10, 1817, and Mississippi became the twentieth of the United States. Within the state's document, however, lay the seeds of divisions which would trouble white residents in the years to come.

On October 18, 1820, Mississippi folk hero Andrew Jackson "accepted" the signature of the Choctaw chief Pushmataha to the

Treaty of Doak's Stand, named for a rest stop on the Natchez Trace north of today's Canton, a clearing where hundreds of Choctaw gathered that day as guests of the United States government. Jackson brought with him twenty thousand dollars' worth of beer, corn and liquor, and an offer to trade thirteen million acres across the Mississippi River between the Arkansas and Red Rivers for five million acres in Mississippi proper. Pushmataha did not want to sign, but as Jackson edged from treaties to open threats, he acknowledged the inevitable. The cession at Doak's Stand resulted in white control of the lower Delta and central Mississippi; but the whites asked for renegotiation, taking away even the new Choctaw lands, when it was discovered shortly after the treaty was signed that settlers were already living on the new Choctaw holdings in Arkansas and Oklahoma. At this time, whites controlled roughly half the land in Mississippi.

In 1829 Jackson became president of the United States. A strong believer in Indian removal, he provided the opportunity for white Mississippians to assume ironclad control of the entire state. In January of 1830, the Mississippi legislature placed all Native Americans within state boundaries under the jurisdiction of Mississippi laws and government. This meant that Choctaw and Chickasaw laws and customs no longer had any acknowledged legal effect, and to avoid being reduced to a condition similar to that of the black slaves, without property or rights, they would have to leave. On September 27, 1830, at Dancing Rabbit Creek in present-day Noxubee County, the Choctaw grudgingly signed a treaty providing for "peace and friendship between the United States and the Choctaw people and perpetual security of the new home." Along with promises of education, land for the Choctaw, less than that provided in the Doak's Stand treaty, was promised in Indian Territory. This third Choctaw Cession granted white Mississippians the rest of the Delta and much of eastern Mississippi. The Chickasaw held on to their lands for two more years, negotiating with whites, including President Jackson himself, and finally succumbed on October 20, 1832, at Pontotoc Creek, west of Tupelo. The Pontotoc treaty gave the whites more than six million acres, and this, combined with the previous and relatively small Tombigbee Cession of 1816, accounted for all the remaining land in present-day Mississippi.

THE 1830s in Mississippi were known as Flush Times. Following the cessions of aboriginal lands came a boom, described in these words at the time by Robert Walker of Natchez: "The feet of thousands press upon the borders of this new purchase to pitch their tents in the wilderness—Kentucky's coming, Tennessee's coming, Alabama's coming, and they're coming to join the joyous crowds of Mississippians." Land was literally dirt cheap, $1.25 an acre from the federal government on a signature, and in ten years Mississippi's total population rose from fewer than 150,000 to more than 350,000—the number of slaves expanding steadily as well, from 66,178 to 196,577, with the price of a healthy young black male reaching $1,600 by 1836.

A century earlier the Mississippi Bubble had occurred, a financial boom fueled by speculation in land and economic development that crashed in scandal in 1731. French investors lost millions of dollars. They had anticipated a thriving colony of sugar and indigo plantations, but these crops were labor-intensive and prey to insect infestations; the export company failed to generate profits and folded. The 1830s saw a similar collapse, as overexpansion led to another inflationary cycle of boom and bust. According to Joseph Baldwin, a landholder of that time, "prices rose like smoke." Speculators signed for the easy land terms, intending to flip their holdings for large profits. But in 1837, Andrew Jackson issued a Treasury order directing federal land offices to accept only gold or U.S. currency for land purchases, and the speculative cycle screeched to a halt. The state legislature, in an attempt to prop up the economy, founded a bank and sold five million dollars' worth of bonds to capitalize it. The so-called Union Bank went bankrupt from defaults within a year, and the state was forced to repudiate the bonds, shedding any legal responsibility for repayment.

Early in this tumultuous decade, in 1832, the Mississippi state constitution had been rewritten to end property qualifications for elective office and to ensure universal suffrage for white males. All offices, including that of judge, were made elective. And though this provision was never enforced, the new constitution outlawed the trafficking of slaves on May 1, 1833, and forbade importation of slaves even by their masters.

In 1845, the United States annexed the territory of Texas, precipitating war with Mexico over the future state and the Rio Grande. The conflict, which broke out on May 9, 1846, is crucial to Mississippi history because, on August 8 of the same year, President James Polk made a simple request to Congress for $2 million to fund peace negotiations with Mexico. To that appropriation, in what would prove perhaps the most fateful parliamentary maneuver in American history, Representative David Wilmot of Pennsylvania attached an amendment demanding that lands acquired in hostilities from Mexico be admitted to the Union as free states. The Wilmot Proviso was never passed; but it assured the issue of slavery a preeminence in American politics and society that would end only with the emancipation nearly seventeen years later. Since the 1820 Missouri Compromise, the country had been tenuously organized around a balance of slave and free states, and the southern bloc feared the admission of additional "free soil" would spell the end of their hold over the House and Senate.

The resultant rupture between slave and free states led to the Civil War. As early as 1850, a Mississippi senator named Jefferson Davis proclaimed a willingness to lead his state in secession. Throughout the 1850s Mississippians argued the issue of loyalty to the Union, with secessionists gaining and consolidating power as the decade wore on. Early in the decade, the slave states held a convention in Nashville to determine strategy with regard to the growing national concerns of free soil, fugitive slaves and abolition.

Adding to the turmoil roiling the South, in 1854 Kansas and Nebraska were admitted to the Union as territories without any explicit slave policy, leading to a vicious war in Kansas between free soil and pro-slavery forces. Bloody Kansas, as the conflict was known, saw atrocities, massacres and merciless search-and-destroy raids committed by both sides. The antislavery soldiers included a man who would loom large in abolitionist history, John Brown.

In 1857, the *Dred Scott* decision of the United States Supreme Court provoked a constitutional crisis. Scott, a slave, had been taken by his master, Dr. John Emerson, from slaveholding Missouri to the free state of Illinois and to the Wisconsin Territory for extended periods of residence. After Emerson's death Scott brought suit for his freedom, claiming that his residence in Illinois and Wisconsin qualified him for free status. Scott won in the lower court, but that decision was overturned by the Missouri Supreme Court. Scott would remain a slave, the court ruled, because he was not a citizen—slaves were barred from citizenship—and therefore did not have the legal right to petition the court. Also, the court said, Scott had petitioned in Missouri and would have to accept that court's jurisdiction.

In Mississippi, planter and yeoman alike were agitated by these events. Secessionist Mississippi senator Albert Gallatin Brown proclaimed abolition a disaster for southern whites: "The Negro will intrude into his [the white man's] presence—insist on being treated as an equal—that he shall go to the white man's table, and the white man to his—that his son shall marry the white man's daughter, and the white man's daughter his son. In short that they shall live on terms of perfect social equality." Not all white Mississippians favored secession. Ironically, many planters favored the Union, trusting Free-Soil Party promises not to eradicate slavery in states in which it was already practiced; and many small farmers felt they had nothing to gain from going to war over slavery, as they themselves owned no slaves.

On October 16, 1859, John Brown of Kansas led a force of nineteen men, including five blacks, in a takeover of the federal arsenal at Harpers Ferry, Virginia. Their plan was to seize guns and ammunition, arm thousands of slaves and foment slave insurrections throughout the South. On October 18 a force of marines commanded by soon-to-be-legendary Lieutenant Colonel Robert E. Lee attacked and savaged Brown's position, killing ten, including two of Brown's sons, while retaking the arsenal.

Brown was tried for treason and convicted on October 31, "quite *certain*," he said, "that the crimes of this *guilty* land will never be purged away but with blood." He was hanged on December 2, with six of his surviving men following him to the gallows. Brown's martyrdom fueled the antislavery cause. Ralph Waldo Emerson said Brown's sacrifice would "make the gallows as glorious as the cross." The stage was set for the now-inevitable conflict of

North and South; as fear and trepidation on the part of the southerners became endemic to them, it was clear that elements in the North would stop at nothing to end slavery, and that secession and war, if necessary, were the only means by which they could guarantee their social and economic security. The entire southern civilization was built upon the foundation of slavery, and Brown's action, however futile, symbolized for the South the gravity of the threat. Southern whites greatly feared the election in 1860 of a Republican, northern candidate. Representative Reuben Davis of Mississippi told Congress in 1860:

> We will resist . . . We will sacrifice our lives, burn our houses, and convert our sunny South . . . into a wilderness waste. . . . We will not be driven one inch beyond where we now stand, we will be butchered first . . . we of the South will tear this Constitution to pieces, and look to our guns for justice.

Abraham Lincoln was elected president in November 1860, confirming the South's worst fears, and southern states wasted no time in responding. Mississippi was the second state to secede from the Union, leaving on January 9, 1861, roughly three weeks after South Carolina. The legislature had authorized in 1860 an election to select delegates for a secession convention, and these delegates voted eighty-four to fifteen in favor of seceding. In the next few weeks, Georgia, Alabama, Florida, Louisiana and Texas followed, and on February 4, 1861, these states met in Montgomery, Alabama, to establish the Confederate States of America. On February 18, Jefferson Davis was elected president of the Confederacy, and in the next two months he oversaw the Confederate takeover of all federal buildings, post offices and military bases in the states he controlled.

On April 12, 1861, Confederate soldiers and artillery at Charleston, South Carolina, opened fire on the federal troops holding Fort Sumter. As described by James McPherson: "After thirty-three hours of bombardment by four thousand shot and shells which destroyed part of the fort and set the interior on fire, [Major Robert] Anderson's exhausted garrison surrendered. Able to man only a few of Sumter's forty-eight mounted guns, they had fired a thousand rounds in reply—without much effect. On April 14 the American flag came down and the Confederate stars and bars rose over Sumter."

The nation was soon plunged into the most severe crisis of its brief history, with war raging from Texas to Pennsylvania. Mississippi's first official battle took place early in the war, at Ship Island off Biloxi, in July 1861. Confederate soldiers had taken control of a fort under construction there and were attacked by the USS *Massachusetts*. The rebels were not dislodged until September, and U.S. admiral David Farragut was then able to use the island as a base in his ultimately successful campaign against New Orleans and Confederate forces on the lower Mississippi River.

Two days after seceding, the state of Mississippi fortified the high bluffs at Vicksburg. Removing those battlements would take Union forces nearly two and a half years, a campaign that would eventually prove to be central to the federal victory.

In February 1862, after unexpected and bruising Union defeats the previous summer and fall at the battle of Manassas (also known as First Bull Run), Virginia; Wilson's Creek, Missouri; and Ball's Bluff (also known as Leesburg), Virginia, Ulysses S. Grant led United States victories at Fort Henry, on the Tennessee River, and Fort Donelson, an important Confederate supply depot. Thus began the campaign for Vicksburg, a bustling river town two hundred miles south of Memphis. Vicksburg was believed to be the back door of the Confederacy, but was so well defended along the riverfront that it could be taken only by land. As long as the rebels controlled Vicksburg, they controlled the Mississippi, depriving the Union of a crucial commercial and military supply route and staking unassailable claim to lands adjoining the river.

By April 6, 1862, Grant had worked his troops down to Pittsburg Landing, Tennessee, where they made camp at Shiloh Church. In a surprise dawn attack, Confederate forces under the direction of Albert Sidney Johnston attacked the Union forces with the most firepower that had yet been seen in the western theater and engaged in what was to that point the bloodiest battle in human history. In two days more than twenty thousand soldiers were killed or wounded, including Johnston himself, who was wounded and bled to death the first afternoon.

Shiloh was a costly victory for the Union, but was a victory nonetheless. News of the Confederate defeat led the nearby rebel garrison at Island Number 10, off New Madrid, Missouri, to surrender the next day, opening the Mississippi as far south as Memphis. On that same day, General Grant's superior, Henry Halleck, took personal control of an army one hundred thousand strong that stalked the retreating Confederates back to Corinth, Mississippi, the junction of rebel north–south and east–west railroads. On May 25, after six weeks under siege, weeks of typhoid, dysentery and pestilence, the Confederates again fell back, abandoning Corinth to the Yankees. In the meantime, Memphis and New Orleans had been retaken by the Union, and for all practical purposes only Vicksburg remained in the west.

The east, however, was a different story. As Corinth was falling, Confederate forces under Robert E. Lee were preparing for a successful summer, bloodying the Federals at Yorktown, Fair Oaks and the series of engagements known as the Seven Days, facing defeat only at Antietam, a battle the Union had to win or else lose the war. The North was facing imminent invasion, and the Confederacy's success was leading European countries to consider recognizing the Confederate States of America as a nation. The pivotal conflict at Antietam took place on September 17, 1862, and five days later Abraham Lincoln issued a statement consisting, in part, of these words:

> On the first day of January, in the year of our Lord one thousand eight hundred and sixty-three, all persons held slaves within any state, the people whereof shall then be in rebellion against the United States, shall be then, thenceforth, and forever free.

This was the Emancipation Proclamation, about which Lincoln himself stated, "If my name ever goes into history, it was for this." The proclamation was primarily designed to weaken the Confederacy by creating chaos within its regions. In August 1862, Lincoln had said, "If I could save the Union without freeing *any* slave, I would do it; and if I could save it by freeing some and leaving others alone, I would also do that." This view reflected the sentiment of much of the country: many Yankees were more interested in preserving the Union and defeating the rebels than in freeing slaves. An editorial in a northern paper ran, "A large majority can see no reason why *they* should be shot for the benefit of niggers and Abolitionists."

In the popular imagination, the emancipation is a discrete event, *the* event that freed the slaves. In reality it was only one more moment in the as yet unresolved history of race relations in this country, like the framing of the Constitution, in which blacks had been declared three-fifths human, or the *Dred Scott* case that had so much to do with the precipitation of the war, or the *Plessy* and *Brown* cases to come. In the incremental progress of black Americans toward legal equality as citizens, the proclamation was the smallest of steps.

Blacks would return to harsh labor after the war in sharecropping, a system that differed from slavery only in degree, and a full hundred years would pass after the advent of that economic system before any real progress occurred in the social position of southern blacks. But emancipation did weaken the Confederacy, as it became harder and harder for the rebels to produce food and commerce or to maintain a semblance of day-to-day life within their accustomed institutions. Some slaves stayed loyal, others fled the plantations, still others refused to work unless paid.

"SEE WHAT a lot of land these fellows hold, of which Vicksburg is the key," Abraham Lincoln had said at the start of Grant's campaign. "The war can never be brought to a close until the key is in our pocket." And this city on the Mississippi was the war's last rebel blockade. But how to take it? The town's fortified bluff guarded a horseshoe bend, a gauntlet through which no ship could pass. The Confederate commander of the city had announced, "Mississippians don't know, and refuse to learn, how to surrender. . . . If Commodore Farragut . . . can teach them, let him come and try." In his memoirs, Grant wrote:

> The ground about Vicksburg is admirable for defence. On the north it is about two hundred feet above the Mississippi River at the highest point and very much cut up by the washing rains; the

ravines were grown up with cane and underbrush, while the sides and tops were covered with a dense forest. Farther south the ground flattens out somewhat and was in cultivation. But here, too, it was cut up by ravines and small streams. . . . The work to be done, to make our position as strong against the enemy as his was against us, was very great. . . .

Having consolidated his victories at Fort Henry and Fort Donelson, Grant took command of the Department of the Tennessee of the Union Army late in 1862. On November 4 he left Bolivar, Tennessee, planning to ride down the Mississippi Central Railroad to the capital of the state, Jackson. The Confederate opposition, led by John C. Pemberton, kept falling back, digging in south of Grenada. Grant was planning to mount a land attack on Jackson and then Vicksburg, but this strategy was thwarted by dissent within the Union command, and on December 20, Earl van Dorn and 3,500 Confederate cavalry sneaked behind federal lines and destroyed the Union's supply depot at Holly Springs. Grant was forced to fall back and wait.

That winter Grant's engineers tried to divert the Mississippi away from Vicksburg by building a new channel to the west that would allow gunboats to get south of town, and also tried to dig canals in the Yazoo River north of town to lower the depth of the Mississippi. All their attempts failed. But the Union soldiers kept busy and were in good condition when spring came. On April 17, 1863, as a diversion, Grant sent Colonel Benjamin Grierson on a raid through the very heart of Mississippi. Starting in Grand Junction, Tennessee, Grierson and his men tore through the Mississippi towns of Ripley, New Albany, Pontotoc, Houston, Starkville, Louisville, Philadelphia, Decatur, Garlandville, Montrose, Raleigh, Westville, Hazlehurst, Union Church, Brookhaven and Summit, destroying rail lines, burning towns and terrifying the civilian population. In addition, Grant sent Sherman to attack Snyder's Bluff north of Vicksburg, and had other Union troops cut Confederate supply lines into town. These actions forced Pemberton to commit rebel troops away from Grenada, and Grant then moved massively with his main force on the western, Louisiana, side of the Mississippi, meeting up with the forces of General John A. McLernand and Admiral David D. Porter. McLernand and Porter had run the guns of Vicksburg by boat late at night on April 16 and were now in a position to cover with heavy guns Grant's crossing back into Mississippi.

On April 30, Grant crossed over into Bruinsburg, Mississippi, and began marching northeast. At Port Gibson, on May 1, his troops engaged rebels and won, as they did again in the next two weeks at Raymond, Jackson, Champion's Hill and Big Black River. On May 17 the Confederates retreated to within the fortifications at Vicksburg.

I SPENT hours riding around Vicksburg and the surrounding countryside, thinking about the Civil War, what it had cost and what it had wrought. Walking through the sharp gullies and close ridges of the battlefield, now a military park, I was struck by the range and intensity of the fighting, how close and dirty and bloody it must have been.

Despite the examples of valor and bravery, however, it became clear to me on reflection that, for the ruling groups, "the War between the States" had been precisely that, a struggle over who would determine the future of North America. Slavery, Lincoln said, had been a tactical factor in the family quarrel. Black slaves and the compromised dimensions of their humanity were never a primary concern. As had been the case throughout American history, black Americans were offstage, regarded as an unpleasant complication to the real issues. The concern at the heart of the Civil War was whether the economic future of the United States would be industrial or agrarian. The North, the industrial power, had decided it would destroy the agrarian South and its resources rather than let it go.

Here at Vicksburg an organized, modern commercial society had struck the older feudal order a harsh blow. I had parked my car just north of the West Virginia Memorial at the spot where, on May 19, 1863, William Tecumseh Sherman sent wave upon wave of Union soldiers against the rebel position at Stockade Redan, only to see each attack bloodily repulsed. A series of charges three days later also failed. The rebels had dug into the green hillsides, shaded by live oaks and maples, with extensive trenches and tunnels, and the courage and dedication of the Yankees who charged are beyond measure. Surveying the scene while considering the larger aspects of the war, I couldn't help wondering what had motivated those foot soldiers. For what did they think they were fighting?

Earlier I'd spent an hour at the Illinois Memorial, a white granite-and-marble rotunda nestled on another of the park's quiet hills. The dome of the memorial is modeled on the Pantheon in Italy, and cast in bronze inside are the names of the 36,325 soldiers from Illinois who participated in the Vicksburg campaign. Ulysses Grant was from Illinois, of course, as was Abraham Lincoln. My parents had viewed Illinois as the vehicle of their liberty—most blacks in Mississippi viewed the Illinoisans as liberators—and our family had risen from sharecroppers to suburbanites because of the opportunity and personal freedom afforded many blacks in that state. The names on the wall in bronze had had something to do with that rise. The domed roof of the rotunda is open to the sky, and on the day I was there, surrounded by all those names and my awareness of what they'd done—enduring a winter in the open, digging trenches and canals to try to divert the river, following the enemy into tunnels for hand-to-hand combat, running miles in the dark in close formation, fording the river twice, throwing siege upon siege at an almost unbreachable opponent—the sky was clear blue through the opening, everything was perfectly quiet and completely still, and in that moment it was a simple thing to feel respect and admiration and awe for all the possibilities of the human spirit.

THE SIEGE of Vicksburg lasted six weeks. After the failure of the assaults of May 19 and 22, Grant decided to settle in and starve out the city. Because Vicksburg was surrounded by hills, ravines and gullies, there existed only seven natural access points to the city, each heavily fortified and defended by Confederates. One of these was the Stockade Redan, attacked with such futility. Another Union assault came from due north, through a tunnel dug by troops under the command of Brigadier General John Thayer, and again the Federals were repulsed by fire from rebels holding higher ground. This high ground, however, made it possible for Grant to isolate the city, and the sufferings endured by its inhabitants, military and civilian, became legend. Southern soldiers had to maintain defensive positions in trenches full-time, eating mule meat, bread made from ground peas and corn and sassafras, drinking sweet potato and blackberry coffee. All this under half, then quarter, rations for forty-seven days. Civilian conditions were even worse, as they were forced by unceasing Union artillery from the river to eat similarly limited rations and to live in caves.

Early on the morning of July 3, white flags began to appear in the Confederate lines. When General Grant entered Vicksburg, he found a city in ruins, described by one survivor in this way: "Very few houses are without evidence of the bombardment." The defense had cost the Confederates more than three thousand men, and the next day the rebels received still worse news from the Virginia theater: Lee had been defeated at Gettysburg. Though the South would fight on for almost two more years, the insurrection was, for all practical purposes, over. Jefferson Davis, Robert E. Lee and the Confederate States of America were caught in a closing vise. The Army of the Potomac held firm in the north as Grant and Sherman drove east, Grant eventually assuming command of the entire Union Army. In that capacity he would accept the Confederacy's surrender from Lee on April 9, 1865. The war was over, but within ten days Grant would be unashamedly weeping over Lincoln's coffin, and Vicksburg and Mississippi would again, in a few years, witness vicious conflict.

AS I WRITE in 1993, the mayor of Vicksburg is a black man. Contemporary Vicksburg is a sleepy river city with a predominantly black population, and race relations are quiet: the residents, black and white, seem to go about their business with a certain peacefulness, even equanimity, that belies the city's history. But though it sits so pretty on the bluffs, it has an atmosphere equally seedy, empty and tired on a quiet summer afternoon. I drove down fabled Catfish Row, a strip of black food shops and juke joints one afternoon, and found it deserted, few pedestrians and no cars. This was true of most of the other streets in Vicksburg, including U.S. 80, the east–west thoroughfare. Most of the city's automobile traffic was on Interstate 20, which crosses the Mississippi on a cantilevered bridge, the twin of the structure at Natchez, and barrels on past the dingy brick buildings and frame houses of Vicksburg for Jackson.

ONE AFTERNOON in the midst of my travels I passed several hours in Jackson with a young black man, Carlton Reeves, who hails from Yazoo City, a Delta town to the northwest. Educated at Jackson State and the University of Virginia, Carlton was an associate in the Jackson office of a large New Orleans law firm. He is tall, well over six feet, and well built, but his imposing physical presence masks an infectious ebullience. We met at his home in suburban Jackson, situated in a collection of seventies vintage apartment buildings of a kind that can be found anywhere in the Sunbelt, in Denver, Houston or Miami—apartments of brick-and-wood frame, with exterior staircases and balconies.

I asked him to tell me about his family and childhood.

"My mother's and my father's roots go back a couple of generations in Humphreys County," he began. "That is Belzoni, the Delta. Down there they call it the Catfish Capital of the World, because they raise catfish on farms. It used to be a bunch of cotton. My father was in the army. I was born at Fort Hood in Texas, but we moved back here when I was four, in 1968. Our neighborhood was a new neighborhood there in the black area of Yazoo City. I can remember the streets still being gravel. We used to play out in the woods.

"I was thinking the other day about how we had a lot of teachers in our neighborhood. That signaled, I think, some kind of class structure: the black middle class in Mississippi in that time was probably the teachers. Of course our neighborhood was all black. I lived at the corner of Ninth and Prentice. You could go down one side of Prentice and that was the black neighborhood. You go down the other way, that was the white neighborhood." He laughed. "As I got older, more blacks started moving in, which encouraged the whites to move out, so now it's all black.

"But growing up in Yazoo City was fine. I mean, we look back on it now as a totally segregated city, and it still is. For example, the summer baseball leagues don't intermingle unless there's a tournament or something. There's a Dixie Youth League and a Babe Ruth League for whites, and ours was the Roy Campanella. We didn't have uniforms—I can vividly remember that, not having uniforms and stuff. When we did get stuff, it would be what the white guys had already used."

"This was the late seventies?"

Carlton nodded. "This was the seventies, early seventies, my third-, fourth-, fifth-grade years. We got some uniforms, wool blend, to use in the summer because that was what had been handed down. We had a swimming pool in our part of town that we went to, but no whites ever came. The most fascinating thing to me right now concerning racial attitudes is that my class, the class of 1982, is trying to plan a class reunion. We were the quote unquote historic class, the first in Yazoo City to start out integrated from first grade on. There was a Supreme Court case, *Holmes County*, where the court ruled that 'with all deliberate speed' means *now*, which meant a swap over from no integration to total integration within a matter of weeks. My class was the first. After growing older and looking back on the way things were and, I guess, still are, I can see how I was fortunate. I went to kindergarten at the Catholic school, Saint Francis, and when I went to public school I was lucky to be put in the top class. The way you knew if you were in the smart class was when you looked around and you were the only black person in there. My classes were always at least ninety percent white. That pattern went on from first grade to twelfth. Especially first through sixth. You always noticed who was taking algebra and biology and college math, and who was taking general science and that stuff.

"You saw that distinction. You go to one first-grade class and you'd see one hundred percent black, all doomed to fail, it just has to happen, and looking back on it, it's extremely tragic." He stopped to look out the window. "Actually, that's probably the most positive thing you can say about it, that it's tragic, that it went on and still goes on." He paused. "Integration has probably been in practice in our community for three generations. We're about to get into the third generation of things. Education is like other things. When you see something out there that you cannot have, you really work to get it. You say to yourself, 'I want that and I'm going to get it.' But now education comes so freely we've got kids dropping out of school. I've seen kids trying to drop out in the sixth and seventh grades. I don't know the answer. When I was in school, there was always a group of students who were just lost out there in the shuffle. Nobody cared about them. Students that show some potential, everybody cares about, everybody wants to help. I was one of them. But those others—the fault, of course, goes some to parents, but we have to do more, the teachers and the administration and all of us, in our perception of how school works."

"That happens in the North as well," I remarked.

Carlton hunched his shoulders in an exasperated gesture. "It's easy now to get a high school diploma. Anybody can get one. I think that's how the children look at it. Education doesn't look like an impossible dream to them. They don't have to strive. They got buses to pick them up, they got meals and recreation at the school. They can get involved with all the sports. It's like I said, you see someone with stuff you aren't supposed to, cannot, have, you want it that much more. Our folks couldn't have education, they weren't supposed to write, they weren't supposed to own nice things or do anything interesting. And because we couldn't, we wanted it all the more."

I asked him to tell me about his high school.

He smiled. "High school was fun, for the most part. For the most part. They had these three tracks, vocational, classical or science. Classical was the general track, you could go through that and go to college. But science curriculum was supposed to get you ready for college. You took your science and your math and all that."

"How many white kids were there, and what social class did they come from?"

"It was about fifty-fifty. Some of the white kids who were there were, in my mind, rich. Some of them were as poor as I was. There was a cross section. There *was* a white academy, which was right across the street from our school. You could see it from our school." He laughed. "It was called the Manchester Academy. There was an airplane runway, a cotton field and the school, all sitting over there."

"How did you all get along in the public school? Was there any, as they say, 'race mixing'?"

He laughed again. "No. As I was saying, we're planning our

class reunion and one of the key things is trying to get white folk involved with the process. That has never happened before. What you do is have separate events and activities for the same students. When I was in twelfth grade, for example, that was the first year we had an integrated prom in Yazoo City. That was 1982. The school had been integrated since 1970, and that was the first year that the school had sponsored a senior prom. In the years before, the black kids would sponsor their senior prom and have it at our community center, and the white kids would have their homecoming dances and proms and everything away from the school because their clubs raised the money to do it that way. Not to say 1982 changed anything. When we had our prom, the white kids didn't show up. You could probably count the white kids there on ten fingers—they didn't show up." Carlton was solemn and then brightened. "Miss McCoy, the choir director, is very close to my heart. She's a black woman and the choir has always been perceived as the black thing. The choir was always ninety-nine percent black, the band was always ninety percent white. That was their activity. They sang in their churches, but not with the school choir. So there were those dichotomies."

I asked if the dichotomies had bothered him.

"One thing," he said, "I did question. I was junior class president, which was no title, believe me, but I went to the principal as class president because we wanted black history recognized in February. We had been to the grade school and they had all these posters and placards on their bulletin boards recognizing black history, and we wanted it at the high school. The principal was generally a good guy, the least of all evils there at the school, but he said 'We recognize black history throughout all our stuff and there's no need to set aside a whole month' and that type of thing. I remember that vividly. Then I started thinking about all the other things. Up until this day, Yazoo City elects black and white favorites in each class, black and white beauties, black and white homecoming queens. Black and white. It's still going on. They're afraid to have a black win anything. They pass out the ballots, you vote for one on each side, black and white."

———

AFTER A BREAK we walked outside, and standing in the bright afternoon light I felt disoriented by the dissonance between what I saw before me—Carlton's nondescript suburban apartment complex with its busy yuppies, black and white, leisurely bustling through Saturday rounds—and what we'd just been discussing. I was assuming that most of these people had been socialized in the same ways and contexts as had Carlton, in the Mississippi of white academies and formally integrated public schools, in segregated neighborhoods and churches; yet here they were living side by side, peaceably, or politely—though, as in Natchez and other places I'd been, they never seemed to do more together than nod hello. Integration, as my relatives in New Albany had pointed out, was mostly, or merely, legal. Would it ever be more? Given the history of the place and the subterranean enmity of its main groups, *could* it ever be more?

Carlton and I decided to take a ride into Jackson, working our way into the city on side streets through tree-lined white neighborhoods of substantial, well-kept homes. Whether these were Greek Revival mansions or one-story ranches, there always seemed to be black people about, maids waiting for buses, gardeners trimming hedges and cutting grass.

As we rode, Carlton talked. "When you see these distinctions," he said, gesturing toward a row of particularly fine houses, "you wonder. You know, intellectually, why these discrepancies exist and you just have to learn how to deal with it. I think black folk are generally strong people, and have convictions, but people do have families and other things they have to do."

I asked what he meant by that.

"When I was growing up, there were things that black folk generally couldn't afford to do. The white folks had the power of the dollar. If you were going to challenge something that was going on at the school, you might as well quit your job. You teach your kids to put up with stuff so you can continue to feed your family."

We worked our way into the black section of the city, ending up near Carlton's alma mater. I was curious as to his choice; he could have attended any college, North or South, and had chosen and done well at Jackson State. Since he was ambitious and planned to live in Mississippi, the obvious question was, Why not Ole Miss?

He winced in response. "There is no way I would've gone to Ole Miss. Didn't even consider it. Jackson State really was good to me, and to a whole bunch of other people in my situation, people like me. And I'm not just talking about the historical problems Ole Miss has had. Simply because I knew that these white kids in my class loved Ole Miss so much. If they loved it that much, I didn't want it. I thought about going to Southern Mississippi, but I decided to go to Jackson State instead. That was the most significant decision I have made. The atmosphere was just what I needed to grow up. You learn so much more about yourself because you see your own people. Jackson State, and being around black students in general, are the best thing for any black student. I went to law school with a lot of black students who would've benefited from a black college. You can learn about yourself. Every black child in Mississippi can get some benefit from a black school. This knowledge of yourself, you need to learn it in school."

I asked him why this couldn't be learned at Ole Miss.

"In high school, the only black man we learned about was Martin Luther King. There was no way they could teach history without mentioning his name. When I was in the fifth grade, we came down to Jackson for a field trip. We went to all the usual places, and when we got to the capitol rotunda there was a statue of Bilbo right there in the middle." For the first time that day, Carlton grew angry. "One of my friends—a white guy who I'd been in school with since the first grade—his father drove the bus down there. He was the tour guide as well. He took us over to Bilbo's statue and he stood on that statue and hugged it and said, to all of us, 'Y'all should be very proud of this man, the greatest Mississippian ever.' I didn't find out who Bilbo was until I was a sophomore in college. Then I found out Bilbo was the worst, the *worst*, racist of them all. There are so many parents out there who *cannot* teach their kids about themselves. And then a lot of parents would like to be able to, but they also want to forget what happened. They don't want to talk about it. It brings back harsh, harsh memories. Plus, my mother was out trying to work, trying to hustle up a dollar an hour. I still remember her making a dollar an hour. She's *still* making minimum wage. We talk about throwing these responsibilities back onto parents, but I don't know if all parents can accept such responsibility. Most black folk in Mississippi, you'll see as you ride up and down 55, you'll see how most of them still live, up in the Delta working for Catfish Pride or whatever they call it, making no money and stagnating. There is no movement up or even across. This race baiting in Mississippi, what's it all about anyway? We don't have any of these jobs that white folks are complaining about. How can they feel threatened when there's no opportunity for them to feel threatened? Besides, all affirmative action means is that race and other things are taken into account when trying to help people get their share, their fair share. Those things should be noticed, because they've always been taken into account before, haven't they?"

I MET a white man, middle-aged and with a very formal bearing, wearing oxford cloth, khaki and a military haircut, in an Oxford bookstore. We both stood browsing through the Civil War section for a long time, and eventually he introduced himself. We talked about various editions of history books—he was a buff—and about their authors, Catton, Foote and Shaara.

When I mentioned I was living in Maine, he excitedly began discussing Joshua Lawrence Chamberlain and the skirmish at Little Round Top at Gettysburg. After many years of study, the colonel's bravery still amazed him. "Chamberlain and the Yankees had run out of ammunition and they figured they were going to be killed anyway, so they charged and the rebels just gave up and ran. That charge probably saved the Union."

We began talking about the forces that had shaped the South since then, leading to a society that, in the past twenty years, had proven unprecedented and unpredictable, the New South of Doug Wilder, Harvey Gantt and Andrew Young. He remarked on how much more liberal towns like Oxford and Raleigh-Durham, his home, were than their surrounding countrysides. "This Jim Crow thing dies hard."

"I don't think it's ever going to die," I said.

"It will."

"How can you say that? It's in so deep, and it's being transferred to the next generation."

He shook his head, fiercely. "But not everybody. In some of the cities, kids are going to school together, their parents are getting to know each other. My son is going to a magnet school that's at least fifty percent black. He's had those children in our home, my wife and I have had their parents over for meals, we've had meals in their homes. These kinds of things never happened before."

"But that's only so many folks."

"It's the start. It's a beginning. It can't ever go back. In the past Jim Crow was a monolith, everybody believed in it, or at least practiced it. That's the way it worked."

THE CONFEDERATE TROOPS in Mississippi surrendered to Union general Edward R. S. Canby on May 4, 1865. On May 6 the Confederate governor asked all rebel officials to assemble in Jackson, and on May 22 the state archives were surrendered to U.S. general E. D. Osband, who had received instructions from Washington to arrest the Mississippians. As news of his orders spread, Confederate legislators fled Jackson, and only the governor, Charles Clark, was actually apprehended and sent to the Union prison camp at Pulaski, Georgia.

William Sharkey was appointed provisional governor of Mississippi to administer Presidential Reconstruction, as it came to be known. The first major act under Sharkey was the assemblage of a state constitution on August 14, in which the ordinance of secession was rescinded and a declaration adopted that "neither slavery nor involuntary servitude . . . shall hereafter exist in this state." (This, however, was not the federal constitutional amendment, which Mississippi did not move to ratify until 1995, the only state which had failed to do so in the intervening years.) The constitutional convention adjourned on August 24, having failed to grant freed slaves any sort of franchise or legal rights.

On October 2, Confederate general and former slave owner Benjamin Humphreys was elected governor, along with an all-white legislature. That legislature convened on October 16, promptly appropriating large sums of money for the legal defense of imprisoned Confederate president Jefferson Davis. The legislature also refused to recognize the Thirteenth Amendment (outlawing slavery) to the U.S.

Constitution, thus contradicting the pledge of the June legislature, and implemented the Black Codes, laws designed to warrant and regulate the activities of the newly freed slaves.

The Black Codes stated that freedmen, not yet citizens, could not vote; could not hold public office; could testify in court only if a black was on trial and only against blacks; could own weapons only by permission of law enforcement officials; and were required to sign a labor contract by January, and every January thereafter. Further, all orphans and blacks under the age of eighteen could be "apprenticed"—in effect, indentured—to white landowners. The official name for these laws was "An Act to Confer Civil Rights on the Freedmen, and for other purposes." Governor Humphreys's speech at the legislative session included this passage: "It is due to ourselves—to the white emigrant invited to our shores—and it should never be forgotten—to maintain the fact that ours is and shall ever be a government of white men. The purity and progress of both races require that caste must be maintained."

The open arrogance of the Mississippi government, together with similar attitudes of state legislatures throughout the South, led to the collapse of Presidential Reconstruction. The North, while not necessarily pro-black, did wish to see contrition and evidence of change from the supposedly vanquished rebels. Radical Republicans swept the 1866 November national elections and in the following year embarked upon numerous reforms, including the Fourteenth Amendment, which purported to guarantee the right of blacks to vote. Also, Confederate soldiers and officeholders who had betrayed an oath to the U.S. Constitution—having previously, for example, been members of the U.S. Army—were prohibited from public office and from voting. Finally, a military governor, General E. O. C. Ord, was sent to Mississippi to enforce these provisions.

Life in postwar Mississippi was brutally difficult, across the social spectrum. Property values plummeted, cash was hoarded, default and repudiation of debt were endemic, land was everywhere confiscated for debt payment and nonpayment of taxes. The cotton market was failing as well, and all Mississippians, white and black, rich and poor, were restless for normalization or change. Rich whites were unaccustomed to such unremitting privation, and blacks clamored for their "forty acres and a mule"—which had actually been administered to some lucky blacks in South Carolina by General Sherman, though they later were forcibly removed by whites.

General Ord arrived in Mississippi in March 1867 with a force of 2,100 soldiers, and before the November elections, 79,176 blacks and 58,385 whites, all males, were registered to vote. In that election, the first in which blacks had voted in the history of the state, delegates to another state constitutional convention were chosen; and, on January 7, 1868, those delegates met and drafted a constitution that contained such safeguards for blacks as property and suffrage rights and maintained the poll ban on Confederates.

In early 1868, the Ku Klux Klan began operations in Mississippi, unleashing a campaign of terror that contributed to the failure of the new constitution at the polls in June. Mississippi was the only southern state that year to fail to ratify a black-and-tan (meaning that blacks were involved in the drafting) state constitution, and as a result remained under military law. This, however, did not hinder the Klan's continued campaign of floggings, burning of property and murder, orchestrated to intimidate blacks and white sympathizers. Simply dealing fairly with blacks was sometimes enough to cost a white his home, if not his life.

War hero Ulysses Grant was elected president in November 1868. Grant endorsed the Republican agenda in Mississippi and, with the aid of the state's new military governor, General Adelbert Ames, secured the 1869 election of James Alcorn as governor. In a separate ballot issue, Confederate disenfranchisement was disallowed. But an open and fair election had taken place, blacks had voted and now held thirty-six seats in the new legislature.

That legislature convened on January 11, 1870, and promptly ratified the Fourteenth (due process) and Fifteenth (black suffrage) Amendments to the U.S. Constitution. The legislature also sent Adelbert Ames and Hiram Revels, a black minister from Natchez, to the U.S. Senate, the latter being the first black in the nation to serve as a senator. By February 23, President Grant was satisfied that Mississippi was "reconstructed" and ready to reassume full fellowship in the United States; two days later, military rule was ended and Mississippi became, once again, a state in the Union.

On March 10, James Alcorn was sworn in as governor. Eighteen-seventy was a tumultuous year in Mississippi. Whites adamantly refused to allow their children to attend school with blacks, so two public-school systems were established. Whites also violently resisted the levy of property taxes to fund schools, and their discontent was evidenced in the resurgence, after a brief respite, of Klan activity. Jack Dupree, a black leader in Monroe County, was murdered in front of his wife and children: his throat was cut and he was disemboweled as he bled to death. The Klan, to quote Eric Foner, "was a military force serving the interests of the Democratic Party, the planter class, and all those who desired the restoration of white supremacy. . . . It aimed to reverse the interlocking changes sweeping all over the South."

According to legend, and with some substantiation in fact, the Ku Klux Klan was organized by Nathan Bedford Forrest, planter, slave trader, president of the Selma, Marion and Memphis Railroad, original Klan imperial wizard and the most successful Confederate commander of the Civil War. Born poor in 1821 in Bedford County, Tennessee, near Shelbyville, and never formally educated, Forrest organized and outfitted a Confederate battalion with his own money. Starting out as a private, Forrest eventually rose to the rank of lieutenant general and was not, as a commander, decisively defeated until April 1865, when he surrendered in Georgia.

Forrest was a solder of mythic stature, wounded seriously several times and capable of inspiring his men to unimaginable feats in pursuit of victory. In February 1862, to avoid surrendering to U. S. Grant, Forrest led a retreat of seven hundred cavalrymen from Fort Donelson through an ice-cold river thought to be too deep to ford. His riders performed well at Shiloh, where Forrest was wounded, turning back a charge of Sherman's men; then, falling back to a base in northern Mississippi, Forrest led raids against Union forces in Tennessee. In July 1862, he captured a Union garrison at Murfreesboro, Tennessee, demolished a crucial rail line and escaped. As Union construction battalions repaired the tracks, Forrest blew up bridges along the same line. Outnumbered twenty to one, Forrest's troops wreaked havoc at will and greatly hindered the federal advance. At Chickamauga, Forrest led the right flank that destroyed the Union forces, fighting under William Rosecrans, on what might have been the bloodiest single day of the war.

Forrest's heroics, however, had a very dark side. He was known for his visceral hatred of blacks, and of northerners, tendencies which culminated in the massacre at Fort Pillow, Tennessee, on the Mississippi River. On April 12, 1864, Forrest supervised the deliberate slaughter of three hundred black and fifty-three white surrendering Union soldiers, many of them on their knees begging for mercy. When questioned about the incident, Forrest stated, "The river was dyed with the blood of the slaughtered for two hundred yards. It is hoped that these facts will demonstrate to the northern people that negro soldiers cannot cope with southerners."

Formed in 1866 in Pulaski, Tennessee, the Ku Klux Klan claimed to support and defend the United States Constitution—but plotted to preserve the class and caste privileges of the antebellum order. Led by Forrest and other Confederate veterans, the Klan became a shadow system of "white justice" and terror, enforcing the old codes of the slave days and brutally punishing any blacks who dared challenge them.

In March 1871, three blacks in Meridian were falsely charged with inciting the large black citizenry there to riot. During the trial several shots rang out, killing the judge and two defendants, and in the riot ensuing, full-scale, thirty blacks—coincidentally, all community leaders—were murdered.

In 1873, Adelbert Ames defeated Alcorn for governor, riding a large black vote to victory in what would prove to be the last election blacks would play a part in for nearly a hundred years. Ames was labeled "the black man's candidate," and his known sympathy for the Republican cause—coupled with another surge in the number of black officeholders, including the president of the state senate and the Speaker of the House—led to an increase in white paranoia.

On December 7, 1874, the black sheriff of Vicksburg, Peter Crosby, tried to retake the Warren County Courthouse from whites who had seized it in order to demand his resignation. Then, under instructions from Governor Ames, Crosby attempted to assert the state's legal possession of the building, and fighting broke out. In the next several days more than three hundred blacks in Vicksburg and

Warren County were killed, most of them civilians. Crosby was re-instated in January, but only after President Grant sent federal troops to Vicksburg.

The Vicksburg crisis was a dress rehearsal for the actions white Democrats would take in the months before the 1875 elections. Various groups, including the Klan, agitated throughout the state, causing riots in several cities. When Governor Ames sent out the mostly black militia to restore order, white anger was fanned. In an attempt to keep peace, Ames disbanded the militia, but this action served, in the end, only to give the white terrorists free rein to lynch, loot, burn and destroy. White mobs marauded in broad daylight, assassinated black leaders and drove sympathetic whites out of the state. The violence was organized, relentless and systematic, as all educated or leadership-inclined blacks were eliminated. In the town of Clinton, a skirmish between Republicans and Democrats led to the wanton slaughter of scores of blacks; in Coahoma County, another altercation ended similarly.

The leaders of the Democratic Party devised the Mississippi Plan to seize the November elections and restore white domination of the state's political system. The plan included the violent intimidation of blacks, ballot stuffing and destruction, automatic Democratic votes for illiterate blacks and miscounting of any election the Democrats lost; and these methods proved successful, with Democrats gaining solid majorities in both the state senate and the state legislature. As a sort of coup de grace, black leader Charles Caldwell, a fearless militia commander in Hinds County, was assassinated at his home on Christmas night 1875.

With their newly gained legislature and in the absence of federal supervision, white Democrats immediately began impeachment proceedings against all black officeholders. The lieutenant governor, Alexander Davis, and the superintendent of education, Thomas Cardoza, were impeached, and Governor Ames was forced to resign. One could say that when Ames left Mississippi on March 28, 1876, Reconstruction was over; and, in the words of white Mississippians, the state had been "redeemed."

Democrats would rule Mississippi unchallenged for the next 115 years, holding the governor's chair until 1991. After the white revo-

lution of 1876, the state's Democratic Party was run by a group of
wealthy aristocrats whose most notable achievement was the demar-
cation of the color line, by means of the 1890 state constitution and
the enactment of segregationist Jim Crow laws.

"MISCEGENATION" is an odd-sounding word, owing perhaps
to its manufacture in the heat of a political moment, directly after
the emancipation—a term created by politicians who wished to gal-
vanize their supporters into concerted action against the newly freed
slaves. The roots of the word are Latin (*miscere*, "to mix," and
genus, or "race"), and the term from its beginning had a negative
connotation: the sexual commingling of the black and white races
would, the term's originators held, lead to the destruction of the
white race. This commingling was therefore to be prevented at any
cost—a tenet which denied, of course, that such interaction had been
occurring for centuries, as a walk down any American street or
southern country lane would prove.

I had heard so many times during my travels, from young and
old, black and white, that the cause of racial violence in Mississippi
was the desire of white men to keep black men from having sexual
access to white women. I'd assumed that this explanation was a tru-
ism, a folk nostrum that explained away all other political and economic factors. But as I pulled at the tangle of Southern history,
culture and custom, it began to occur to me that those potential ex-
planations—folk, social, economic, political—might all be true, and
essentially connected.

Less than 20 percent of American blacks are of unmixed African descent, the ancestors of the remainder having intermingled
primarily with whites and Native Americans to such an extent
that there exists an infinite gradation of skin hues, hair textures and
physical characteristics within the broad category of African-
American. Cross mixing of these racial groups first took place within
the slave system and among free blacks: strict, violent enforcement
of miscegenation laws did not occur until Reconstruction. Before
the Civil War, it was common to refer to "Negroes" (full blacks),
"mulattoes" (half), "quadroons" (one-fourth) and "octoroons"

(one-eighth), and laws often differentiated among these groups. Each term denoted a state of nonwhiteness, but this careful delineation was in itself an acknowledgment of the sexual activity occurring between races.

Many of the American colonies, including Massachusetts, Pennsylvania, Virginia, North Carolina and Georgia, passed antiamalgamation laws, some doing so as early as the seventeenth century. From the time of the first white settlements in Mississippi, considerable numbers of racially mixed children were born, almost all to slave mothers by white fathers. Between the end of the Civil War and the constitution of 1890, there were a number of legally recognized marriages between white men and black women. Section 263 of Article 14 of that Redeemer Constitution, however, reads: "The marriage of a white person with a negro or mulatto, or person who shall have one-eighth or more of negro blood, shall be unlawful and void." This line was to become virtually indelible for a century, as it took a referendum vote in 1987, twenty years after the landmark Supreme Court case *Loving v. Virginia* declared all antimiscegenation laws unconstitutional, for Mississippi to remove the provision from its state constitution. The *Loving* decision stated clearly, "The freedom to marry, or not marry, a person of another race resides with the individual and cannot be infringed by the state."

Antimiscegenation laws were constructed on the idea of "race": that there are quantitative and qualitative differences between groups that manifest themselves in physical appearance. Eighteenth-century German anthropologist Johann Friedrich Blumenbach and nineteenth-century French philosopher Comte de Gobineau were significant proponents of the theory that there were distinguishable groups of humans, and that Caucasians (a term first implemented by Blumenbach) were superior to all others and destined to rule over them. Later, these ideas mingled with those of Spencer and Darwin to become an ideology that reigned throughout the American South and, in the twentieth century, in Germany and South Africa. In America, the stigma created by the racist view of blacks justified first slavery, then Jim Crow; and, by circular reasoning, proved conclusively why the tainted blacks would never be worthy of inclusion as family members or social equals.

The question becomes, What was, and is, at stake in the ideology of antimiscegenation? Can simple racism, or sexual jealousy and paranoia, explain this twinning obsession of sex and race? What is intriguing about the larger battle over miscegenation is that so many of its constituent struggles end up being about neither sex nor race, but about property. In a circuitous manner, miscegenation laws ensured white supremacy. By barring black–white marriage, whites kept blacks, who already had been deprived of property rights by slavery, from gaining property through marriage or inheritance. This constant exclusion of blacks had also the effect of circumscribing the lives of white females, reducing them, too, to de facto status as property, as they were limited by law and mores to white men, while privileged men essentially did as they pleased.

When the actual killing and mutilating in the name of white womanhood and racial integrity was done, however, its agents were often poor white men, those without property or station who were struggling to stay ahead of blacks. Their obsession with miscegenation—"mongrelization," in the words of one Mississippi politician—can be seen either as some sort of atavistic impulse toward racial "integrity" or as a brutal maneuver to preserve a wall of privilege, however slight in material terms, between themselves and blacks. Proclaiming white women off-limits kept poor whites from "becoming black," as it were; it gave them a tenuous niche above blacks in the caste system. These codified "differences," moreover, kept poor whites and blacks from joining together in common economic cause, reinforcing the power and privilege of well-off whites, who often exploited both groups.

The furor over "miscegenation" thus had several purposes, all in service of the status quo of southern aristocracy, among them the establishment of a rigid caste system which greatly lessened the competition faced by white males for property. After Reconstruction, violence based on alleged violations of race–sex taboos by black men would become commonplace in Mississippi; eventually, national disgust with this violence would bring scrutiny and force change. In the meantime, the practice of racial classification, based on bad science and demagoguery, would consign generations of blacks to the margins of society and would become such an integral part of folklore as to scar society, and blacks in particular, in inescapable ways.

THE 1890 state constitution, in addition to codifying racial taboos, instituted suffrage requirements designed to disenfranchise blacks. A literacy test and poll tax were required. The number of registered black voters fell from 142,000 to 8,615 in the next election. In an ironic twist, the implementation of the color line ultimately led to the demise of aristocratic control of the Democratic Party. Since blacks no longer had a voice in state issues, white racial solidarity began to fracture along economic lines, and white "yeoman" farmers formed their own political movement. Known as "the revolt of the rednecks," this movement reached its apotheosis in James K. Vardaman, who, along with his protégé Theodore Bilbo, would come to symbolize racist Mississippi in the memories of my father, Carlton Reeves and many other black people.

Vardaman. One afternoon when I was house-sitting for some friends in the hills north of Oxford—a neighborhood of houses so splendid it felt more like the Connecticut suburbs of New York City than the Mississippi I had known to that point—I answered a knock at the back door to be greeted by a gregariously polite and friendly young white man reporting to do yard work. As we stood there chatting—the young man told me he was a student at Ole Miss—I couldn't help staring at the name emblazoned across his T-shirt: Vardaman. Apparently this was the name of his high school: the shirt, in athletic gray, read VARDAMAN FOOTBALL. I felt a pang in my chest because I simply couldn't see how that name could be so casually appended to a town or school. To me, Vardaman was the man who had used Reconstruction and white fear to seize the Mississippi Democratic Party and then had used his power to nail the coffin shut on the hopes and dreams of black Mississippians for one hundred years. Vardaman, along with Bilbo, could be called the inventor of modern racism; and there I was, standing in the bright afternoon light of Oxford, amicably instructing a white Ole Miss student in a Vardaman T-shirt on how to mow the grass.

Vardaman was a politician who wanted, and acted, to keep blacks disenfranchised, dispossessed and barred from schools. He proposed to cut taxes by closing down the black educational system, saying flatly, "When I speak of educating the people, I mean white people. Educate a nigger, spoil a good farm hand." A populist, Vardaman felt that a great world for all whites could be built on the backs of blacks: "The Negro is necessary in the economy of the world but he was designated for a burden bearer." Buttressing this logic, Vardaman claimed blacks were lazy, dishonest, mentally infirm and congenitally prone to criminality.

For all his populist rhetoric, Vardaman had wanted initially to be a planter, but failed at this in Greenwood before becoming a newspaper editor. Vardaman eventually became a legislator from Greenwood and in this guise began to organize the farmers' movement he rode to power in 1903. His speeches and many of his actions as governor earned him the title "the Great White Chief." Strangely and, if true, sadly, Vardaman may not in his private beliefs have been the virulent racist he was so adept at publicly portraying. As governor he ended the brutal convict-lease system under which thousands of convicts, most of them black, died, and he put down a Klan insurrection against black landowners. He also personally led a National Guard unit in stopping a lynching.

Still, regardless of his true sentiments or occasional nobility, Vardaman is destined to be remembered as the man who defined the redneck, race-baiting style in Mississippi politics. He was succeeded by politicians who did not share his qualms about penal reform, lynching or black property rights; and these politicians had learned from him how to get themselves elected. Foremost among these was, to blacks, the worst white man of them all: Bilbo.

Bil-bo. The falling first syllable into the hammering second; even the name sounds brutal and oppressive. In my childhood, whenever my father became weary of or angry at white folks, that's the name he would use, Bilbo. According to my father, no one had ever hated blacks more.

Bilbo's nickname was "the Man." Among whites this symbolized his stature as cock-of-the-walk, the one who would keep-them-niggers-down, the redneck's redneck. Among blacks it described his position as the ultimate authority figure, with a negative connotation continuing to this day. If you hear contemporary blacks deriding the injustice of "the man," the memory of Bilbo is tied to their words, a fury in their collective unconscious.

Theodore Gilmore Bilbo was born October 13, 1877, in Juniper Grove, Mississippi, the son of a yeoman farmer who later became a bank executive. After attending Vanderbilt and the University of Michigan (no degrees), Bilbo toyed with preaching, then taught school before running unsuccessfully for circuit clerk of Pearl River County in southern Mississippi. Bilbo ran again, in 1907, for state senator and won, and was soon embroiled in scandal. Accused of taking bribes, he was nearly expelled from the state senate. He managed, however, to turn this near disgrace to his advantage by claiming he'd been framed by Delta aristocrats, a stance that enabled him to portray himself as the champion of average and poor whites. Bilbo would be ensnared in one controversy after another over the course of his career. He was accused of conflicts of interest, trading influence for sex, contempt of court, assault and battery. He also, as governor, almost destroyed the University of Mississippi in a fit of pique, trying to make the administration and faculty bow to his will. But his visceral hatred for and unrelenting oppression of blacks, coupled with his mastery of poor-white rhetoric, allowed him to escape all reckonings and win election as governor twice and senator three times.

In the U.S. Senate, Bilbo distinguished himself as the implacable foe of any federal assistance to blacks. He portrayed himself as the last defender on the ramparts of white purity and began a national crusade to send all blacks "back" to Africa. In the 1946 election, Bilbo called "on every red-blooded white man to use *any means* to keep the nigger away from the polls. If you don't understand what that means you are just plain dumb." In addition, Bilbo used filibusters and other legislative tricks to stall passage of an antilynching law for years and gradually became an embarrassment to the national Democratic Party.

In 1947, the Department of Justice opened an investigation of charges that Bilbo had obstructed blacks from voting. In addition, Congress announced a probe into alleged war profiteering by Bilbo and his supporters, and Republican senators led by Robert Taft maneuvered to bar Bilbo from his seat. Bilbo was suddenly stricken with cancer of the mouth and forced to travel to New Orleans for treatment. As a result, he was not sworn in as senator for that term and, after an agonizing eight months, died on August 27, 1948, never having returned to Washington.

WITH THE collapse of the antebellum order, Mississippi was in dire need of a new method of organizing agricultural production and, by extension, its society. Several different systems were tried, but gradually a form of employer–employee relation known as sharecropping became standard. In this system, as described by Eric Foner, "sharecroppers retained one-third of the year's crop if the planter provided implements, fertilizer, work animals, and seed, and half if they supplied their own." The first record of this arrangement comes in 1866; by the 1870s the system had spread throughout the state.

Sharecropping would continue through the 1950s, and, while it seemed at its inception to be an improvement over slavery, came in time to be recognized by southern blacks as yet another form of bondage. Sharecroppers, who lived on the planter's land, often in ramshackle quarters, were quickly locked into permanent debt as the seed, livestock and equipment needed for farming were obtained on "credit" and counted against each new crop. The planter usually had a store, or commissary, as it was known, which was the only place for miles around where blacks could purchase groceries, clothes and household supplies. Since, again, the farmer often had no money for most of the year, if at all, these routine purchases on credit exacerbated his debt to the planter.

On one of the largest Delta plantations, tenants did not see cash even if they somehow managed to avoid debt because they were paid in scrip, private money that could be used only at the planter's commissaries and doctor's office. This plantation, in Sunflower County, east of the town of Cleveland, was called Dockery's and was owned by William O. "Will" Dockery and later by his son Joe Rice Dockery. It was built on ten thousand acres of premier Delta farmland, which Dockery cleared with black work gangs before the turn of the century.

The son of wealthy slaveholders dispossessed by the Civil War, Dockery graduated from Ole Miss and, according to legend, rode to the Delta on horseback. He started with a store in the small town of

Cleveland and then, as nearby land was cleared by drainage and lumbering, secured mortgages on succeeding plots. Gazing across the infinite, empty fields and horizons of today's Delta, I found it hard to believe William Faulkner's description of that land as once a "vast, flat alluvial swamp of cypress and gum and bake and thickets lurked with bear and deer and panthers and snakes."

In its prime, Dockery's was home to four hundred black families, a self-sufficient town with a post office, two churches and two elementary schools. And there was a physician on the premises at all times. Although Will Dockery ran a much more extensive and even benevolent (in a day-to-day sense) operation than did the average planter, his actions were taken in his own interest. He had his crop to tend and harvest and needed his large captive labor army to accomplish these tasks. The happier those thousands of blacks were, the more cotton Dockery could mill. As Joe Rice Dockery stated, "Many a day has been worked down here for fifty cents a day. We didn't rob 'em blind like some of them did. I'm not saying that we didn't follow the system—if you tried to buck the system in those days you woulda been put outa business."

Until the Depression, the Dockery plantation was unparalleled. Perhaps "empire" is the best way to consider its extent. Driving south on U.S. 61, you enter Cleveland, a windblown town of fast-food restaurants and prefabricated factories, and go through several lights before crossing Mississippi 8, where a left turn will take you east toward Ruleville. After about five miles you will cross the Sunflower River, and if you look closely to your left, you will see a small frame building with a sign reading DOCKERY'S. Behind it is a large barnlike building, the cotton gin, with a fading sign that reads:

DOCKERY FARMS
EST. 1895 BY
WILL DOCKERY
1865–1936
JOE RICE DOCKERY, OWNER

Dockery Farms is now a ghost town, worked by a few men with tractors. But the plantation once spanned forty square miles, which means that, driving at fifty miles an hour, by the time you see the sign you will have been on Dockery's land for approximately ten minutes, and continuing east through fields empty save for soybeans and cotton, you'll be on his land for ten minutes more.

RULEVILLE, Mississippi, is, like most other Delta towns, a dusty collection of utilitarian stores, empty buildings and houses widely varied in type and quality—all scattered around the intersection of U.S. 49w and Mississippi 8 about ten miles east of Cleveland. I rode through late one terribly hot August Sunday afternoon, looking for nothing in particular but impressions, taking in the scenery and hoping to find a road sign to direct me toward Grenada and I-55. The town was deathly still, nothing moving except for a group of black teenagers hanging out, barefoot and simply dressed, talking and slapping palms in front of the general store. As they nodded and waved, I lazily returned their greeting, unaware that I was in the hometown of Fannie Lou Hamer.

Most Americans became familiar with Fannie Lou Hamer on August 22, 1964, when she testified at the Democratic National Convention in Atlantic City about her struggle to register to vote in Mississippi and about the complicity of the state Democratic Party in preventing her from doing so. Mrs. Hamer was a member of the Mississippi Freedom Democratic Party (MFDP), a largely black alternative to the all-white regulars, and the MFDP delegates were petitioning the credentials committee to admit them as the true Mississippi delegation. Millions watched on prime-time television as Mrs. Hamer told the story of her incarceration for voter-registration activities: "I was carried out of that cell into another cell where they had two Negro prisoners. The State Highway Patrolman ordered the first Negro to take the blackjack. . . . I was beat by the first Negro until he was exhausted . . . The State Highway Patrolman ordered the second Negro to take the blackjack."

Who was this short, squat, chocolate-brown woman, relating these horrors with so much dignity and courage? And how had an unschooled daughter of sharecroppers, a sharecropper herself, brought the routine injustices of the Delta to world attention with the clearheadedness and fearlessness required to say, without rancor,

"America is sick and it needs a doctor," while remaining in a small Mississippi town under scrutiny and threat until her death?

Fannie Lou Hamer was born October 6, 1917, in Montgomery County, near the town of Winona, the youngest of James and Ella Townsend's twenty children. As was customary at the time, Hamer's mother was paid a fifty-dollar bonus by her employer for producing the healthy child, who was expected to be a future laborer. In 1919, in search of steadier work, the Townsend family moved to the Brandon plantation in Sunflower County, the home of such cotton and land barons as Will Dockery and the notorious James O. Eastland, longtime segregationist and U.S. senator.

In this county, in 1904, Eastland's uncle and namesake James was allegedly murdered by Luther Holbert, a black man he was attempting to discipline for harassing another black man. In the ensuing frenzy, several innocent blacks were killed as a posse of more than two hundred men hunted Holbert and his wife with bloodhounds for four days through the bayous and fields of four Delta counties. Once captured, Holbert and his wife, who was not involved in the murder, were tied to stakes and tortured. According to the Vicksburg *Evening Post*, "the blacks were forced to hold out their hands while one finger at a time was chopped off. The fingers were distributed as souvenirs. The ears of the murderers [the newspaper did not distinguish between Holbert and his wife] were cut off, Holbert was beaten severely, his skull was fractured, and one of his eyes, knocked out with a stick, hung by a shred from the socket. . . . The most excruciating form of punishment consisted in the use of a large corkscrew in the hands of some of the mob. This instrument was bored into the flesh of the man and woman, in the arms, legs and body, and then pulled out." More than a thousand watched as the pair was soused with kerosene, placed on pyres and burned.

When the young Hamer moved to the area fifteen years later, little had changed. She recalled: "I never will forget, one day—I was six years old and I was playing beside the road and this plantation owner drove up to me and stopped and asked me, could I pick cotton? I told him I didn't know and he said, 'Yes, you can. I will give you things you want from the commissary store,' and he named off things like Crackerjacks and sardines. . . . So I picked thirty pounds of cotton that week, but I found out what actually happened was he was trapping me into begging the work I was to keep doing, and I was never to get out of his debt again."

At the age of twelve Fannie Lou Townsend was baptized in a Delta river, a crucial moment in her life. Deep religious faith and pacifist conviction would guide her actions whatever the circumstance. "Ain't no such thing as I can hate anybody and hope to see God's face," she said. In 1944, she married sharecropper Perry Hamer and moved with him to the Marlow plantation outside Ruleville. One feature of that farm was that the Marlow dog had his own bathroom with running water, while none of the plantation blacks had any plumbing, indoor or out.

In 1961, after two miscarriages, and at a time when she was raising two informally adopted daughters, Hamer was sterilized while undergoing routine surgery. The procedure was performed without her knowledge (she thought she was having a small tumor removed), and she didn't learn of it until she heard gossip started by the plantation owner's wife. After World War II, the sterilization of young and poor black women was a common occurrence in the rural South—a practice not widely known until a twelve-year-old girl and her fourteen-year-old sister were sterilized in Alabama in the 1970s, and filed suit against the doctors involved. Hamer was outraged and heartbroken at how cruelly she had been treated and at the impossibility of legal redress. "Getting a white lawyer to go against a white doctor? I would have been taking my hands and screwing tacks in my own casket."

In the summer of 1962, Student Nonviolent Coordinating Committee (SNCC) worker Charles McLaurin came to Ruleville to help blacks try to register to vote. In Sunflower County, registration involved going to Indianola, the county seat, and enduring a hazing designed to forestall successful black applications. On August 31, when Hamer went to Indianola with a group of civil rights workers and tried to register, all the group's applications were denied. Hamer had to fill out a long questionnaire that asked, among other things, where she worked. As she related, "Well, see, when you put by whom you are employed, you fired by the time you get back home." She was given the infamous Mississippi constitutional exam, subject to the grading and interpretation of the clerk, and thus designed for any black to fail.

On the way back to Ruleville, the sheriff pulled over the bus carrying Hamer and the others. After the driver was arrested and taken away, Hamer calmed her companions, mostly women, as they sat by the road in the hot vehicle and waited. She sang gospel songs and spirituals and clapped, getting the others to join in. When Hamer returned to the Marlow place, she was confronted by the owner and ordered off the farm where she'd lived for eighteen years. She left that night, never to return. Interestingly, Marlow later reconsidered and asked Hamer to come back, but she refused.

Inspired by her example, several poor blacks in Ruleville rallied to Hamer's side, offering food and shelter and anything else they had. The "middle-class" blacks, by contrast, mostly teachers, thought Hamer was recklessly endangering the community. Ruleville blacks were punished economically that fall, as the loans on their businesses were called in and their businesses forced to close, the black church mysteriously lost its tax exemption and the token black city worker was fired.

In September, when the U.S. Supreme Court ordered the admission of James Meredith to Ole Miss, several Ruleville families active in civil rights were terrorized with shots fired into their homes. At the home of Herman and Hattie Sisson, a granddaughter and another young woman were seriously injured. Sisson, a man of high standing in the black community, was accused by Ruleville authorities, including the mayor, of having done the shooting himself. This became a regular pattern in Ruleville, as blacks and SNCC workers were frequently arrested and falsely charged.

That winter, the whites of Sunflower County changed tactics from physical back to economic violence. Blacks were systematically denied federal surplus food (often a sharecropper's principal winter supply), refused bank loans and made to face taxes and utilities raised to confiscatory rates. Fannie Lou Hamer was sent a nine-thousand-dollar water bill for a house that had no running water.

On December 4, Hamer again tried to register, having carefully studied the state constitution. She passed her exam but later was denied registration because she hadn't paid poll taxes, which could not, of course, be paid unless one was already registered.

In March 1963, Hamer entered the Southern Christian Leadership Conference's (SCLC) training course, learning how to teach others to read, take voter-registration tests and understand their rights as citizens. Her training began at the Highlander Folk School in Appalachia, and Hamer took further instruction at Dorchester, Georgia, and Charleston, South Carolina. According to instructor Dorothy Cotton, "Our purpose was to see how people could unbrainwash themselves. . . . We taught them how to make long-distance phone calls. A lot of people did not know how to do that. We taught them how to use bank drafts. These were people who, when they got any money, they put it under the mattress. We needed to teach them to use banks. We introduced them to political officials. We wanted to demystify the political process and build a base from which folks could operate." While in Charleston, Hamer visited the Old Slave Mart and was deeply moved. She was also angered; seeing a stump from which blacks were sold, she remarked, "They keeps it nice and shellacked," and resolved to redouble her efforts.

Returning from Charleston, Hamer was incarcerated and savagely beaten; she later, in 1965, spoke of this beating before Congress. The bus carrying Hamer and others had stopped in Winona, Mississippi, late on a Sunday morning. Several SCLC workers entered a Winona café, sat down and attempted to order, but were refused service. The highway patrol tried to make them leave and, failing at this, arrested them. While organizing the remainder of the group, Hamer was singled out by officers who seemed to know who she was, and was also arrested. Cuffed and taken to the Montgomery County Jail, Hamer was held for several days, terrorized and beaten. (During this stretch, on June 11, Medgar Evers was assassinated in Jackson.) A federal civil rights trial concerning the incident was held in December 1963, but the police were acquitted and white Mississippians portrayed the entire series of events as a challenge and affront created by "outside agitators"—though Hamer and the others had never left the state before the Dorchester, Georgia, trip. These "agitators" had gotten, whites claimed, what they wanted: trouble and then some. The ferocity of the state's representation in court was meant as a warning, or a threat, for the future.

That future came quickly. In February 1964, sympathizers in Boston and Cambridge shipped fifteen tons of food and clothing to help sharecroppers through an unusually cold Mississippi winter, made even harder by economic pressure from the white power structure. Hamer controlled the distribution of these supplies, which became a strong weapon in her arsenal. In order to get dry goods and food, blacks in the Delta had first to meet with her approval; to win her approval they had to attempt to register to vote. Thus white pressure backfired and led to more, not less, black activity, and activity that did not subside despite myriad attempts to disrupt and sabotage Hamer's movement. In a humorous incident which is also testimony to Hamer's genius, the mayor of Ruleville, Charles Dorrough, announced over the radio that "everyone" should immediately go to Hamer's house for free goods, hoping through this to start a panic that would exhaust Hamer's resources and credibility. Hundreds converged, but Hamer and her associates—they called themselves the Citizenship Club—turned the mob scene into a voting-rights seminar.

In March of that year, Hamer ran for Congress. Her opponent was, like most Democrats statewide, an incumbent of several decades, Jamie Whitten. Hamer had, of course, no chance of winning, but her dare proved successful as another catalyst for blacks throughout the Delta. Allegedly there was at this time a contract on Hamer's life, and she continually received threats and hate mail. When questioned about the threats, all she said was, "Sometimes it seems like to tell the truth today is to run the risk of being killed. But if I fall, I'll fall five-feet-four inches forward in the fight for freedom."

In the summer of 1964—Freedom Summer—Hamer went to Oxford, Ohio, to help organize and train civil rights workers. Back in Mississippi she sheltered and advised young SNCC workers, while her house was shot at and her church firebombed. In an ever-escalating conflict, blacks involved in the movement were fired, registration workers tailed, harassed and jailed—and in May, three Freedom Summer workers, Michael Schwerner, James Chaney and Andrew Goodman, disappeared from a jail in Philadelphia, Mississippi.

This terror led to the formation of the Mississippi Freedom Democratic Party. The MFDP was thought necessary by Hamer and others because blacks had been fully barred from the existing Democratic Party, whose regulars controlled the state political apparatus and were authors of the monolith of racist laws and institutions that precluded any hope of real change for blacks. The MFDP developed an internal structure, a slate of state office candidates and delegates, and, in the summer of 1964, petitioned the national Democrats to unseat the regulars at the 1964 convention.

On August 22, Fannie Lou Hamer opened her testimony before the credentials committee with a statement that has become legendary: "My name is Mrs. Fannie Lou Hamer, and I live at 626 East Lafayette Street, Ruleville, Mississippi." Hamer told her story in vivid and excruciating detail, then concluded: "All of this on account we want to register, to become first-class citizens, and if the Freedom Democratic Party is not seated now, I question America, is this America, the land of the free and the home of the brave where we have to sleep with our telephones off the hooks because our lives be threatened daily because we want to live as decent human beings in America?"

After much wrangling, with negative pressure applied by President Lyndon Johnson, who wanted a problem-free and unified convention to nominate him in the crowning moment of his long career, the MFDP was offered a "compromise" of two at-large seats and the promise that all future delegations would be forced to embrace color-blind modes of selection and participation. The MFDP refused. Mrs. Hamer explained: "We didn't come all this way for no two seats when all of us is tired." The end result was that no Mississippi delegation was officially seated at the 1964 convention.

In September 1964, at the behest of Harry Belafonte, Hamer traveled to Africa with a group of civil rights workers. There she met the president of Guinea, Sékou Touré. "I had never seen nobody black running the government . . . so it was quite a revelation to me . . . because then I could feel myself never, ever being ashamed of my ancestors or my background."

That December, Hamer met Malcolm X. At a rally in Harlem she told her life story and spoke of the need for nonviolent tactics when pursuing social change. Malcolm followed her, saying, "When I listen to Mrs. Hamer, a black woman—could be my mother, my sister, my daughter—describe what they had done to her in Mississippi, I ask myself how in the world can we ever expect to be respected as *men*, when we allow something like that to be done to our women, and we do nothing about it? . . . We *need* a Mau Mau. If they don't want to deal with the Mississippi Freedom Democratic Party, then we'll give them something else to deal with."

Back in Mississippi, Hamer, with her ever-loyal allies Annie Devine and Victoria Gray, formally challenged the seating of the five white congressmen from Mississippi on the grounds that the state's elections excluded blacks and were therefore illegal. Hamer filed their motion with the clerk of the House of Representatives, and William Fitts Ryan, the congressman from the Upper West Side of Manhattan, stood in House chambers on January 4, 1965, and supported their objection. This protest forced a roll-call vote on the issue, which ended in the swearing in continuing as planned but also led to a congressional investigation of Mississippi election practices.

Simultaneously, the marches, riots and negotiations in Selma, Alabama, often broadcast on national television, built public support for the Voting Rights Act, the most important federal civil rights legislation since Reconstruction. Even with the passage of that watershed act, however, another twenty years would pass before real political and social change was seen in Mississippi.

In the remaining twelve years of her life, Fannie Lou Hamer receded from the national stage, but continued, tirelessly, to advocate racial change and reconciliation. In 1965, one of her lawsuits, *Hamer v. Campbell*, an attempt to block local elections in Sunflower County, succeeded when a federal court, on appeal, overturned two previous elections. In 1967 she suffered a dreadful setback when her daughter Dorothy died en route to a Memphis hospital after being denied treatment in Mississippi. The next year, she saw Robert Clark elected to the state legislature, the first black person elected in almost one hundred years.

In 1968 she helped found a bank, the first step in her strategy for increasing black economic independence. The next crucial step in this plan was the purchase of forty acres for Freedom Farm, a cooperative venture in which black farmers (and, eventually, a few poor whites) could fully share in the profits of Mississippi agricultural enterprise. At its height Freedom Farm contained more than 680 acres, but it was plagued by inexperience, poor management and bad weather; at Mrs. Hamer's death only forty acres remained. Still, these activities had a considerable psychological impact on Delta blacks, intimating if not proving that true economic emancipation was possible.

In 1970, Hamer filed *Hamer v. Sunflower County*, which demanded school desegregation, and in 1971 she pressed for a full investigation of the murder of Jo Etha Collier, a seventeen-year-old black girl slain on the street in the neighboring town of Drew by drunk and joyriding white teenagers. In 1972, her health began to deteriorate, and she was hospitalized for exhaustion, two years later suffering a nervous breakdown and two years after that undergoing a mastectomy before dying in 1977 of heart failure caused by cancer, diabetes and hypertension. Near the end, she told her friend June Johnson that she was "so tired."

At her funeral, on March 20, such civil rights figures as Andrew Young, Stokely Carmichael and Hodding Carter III gave eulogies; but the truer tribute lay in the presence of thousands of poor Delta blacks who stood outside the church and filled the high school gymnasium when the church could hold no more. Like most sharecroppers, Mrs. Hamer was buried in her hometown, not far from where she started, but having traveled light-years past where she had been intended to go. And she carried millions with her, first a few to Indianola, just down the road on 49w, and eventually blacks and whites across the country, inspiring them with the words she so often said and that are now engraved on her tombstone: "I'm sick and tired of being sick and tired."

I WENT for a drive one fall afternoon with my friends Richard and Kristina Ford. Richard is a fiction writer, the author of such books as *The Sportswriter*, *Rock Springs* and *Wildlife*, while Kristina, an urban planner, was at that time a professor of political science at the University of Mississippi. I was using their home in Oxford as my base of operations in that part of the state, and one slow Friday we set off west down Highway 6, toward Batesville, Panola County and the Delta.

We rode first to a soybean farm north of the town of Marks, eight miles off the highway down a gravel county road. We left the car and walked a short distance to a stand of trees.

I asked Richard about something I'd found curious. "You said the other day that when you were growing up in Jackson, the Delta represented something exotic, even like another country to you. What did you mean by that?"

He looked past me toward the cotton and soybean fields. "It's so different, geographically, from where I lived. It's flat, and has a sort of profound quality to me. It's completely under agriculture, under cultivation. It seems like the landscape has been fought back into the shape it's now in. If you read Faulkner, you see that's true, it was a struggle to establish this big agricultural belt, and that was always appealing to me. It wasn't romantic; it has a kind of almost relentless quality. And what comes along with that is a kind of tedium. When I got older and had gone away from Mississippi, in fact had gotten much older, I found that it was the place in Mississippi that had the most visceral appeal to me, and I was just drawn to it. Also, my friends and I used to hear lots of stories of wild things going on in the Delta, wild girls, wild parties."

Kristina laughed. "Lots of drinking."

Richard agreed. "Lots of drinking, eccentric landowners, big rich people, big cotton barons."

"This was the part of the state that made the state rich," Kristina added. "This was the economic power."

"They held the rest of the state hostage for a long time," Richard said. "There was a lot of money over here, so a lot of little mysteries got expressed toward the rest of the state. For example, a small example, I used to listen to those old bluesmen all the time. I think I told you, I would go to fraternity parties at Ole Miss and Howlin' Wolf would be playing." Richard laughed. "When I used to go to those parties, we knew where the guys who threw those parties were from. They were from the Delta. The Delta had a real mystique."

The Delta, according to my parents, had a mystique for blacks as well, but a negative one. "My father says he was told by everybody, 'Stay the hell out of there unless you got some serious business to attend to, unless you had some purpose.' My mother's father said the same thing, 'Don't go over there.' That was their view."

Richard nodded. "Well, I know people who live in the hills, black people, and black people who live in the Delta, and I think people got worked hard over here in the Delta in a way that they didn't get worked hard in the hills."

"Like chopping cotton," Kristina said.

"Chopping cotton is probably the hardest job they could do."

I had heard the term often in my childhood, but still wasn't sure exactly what it meant. "Chopping is weeding?"

"Yes." Kristina nodded. "The cotton needs this bright sun, no shade. You've got to keep the plants clear. They mostly do it in June and July, when the plants are young. When the cotton gets big enough, I guess then it will choke out the weeds. It's ninety-eight degrees out here and they chop cotton all day long. They still do it."

There were no workers in the fields this late September day. The bolls were beginning to burst, in the process of forming seas of white, a few weeks away from the mechanical harvester, which allows several men to do the work that once took two hundred. I had thought the entire process was now mechanized. "They still do it?"

Kristina stared across the field. "They still do it."

"And if they can," Richard added, "they still pay about three dollars an hour."

"And they complain about people leaning on their hoes," Kristina said. "They say, 'That's not what I'm paying you for. If I see you twice, I'll fire you.' The first summer we lived here, I'd drive by the fields and there'd be women out chopping cotton. It was the first time in this country where I've seen a life so alien: I knew I didn't know anything about the kind of life they have."

Outside the hamlet of Jonestown, we stopped and visited for a while with Joe Campbell, an elderly black man and a family friend of the Fords. He was living in an old tenant house on a back road that bisected two more endless cotton fields. Mr. Campbell and the Fords didn't discuss much of any consequence besides Mr. Campbell's health, and plans for that week's bird hunting and feasting. The very ordinariness of the encounter surprised me; it was yet another example of how black and white Mississippians had forged accommodations and even affection amid the irrational tangles of the state's public life.

When we were back in the car, I asked Richard about Joe. "Do you ever wonder how a guy who has lived his entire life around here has been able to keep that much equanimity?"

"I don't *wonder* about it, but I'm very aware of it."

"Did you think things would ever change here?" I asked.

Richard nodded. "It was clear to me when I left in 1962 that things were going to change. There were two strong reasons, in my estimation. One, it seemed right that it should change, and two, it wasn't great in the South. There was never any reason for anybody who lived in the South, that I can see, to want things to remain the way they were. By the time I got out of high school, 1962, I was distinctly aware things were in a state of disruption, that everything was about to change. Now I couldn't have said *how*, that the civil rights movement was going to flower the way it did, that equal opportunity was going to become an attainable goal. But I grew up with a sense that something was wrong—let's not say 'wrong,' let's say 'did not make sense.' I mean, you drove around in a countryside that was racially separated, that tension all around you—it was not a natural state. I had an instinct for relations between human beings being amicable, particularly between whites and blacks; the culture around me was at war with that. I trod both sides of the line, one side a great deal more than the other. My white societal dictates I followed pretty well, but I was in arguments with my family about race relations as early in my life as fourteen. Such things as, my grandfather ran a hotel in Little Rock and he had a lot of black employees, and when I came to visit, I'd shake hands with the guys he employed. My grandfather would never say 'Don't,' but he'd say, 'Why do you shake hands with Cedric Bowe, why do you shake hands with Chester Matthews?' I'm only saying this as the tiniest example."

"But wasn't that what the whites' conception of themselves was based on, that notion that they were on top, that they had to be on top?"

Richard considered my question before answering. "Yeah, but I think my generation—we inherited it. Maybe in the generations prior to ours being on top meant something. But frankly, for a lot of white Mississippians like my parents, being on top didn't mean anything."

"In our generation," Kristina interjected, "you didn't know anybody. The high schools were segregated. Black people were near us, but I didn't know them as individuals."

Richard continued. "I didn't feel myself superior to blacks. I just thought, 'They're someplace else.' And by and large they were. I didn't feel myself on top at all. Looking back, I think I was, but it just wasn't anything that meant anything to me. Likewise with my parents. I never heard my parents make a racist remark. And they were country people. Mississippians."

I wasn't satisfied. "Well, what about when you go down another level, psychically? What incites the rednecks to do the things they do? Ellen Douglas said to me, and most of my relatives agree, that the goal is to keep me and Kristina from knowing each other."

Richard nodded his head in acknowledgment, then questioned, "To keep white women and black men apart?"

"Yes."

After a moment of reflection, Richard said, "That's something I don't know about. It's in Faulkner, but it has the ring to me of convenient conventional wisdom which needs to be explored as to its absolute truth. Now, I'm sure there's truth to it, but I don't know how basic it is."

"But," I said, "the violence surrounding that stuff is just so much more vicious here in Mississippi than anywhere else."

Kristina was startled. "Worse than Alabama?"

"Yes," I said. "Even black folks in Alabama will say, 'Forget Mississippi.' "

Kristina pressed the point. "Are they saying that from knowledge or from hearsay? I don't know. When I think of ugliness, I think of Birmingham."

"But that was like a flare-up," I said, "whereas in Mississippi, well, the majority of people that were lynched were lynched here. You had things like Mack Charles Parker being dragged out of jail in 1959 and killed. You had Emmett Till, a little boy, a little boy killed. You just say 'Mississippi' to a black person and it's like the whole thing, a symbol of everything that's happened to us, at least until the last ten years and what's happened in urban centers."

Richard thought for a long moment, then circled back to a previous topic and spoke as if he had reached a conclusion. "I think a lot of people, particularly your ordinary, everyday Mississippian, were for the status quo. The status quo happened to be segregation. But I don't think they thought much about it or could have said what they had to gain from it. The white power structure gained, white politicians gained, so they wanted to maintain it."

"It has always amazed me," I said, "that poor white folks, probably plowing the next field over from my grandparents, thought that their interests were with Will Dockery and not with blacks who were tenants like them."

Richard shook his head. "That's getting it down to the level of irrationality and I don't understand that."

I protested. "But it happened for years. I think it's something that goes over into the human heart, how people are."

"I don't think it's the human heart," Kristina said. "I think it's the American heart, the way of seeing the unknown as dangerous."

"Yes," Richard continued. "The unknown as adversary. Seeing the things that are different from yourself—what looks different in the mirror—as your opponent."

By this time we had reached the river, crossing over the bridge at Helena, then doubling back across and riding south along the levee, so huge and silent, holding back the river and looking like nothing so much as a larger version of the burial mounds of the Natchez empire. The levees are, in truth as well as appearance, mounds of that kind, for many laborers, convicts and black men with nowhere else to turn, are buried in those levees, buried where they fell in accidents while working, some alive, the project of building too important to delay to rescue them.

AS EVENING came on, we turned back north, and I asked Richard if he thought history had passed Mississippi by. "That's a kind of a cul-de-sac," he said, "an intellectual cul-de-sac. I can start thinking of the world as just this cupcake with ants swarming on it, each one trying to get a piece—and nothing mattering, as if all of it is outside of time, so that anything we do, our notions of progress, our notions of salvation, however we imagine making our lives bearable on the planet, are all irrelevant in a way. Once I think that, then I come back to that notion of time, about Mississippi, and I say, 'Well, this is my little plot of ground and I don't want to think things about my little plot that will make me become uninterested in it, because it's all I've got.' What we've got happening here is just a running out of a tradition, a very time-constrained and limited tradition, the liberal last gasp of southern tradition. Maybe its last little squeak is this streak of being conservative, this retrograde conservatism, it's all part of the same tradition. It isn't like, 'Well, the South used to be bad and now we're enlightened,' it's all part of the same gasp."

By this time we were bearing east, back toward Oxford, and as the sun went down we approached the town of Crenshaw, which seems to sit almost exactly where the hills meet and end the flat plains, and we left the Delta.

IN THE early 1960s, Claude Sitton of *The New York Times* described Mississippi with words still close to accurate in Delta towns like Tunica, Friars Point and Indianola:

> Mississippi offers a study in contrasts, especially in the Delta. Greek-revival mansions and rambling ranch houses in groves of shade trees look out on weather-beaten rows of clapboard cabins and tarpaper shacks, most of which have open privies and some which lack even running water. A planter dressed in expensive western boots and hat gets up from a leisurely meal in a restaurant and displays a rare dime valued at $90 from his coin collection. Less than a mile away, a Negro mother arises and prepares a breakfast of sugar syrup and hoecake for her children, some of whom cannot attend school because they have no shoes.

The gulf between these two Mississippis is the metaphoric landscape that has been fought over since the first settlement at Natchez, and it was weighing on my thoughts as I stood before one of those Greek Revival mansions in Clarksdale on a Friday in November, about to knock and go inside to have tea with Celeste Luckett, the owner of the house.

Mrs. Luckett was eighty-four years old, the widow of Simms Luckett, a prominent Clarksdale attorney. I wanted to meet her because I had often perceived Mississippi whites as a monolith—excepting my few personal friends, who were liberals, to put it mildly—and I wanted to get behind the facade of those mansions and meet someone who belonged to that other history. Mrs. Luckett was the old friend of one of my friends, and she offered cheerfully to talk with me. We sat down late that afternoon for what became a three-hour conversation.

Mrs. Luckett lived, to my mind, in a Mississippi based on the exclusionary fantasy of the kind I'd seen in *Mississippi Magazine*, a glossy bimonthly put out by Downhome Publications in which there are no shacks, no fish factories, no battles over school integration. The ads the magazine contains are for department stores, banking services, interior designers, Oriental rugs and lock and alarm systems. Flipping through a recent eighty-page issue, with photographs on almost every page, I saw only two black faces, one a young girl learning quilting in Port Gibson and the other a man, a quadriplegic, in a testimonial for the Methodist Rehabilitation Center.

What I did see was the Mississippi that lives on the quiet streets of many towns, in brick ranches and frame Victorians, that worships in the ubiquitous well-kept Baptist churches. This particular issue of *Mississippi Magazine* celebrated families who had owned their farms for at least a hundred years; interviewed Miss Mississippi of 1933, the "very first" one; ran thirteen pages of photos of American flags around the state; and contained "Mississippi's Best-Selling Attorney," a puff piece on the novelist John Grisham. I suppose what astonished me most was the ordinariness—I'm tempted to say banality—of it all, the unconscious enjoyment of the symbols and privileges of the tragic past. This same vacuity is everywhere apparent: in the lack of irony in a *Condé Nast Traveler* article, "Spring Flings," in which Ellen Gilchrist praises Natchez "style"; in the romanticism of the state travel bureau's guide and its featured theme, "Vintage Vicksburg." Now *this* Mississippi is strange indeed to someone with a head full of slave tales, Sherman's March and Medgar Evers.

I WAS met at the door of Mrs. Luckett's pillared house by the maid, a young white woman, and shown into the den. Mrs. Luckett rose from her chair, a tall, white-haired and clear-eyed woman who could have been twenty years younger than her age, with a vigorous constitution of which she is very proud. She offered me a chair, and we chatted briefly about current events—Bill Clinton had been elected three days earlier—and worked our way into other topics.

I asked her if she had been born in Mississippi.

"Yes, in Pontotoc, in 1910. The reason I was born there was that my father was a student at Ole Miss, and his parents owned a hotel there. He rode from Pontotoc to Oxford on a mule, and he had two shirts, the one on his back and one in a package. He worked his way through Ole Miss and after he graduated he went to Winona, Mississippi, where he met my mother. They got married in October and I was born the following July. My father went back to law school, and I was the first baby at Ole Miss!"

We laughed, and then she sobered to make sure I knew what she'd said was true. I was curious about her family's history at the university. "What years did your father go to Ole Miss?"

She cocked her head and thought. "I was born in 1910 and he had finished his undergraduate work. So subtracting, that's 1905 or '6 and then after I was born he was there for three years." She sat up in her chair. "My grandchildren have gone to Ole Miss, and we are one of two families in Mississippi who have had six successive generations there. My great-grandfather was a United States senator named Hernando de Soto Money, M-O-N-E-Y. My daughter is named Claudia Money Luckett, but the Money is a family name, it doesn't have anything to do with finances. Unfortunately. My great-grandfather's portrait hangs in the law library at Ole Miss, and my husband was a graduate of Ole Miss. I have two brothers that both went to Ole Miss, and my grandparents. We've been interwoven, my family, with the university."

"You went to Ole Miss?"

"Two years. This was *the* Depression, and we did not have enough money to have me and my brother in school, so I went two years and then I came back and my brother went. He played football, and also got a law degree."

I wondered how long she had lived in the Delta.

"I was five years old when my family came here, and I have been living in this house," she pointed to the floor, "for fifty-something years."

"In your lifetime," I said, "the world has in some ways turned."

"In *every* way," she corrected.

"When you were young, did you ever think it could change this much?"

"*No.* Not even when I was older did I think I'd see the changes that have come in the last twenty years. Drastic changes. I was in prep school in Maryland the year Lindbergh flew, and we didn't know he'd come and gone until he'd been there and been hailed a hero. But, of course, *everything* has changed, I don't know one thing that hasn't changed." She shook her head. "We are all still human beings, but relationships and activity and production and a way of life and your fundamental precepts of value, everything's changed. Why, when I was a child, the first airplane came to Clarksdale and they told us that the first one my age who got there got to go up for a ride. I got there first." She smiled. "I have seen some changes. There were no airplanes. There certainly wasn't television."

"Do you think," I asked, "that television and airplanes have made Mississippi more like other places?"

Mrs. Luckett frowned. "I think television has changed everybody everywhere. It's a terrible influence. It certainly has brought us all together, I mean, we know everything that happens to everybody in the world, but I know too much, really. They tell me things I don't want to know. Certainly, in my lifetime the world has changed, almost—what is it?—about three hundred forty degrees around the circle."

"How have these changes worked regarding black folks? It seems to me that black people can come and go as they please, but there doesn't seem to be a lot of, shall we say, socializing, or personal—"

"Associations?"

I nodded. "Yes. Interactions."

She settled back in her chair. "I think you're right about that. There's more than I ever thought I would see, and it came quicker than I ever thought. Things have a way of evolving. Sometimes when a great push is put on, it does more harm than good. We in the Delta here have been kind of thrown away, and we have a preponderance of people who are unskilled and uneducated and some of them are two and three generations on welfare. It's tragic for them, for the state, for the whole picture. But this is the breeding place in Mississippi for lots of Medicaid, lots of food stamps and children born out of wedlock.

"A lot of bad things happen here and I don't know why. We are the fertile part of Mississippi, and we had the plantations. I saw the first cotton picker when I was a grown woman, and it totally changed the place—all the technical advances have in a way destroyed the families that lived on places with a cow and a garden and whatever, and then they weren't needed anymore. It's been a sad transition. It's taken longer than it would have in a place with more diverse ways to make a living."

"Did you think the cotton picker would change so much?"

"No. I don't think they had any idea. I remember going to see it. It was out to Hobson's place. That was when we had German prisoner-of-war camps here, and they sort of helped put it together. It's placed a hardship on poor people because they can't get a job chopping cotton, for instance, farmers can't pay them minimum wage. The farmers have substituted all these horrible chemicals that they have to put down before planting the cotton and to kill the bugs and to make it grow and to defoliate it. It's been a revolution down here, almost like the invention of the wheel, in what it's done to the population—the poor population."

We were quiet. Then I asked her if she had any theories about how all of this had occurred. Did World War II have anything to do with the changes in the position of blacks in society?

"I never really thought about it a whole lot, if you want the real truth, and I don't know. Maybe after you've been serving in the army and there are certain privileges and maybe access to money that maybe you wouldn't have had if you hadn't been in the army, maybe that's made a difference."

I asked if there had been a time when she knew that blacks would no longer be pacified or placated.

"For example?"

"The late fifties or the early sixties."

"Was that when James Meredith was at the university?"

"Yes."

She frowned deeply and looked away. "I don't know. That was such a horrible travesty in so many ways. Sometimes if you change too fast, it's like two steps forward and five steps back. And now what they're going through is almost equally as ridiculous. Before integration came on the scene there were black colleges and white colleges, and what they wanted then, the whole push of the movement, was to integrate the white and the black, and now when it comes a time they might be brought together through force of finance as much as anything else, they say they don't want it. But there gets to be a point where preference has to give way to reality, and it's a problem. Not only in Mississippi. It gets back to money. This poor state has eight universities and everybody knows you cannot fund them. You cannot pay the teachers. Sometimes the students who get there haven't learned to read or write in high school, and I just don't know what's going to happen. Unless we can get a sound educational program for both white and black—the whites are just as ignorant as the black, most of them, a lot of them, because we have not had the teachers. You cannot teach if you don't have good teachers and that's a great lack that we've had. We can hardly compete with Arkansas." She changed direction. "It happened so fast. I never went anywhere in my life that was integrated, a party or a tea or a reception or anything like that until maybe five years ago."

"Why?"

"I don't know. I've always got along just fine. We have always— I have never in any phase of my life been without Afro-Americans in my house with me. But they were in my house helping me. They were not in as my companions, though they nursed my children and cooked my food and were closer to me than a lot of people, but there was not the feeling of equality between us. It was just what you'd always seen, always done, and in many ways people were a lot nicer than they are now. White and black. They had more respect for each other, and good manners were more a part of a person's behavior, and moral values were certainly more fully ingrained. For both. The family meant a great deal more. I don't know what makes these things happen, I've watched as sort of a spectator most of my life. A whole lot of things have happened that I never thought would happen, I never dreamed it. But they certainly happened. Sometimes when you're wrapped up in the daily life of a place, you're isolated and you don't see things happening around you unless there's this huge crack."

Mrs. Luckett walked me through the first floor of her home, a guided tour of the most splendid house I'd been in during my travels through Mississippi. There were seven or eight exquisite rooms, and she proudly showed me the carefully chosen and arranged furniture, artwork and objects, much of which, she said, had been culled from garage sales and flea markets in the Delta. We lingered and talked a minute more, then she opened the great front door and I walked down the brick steps of the circular portico into the night.

LEAVING Clarksdale that evening, I drove again across the Delta, down Highway 6 toward Oxford, on a clear night with a full moon, the burst and ready-to-be-harvested cotton bolls soaking up moonlight and seeming to give off an odd, phosphorescent glow. I was headed back to Ole Miss to spend homecoming weekend with friends. Listening to Mrs. Luckett, I kept thinking of how my mother had pined for Ole Miss just as much as the Moneys and the Lucketts had gloried in it; and I realized that my mother's exclusion from the university and what it represented had been as personality forming as had Mrs. Luckett's familial embrace.

Ole Miss seemed to be a theme throughout my journey, touching in one way or another most of the people I talked to, surfacing again and again in historical accounts and looming in my imagination as a symbol of Mississippi's social culture. Ole Miss, with its redbrick buildings (some built by my mother's relatives), its groves of trees, its winding roads and pretty coeds, seemed to represent "the South" and all its preoccupations with history, romance and order.

The University of Mississippi was founded in 1844, the first college in the state. In 1861 the entire student body left school and enlisted in the Confederate Army. No classes were held during the Civil War, the college reopening in 1865. Aside from a conflict with Governor Bilbo, who in 1928 tried to move the campus to Jackson, Ole Miss remained a quiet and stately place, as befit its status as the finishing school for the scions of the South, until September 1962, when James Meredith gained admission as its first black student. The name "Ole Miss" comes from an early student yearbook and is not official. Today, roughly ten thousand students attend the university from across the United States and the world. Four percent of them are black.

AFTER ARRIVING in Oxford that night, I met a friend, Mona Crockett, for a drink, and we walked from her small apartment in a Victorian house near the university to a faux working-class bar (many more frat boys in attendance than mechanics) on a side street off the town square. I was aware that by being together in public on what could be construed as a date, we were breaching the traditional continental divide of Mississippi culture, that of black men and white women "socializing." Before we entered the bar I mentioned my trepidation to Mona, but she just waved her hand, sighed wearily and said in her heavy southern accent, "These folks *need* something to talk about."

Mona and I had become friends several years before at NYU, where she and my wife studied law together. Now she was a non-practicing lawyer, surviving in Oxford on the margins, a part-time waitress, baby-sitter and librarian, thinking about becoming a writer and keeping, generally, a low profile.

The place was overfull, so we squeezed in and worked our way to the bar, where we ordered drinks. We settled in and listened to the band, which appeared to be composed of Ole Miss students performing adequate covers of southern rock songs, Allman Brothers, Lynyrd Skynyrd and Marshall Tucker. The dance floor was crowded, and the general atmosphere was festive, with lots of war whoops, hollering and merrymaking. It was homecoming weekend, a traditional three- or four-day party on the campus. I was the only black person in the bar, something I couldn't help being acutely conscious of, but something that didn't seem to attract much notice. If anything, several "good old boys" went out of their way to acknowledge me, nodding and pointing their long necks in my direction as a toast. Later on, one of them, a friend of Mona's, walked over with a fresh beer and handed it to me with a smile.

I asked Mona why there were no blacks present.

She shrugged. "They're probably at their fraternity parties. Tonight is their Greek night."

"Do they ever come out?"

"Now that you mention it, no." She grimaced. "I don't know. I don't think they'd be unwelcome. They just don't come."

We left the bar and walked back up to the square. Looping around the courthouse, we stopped for a minute in a club where a New Orleans band, the Subdudes, was playing, then walked down another hill to a coffeehouse. Mona introduced me to several people there, including the owner, Ron Shapiro. The Hoka, a bohemian hangout complete with a folksinger and posters of old foreign movies, was the first place I'd seen any other blacks during my night tour of Oxford—a few working as busboys and waiters, but more sprinkled throughout the restaurant at tables, eating and drinking. When I asked Mona if she'd brought me there to show off progressive Mississippi she laughed, but then said, very seriously, "You know, I think people are just doing the best that they can." The owner came over and sat with us, and we talked about new books and movies for some time until, at 1:00 a.m., the coffeehouse filled up with the denizens of the closing bars and clubs. I made a date with Mona for breakfast on Sunday, bade them goodnight and climbed back up the hill to the square. I looked for Lamar Street— named for L. Q. C. Lamar, rabid secessionist and segregationist, I couldn't help remembering—where I oriented myself toward north and my lodgings.

I woke the next morning in brilliant sunlight, half hungover and unsure where I was, then realized I was in Oxford, in the guest room of my friends Richard and Lisa Howorth. I'd been awakened by the Howorth children playing in the yard, and as it didn't seem they were going to stop anytime soon, I gave up the contentment of blankets and shoved myself into the day. I was going to the homecoming game as Richard's guest, hitting the tailgaters before the game and a series of parties that night, a sequence Richard felt would give me a feel for "a real live football weekend," and I figured he would know, given his status as a twenty-year Ole Miss alum and a fixture of the Oxford business community.

We parked the car about a mile from the stadium, cut through a gully and some woods to emerge onto University Avenue, melding with a tremendous crowd of students and alumni, chanting and singing as it surged toward the campus. With us was Richard's old-est daughter, Claire, who was ten, and Richard's classmate Homer Best, a lawyer up from Jackson for the weekend. We had met Homer on the way, and I recognized him as one of the men who had greeted me warmly in the bar the night before.

We walked onto "the Grove" at the circle, past the Confederate Memorial I'd seen the year before with my mother. Again I was jolted by the surreal character, or so it seemed to me, of my presence at Ole Miss. Though I was enjoying myself with my friends, I was unable to escape Mississippi's unsubtle reminders of past pain; and that sense of the blood of history that at times seemed would be with me all day—from tailgate parties there in the Grove, with molasses-accented belles offering me hors d'oeuvres and barbecue, to the Ole Miss Marching Band's playing of "Dixie" to celebrate the day's vic-tory—clashed in a kind of double vision with the festivities and high spirits. With the exception of the two football teams, there were very few blacks in sight.

From the tailgaters we worked our way over to the stadium, claiming our seats in the south end zone. It was a gorgeous fall day, clear skies and about fifty degrees, and when I noted the large num-ber of black players warming up on the field, Richard remarked slyly, "Well, you know the *real* reason Ole Miss integrated?" I shook my head. "Well," he said, "in 1969 Ole Miss lost for the first time to Southern Mississippi. Southern had black players, Ole Miss did not. The next year Ole Miss recruited blacks."

The game itself was a slow and fitful affair, Ole Miss climbing to a 27–9 defensive victory over Memphis State, most of the scoring coming in a wild third quarter bracketed by great stretches of bore-dom. I was more interested, though, in the activity surrounding the game, the combination fashion show, networking event and celebra-tion of privilege that seemed to circle in concert the pagan ritual of young men struggling on the field. Virtually all the spectators were sharply, richly dressed, women in barn jackets and riding boots, men in flannel blazers and loafers, everyone shouting hello and shak-ing hands and trading phone numbers. I was disappointed to see the Confederate battle banner everywhere, everywhere, particularly among the alumni.

Richard explained that the university, responding to black protest, had disavowed use of the flag at games; but the alumni half of the stadium seemed filled with the Stars and Bars, and the student section, while less populated, at times displayed hundreds. The flag has been a casus belli for years at Ole Miss and throughout the South. Georgia governor Zell Miller set off acrimonious debate when he proposed removing the emblem from the state flag, and in the summer of 1993 the issue spilled onto the floor of the U.S. Senate, as Illinois senator Carol Moseley Braun argued down a motion by North Carolina senator Jesse Helms to renew the patent on the insignia of the United Daughters of the Confederacy, a different Confederate flag.

The whites claim the rebel flag represents history and heritage whereas blacks see it as a totem of their subjugation; and it was astonishing to see fifty thousand whites waving Confederate flags to urge on their black gladiators. This flag was not, in fact, the South's official flag, and it never flew in Confederate offices. The flag wasn't widely seen until the 1950s, which indicates there might be something more at stake in its use than remembering history and respecting tradition.

The struggle over the battle flag is symbolic of the next phase in the South's evolution, and seeing the Stars and Bars so proudly displayed clarified for me the question that had dogged me since Natchez, that I had wondered about the night before with Mona and had carried with me that morning into the Grove. I suddenly knew why blacks would not be present at the football stadium or, in significant numbers, at Ole Miss itself. This was not their place, it seemed to me; they did not belong and were not missed. Blacks in Mississippi had simply continued the society my parents had grown up in, and that society was separate, if somewhat more equal than it had been before. This was the division that stood at the heart of the court cases and battles over state educational funding and all-white academies and the rest. Mississippi contains two cultures, mutually suspicious if not hostile and, on a good day, indifferent. Whites waving the Confederate flag see that flag as *who they are*, whereas to blacks it is by definition an insult and humiliation.

That day in Oxford at Ole Miss brought me back to the beginning of my journey, when my mother, in what I took to be naïveté, had asked me about William Faulkner. I had traveled through Mississippi for two years doing my best not to think about Faulkner, not wanting him to overshadow my thoughts and even convincing myself that his words didn't really apply to me. What could this white man, a celebrator of the Confederacy and the owner of a "big house" out on Old Taylor Road, say to a descendant of those who had been the slaves of his Sartorises, Compsons and Sutpens, who had suffered enormously under the Snopeses? I wanted very badly for the answer to be "nothing at all," but that response would be far from true. Faulkner was everywhere I went in Mississippi, often coloring if not creating how I saw things.

Reconsidering my feelings in light of what I'd learned about the state, I realized that Faulkner had presented one way of analyzing everything I'd seen. I began to extrapolate on the metaphors in his novel *Absalom, Absalom!*, the story of Thomas Sutpen, the mysterious planter who appears in Jefferson (Faulkner's name for Oxford) one day to buy land and build a kingdom. When I started in Mississippi, I had thought this a parable of the futility of ferocious ambition: Sutpen building an empire he could rule absolutely, only to see it fail because of his vanity. And that is one way of reading the tale.

But Mr. Faulkner wasn't that simple, and the more time I spent in Mississippi and the more I learned of its past, the more I came to see *Absalom, Absalom!* as a short history of the Deep South and a prediction for its future. Thomas Sutpen had two sons, one by a black woman and one by a white. Sutpen disowned the former and embraced the latter; and when the black son returned in search of patrimony, Sutpen refused to recognize him. That failure of recognition, in every sense of the word, set off a chain of events that led to the destruction of the entire Sutpen family and plantation.

Contemporary Mississippians refuse, in the same way, to "recognize" each other, to acknowledge their commonality. The state's tragic history is testimony to what this refusal has wrought. And it is now likely that the members of the two racial groups are permanent strangers, doomed to gape and stare but not see, blind to each other as siblings, humans, Americans.

"The past," Faulkner said, "isn't dead. It isn't even past yet." He understood, in a way that seems profoundly foreign to Americans, that a person is infinitely more than what happens to him or her, the specific events and places of one lifetime. Men and women are also the product, or prisoner, of all the things that happened and were thought generation upon generation before their births. Freeing oneself from this psychic and cultural web can take superhuman effort; few manage to do so.

Faulkner's lifework was to explore and delineate how the web played itself out in Mississippi, and his account has proven largely accurate. He was a descendant of the early planters and thought of them as heroes, like his great-grandfather Colonel William Falkner, who distinguished himself in the Civil War, and his grandfather John Falkner, the local big man. Faulkner's father, Murry, was unable to sustain the energy of his forebears, and that allowed the Snopeses— the Bilbos and the Vardamans—to take over and exercise their rapacious greed. These Snopeses, the poor whites, had always seen blacks as the greatest threat to their prosperity, and therefore as their greatest enemies. When they came to power, they ruled without mercy. The story of Faulkner's family was the story of Mississippi.

Faulkner was the first artist in the South to understand and question those myths and legends people carry as the justification for what they do and how things are, the first to question the way humans experience life by moving forward through history while always looking back toward where they have come from. He called this blinding preoccupation the burden of the past, and though most people never made this connection in their own daily lives, Faulkner knew that there were no such things as happy slaves, that the mansions amid the magnolias were often decrepit and verminridden, that the self-appointed aristocrats were often conscienceless and incestuous brutes. He knew that many an old colonel had proved cowardly in battle, and that many a public racist turned to the arms of a Negro for comfort, pleasure and release, unions that resulted in children, white and black, bearing the same last name. He knew how the past and the present intertwined, blinding Mississippians to both.

I think Faulkner understood this conflict in the hearts of Mississippians because he understood, or at least acknowledged, the conflict in his own. Faulkner was a white man, a southerner, a Mississippian, as full of rebel legend and as much a prisoner of the past as anyone. Yet he also loved Caroline Barr, a black woman he called

Mammy, perhaps more than he loved anyone in his family. In his dedication of *Go Down, Moses* to her, he describes her "immeasurable devotion and love." At her funeral, Faulkner praised her as "a fount not only of authority over my conduct and of security for my physical welfare, and of active and constant affection and love. . . . From her I learned to tell the truth, to refrain from waste, to be considerate of the weak and respectful to age. I saw fidelity to a family that was not hers, devotion and love for people she had not borne. She was born in bondage and with a dark skin and most of her early maturity was passed in a dark and tragic time [Reconstruction] for the land of her birth. She went through vicissitudes which she had not caused; she assumed cares and griefs which were not even her cares and griefs . . . if there is a heaven she has gone there."

Perhaps Caroline Barr led Faulkner beyond the day-to-day structures of life and racial relations—in Mississippi, so much of life *is* racial relations. But most of his white contemporaries of any means knew someone like her, with little visible effect on their behavior; and even Faulkner's beloved "Mammy" slept out back and ate in the kitchen. There are no pictures of her in the biographies.

This is not to discount Faulkner's obvious and deep affection. Rather, the complex interweaving of his love for Caroline Barr and the context of Mississippi society becomes yet another shake of the kaleidoscope. If you go to Faulkner's estate, Rowan Oak, you are likely to be impressed, if not awed, by the beautiful white house, the grounds well preserved and wooded. You nod at the stables and barn, then go inside to the dining room, then the study; you might even notice *Invisible Man* on the windowsill and remember that Faulkner praised the book on the jacket. But would you remember to look for Callie's shed? What would remind you that she'd even been there?

These questions, which become the questions of the history of Mississippi, and the history of the United States, come back to Faulkner's metaphor of recognition. Who is acknowledged as a member of the family? Will the failure to acknowledge lead to destruction? It's an old story, Abraham Lincoln's "house divided against itself," or an even older one, King David on the roof, weeping: "Would that I had died instead of you, O Absalom, my son, my son."

ON A CHILLY Sunday afternoon we had a late lunch at the Ho-
worths', Richard, Lisa, Mona and I, along with several other friends
of theirs. We sat quietly in the large kitchen, everyone tired from the
night before but enjoying a meal of eggs Benedict, fruit, cheese and
croissants, savoring the last few hours of the weekend. Richard and
Lisa's friend Ira, visiting from Los Angeles, mentioned that he
wanted to see Faulkner's grave, and it occurred to me that I hadn't
ever been there. Richard said it was within walking distance, took us
to the porch and pointed to a cemetery down the hill. Four of us
walked down the hill, followed the green historical society signs, and
found the grave, a simple concrete tomb under a large oak tree at the
bottom of a ridge with WILLIAM CUTHBERT FAULKNER 1897–1962
carved on its face. Lisa knelt down and carefully brushed an accumu-
lating coat of clay dust from his name. While we stood there other
tourists walked up, but nobody said anything. On the other side of
the ridge above us the sun had dropped behind the houses to the
west, and we stood there in falling November light. I remembered
then something I'd seen the day before, at the game. A little girl,
about four years old, dressed up in a miniature Ole Miss cheerleader
uniform had led a section of the stands a few rows in front of us in a
bowdlerized version of the Ole Miss battle chant, "The Hotty
Toddy." She was blond and fierce and cute, stomping and yelling as
hard as she could:

> *"Are you ready?"*
> Hell, yes, damn right
> Hotty, toddy
>   Gosh A-mighty
> Who in the hell are *we*?
>   HEY!
> Flim flam, bim bam
> *Ole Miss,* by damn!"

Clutched in her right hand was a tiny rebel flag.

Reconstruction

Free to plant
Free to hoe
Free to chop
Every row

Free to harvest
Free to pay
Free to borrow
Free to stay

Letter to a White Friend in Mississippi

The images scroll through my head,
in black, in white, in color,
the face of Emmett Till, a forest
of rebel flags, Martin Luther King
walking down Highway 61, that week's
lonely road toward death.
I look in the crowds for you,
for me, but we are not there.
We are in the future
and there is so much
that has already happened,
that has gone on ahead of us
into what we strangely
call the past.

Then there are the memories,
in black, in white, in color,
too much to remember,
too much to forget,
we couldn't learn the algebra
if we tried. Things change
and add up—blood, sin,
skin—the answers
bleed out of the equation
and leave too much to carry,
to get past, the borders
between history and me,
history and you, history
and us. Then there are the borders
history has placed between
and around us.

The sum of black and white
is gray, ambivalence, doubt.
And sometimes love,
which is why it has everything to do
with us, and nothing.
We wander this empty afterward,
this present that is the ghost
of the past, if not guilty
then not exactly innocent,
but here,
while the river
does what it does,
the levee holds or breaks,
machines furrow the bristling
fields and the empty towns yawn
and bake and fade in the sunlight.

for Richard Ford

Levee

I

No one knows how many
slipped, their final breaths
spent swimming—sucking
fill as it fell in upon them.
Out-of-luck working men, vagrants
and leased trusties, the fill
had to keep flowing to stay the flow
of the river, to save the fields
and crops and progress.

II

Mississippi is dry, and quiet,
absent the grinding pestle of material
and screams, the mortar of bones
and gravel, dirt and cement
knitting these mounds as they channel
the lazy fury south, the water
and the weather the only two things
a white man in the delta
has to be afraid of.

FOUR

A Sort of Chorus

It is a complex fate to be an American.

—HENRY JAMES

People think that Negroes just take whatever the white man puts out and likes it. Well, I know different. I remember one time when I was a little girl. There was this man who lived on a plantation out from Drew. His name was Joe Pullum and he had worked on this man's plantation for quite a little while, but the man never would pay any money. So one day this white man wanted to send Mr. Pullum to the hill country to bring some families down to work on his plantation. Mr. Pullum said he would go and the man gave him a hundred and fifty dollars.

Mr. Pullum didn't go to the hills to get the people. He just figured that since the man had never paid him, he would use this money to fix up his house and do different things he needed to do. So after a while, the white man noticed that Mr. Pullum hadn't gone to get the people. He drove up to Mr. Pullum's house one day in his horse and buggy with another white man. He went up to the house carrying his gun with him and asked the Negro about it. Mr. Pullum told him what he'd done with the money and that he considered it his money 'cause the man had robbed him out of more than that anyway. The white man got mad and shot Mr. Pullum in the arm.

Mr. Pullum ducked in the house and got his Winchester and killed that white man dead. Well, the white man that was sitting out in the buggy saw this and he lit out for town, which was Drew.

The Negro knew he'd be coming back with a lynch mob and they would hang him. So he got all the ammunition he had and went out to Powers Bayou and hid in the hollow of a tree.

The lynch mob came. I ain't never heard of no one white man going to get a Negro. They're the most cowardly people I ever heard of. The mob came to get Mr. Pullum but he was waiting for them and every time a white man would peep out, he busted him. Before they finally got him, he'd killed thirteen and wounded twenty-six, and it was a while in Mississippi before the whites tried something like that again.

The way they finally got him was to pour gasoline on the water of the bayou and set it afire. When it burned up to the hollowed out stump, he crawled out. When they found him, he was unconscious and was lying with his head on his gun. They dragged him by his heels on the back of a car and paraded about with that man for all the Negroes to see. They cut his ear off and for the longest time it was kept in a jar of alcohol in a showcase in a store window at Drew. I was about eight years old when that happened.

—Fannie Lou Hamer

Chopping cotton, Knowlton Plantation, Perthshire, Mississippi, 1940

I stopped and questioned her, asked her what was wrong.

"I dearly loved my master, son," she said.

"You should have hated him," I said.

"He gave me several sons," she said, "and because I loved my sons I learned to love their father though I hated him too."

"I too have become acquainted with ambivalence," I said. "That's why I'm here."

"What's that?"

"Nothing, a word that doesn't explain it. Why do you moan?"

"I moan this way cause he's dead," she said.

"Then tell me, who is that laughing upstairs?"

"Them's my sons. They glad."

"Yes. I can understand that too," I said.

"I laughs too, but I moans too. He promised to set us free but he never could bring hisself to do it. Still I loved him. . . ."

"Loved him? You mean . . . ?"

"Oh yes but I loved something else even more."

"What more?"

"Freedom."

—RALPH ELLISON

Representatives and direct Taxes shall be apportioned among the several States which may be included within this Union, according to their respective Numbers, which shall be determined by adding to the whole Number of free Persons, including those bound to Service for a Term of Years, and excluding Indians not taxed, three fifth of all other Persons.

—CONSTITUTION OF THE UNITED STATES,
Article I, Section 2 [3]
(proposed in 1787 and ratified in 1789)

Plantation store, Marcella Plantation, Mileston, Mississippi, 1939

Neither slavery nor involuntary servitude, except as a punishment for crime whereof the party shall have been duly convicted, shall exist within the United States, or any place subject to their jurisdiction.

—CONSTITUTION OF THE UNITED STATES,
Amendment XIII, Section 1
(proposed in 1865 and ratified in 1865)

All persons born or naturalized in the United States, and subject to the jurisdiction thereof, are citizens of the United States and of the State where they reside. No State shall enforce any law which shall abridge the privileges or immunities of the citizens of the United States; nor shall any State deprive any person of life, liberty, or property, without due process of law; nor deny to any person within its jurisdiction the equal protection of the laws.

—CONSTITUTION OF THE UNITED STATES,
Amendment XIV, Section 1
(proposed in 1866 and ratified in 1868)

All freedmen, free Negroes, and mulattoes in this state over the age of eighteen years, found on the second Monday in January, 1866, or thereafter, with no lawful employment or business, or found unlawfully assembling themselves together, either in the day or night time, and all white persons so assembling with freedmen, free Negroes or mulattoes, or usually associating with freedman, free Negroes or mulattoes on terms of equality, or living in adultery or fornication with a freedwoman, free Negro or mulatto, shall be deemed vagrants, and on conviction thereof shall be fined in the sum of not exceeding, in the case of a freedman, free Negro or mulatto, fifty dollars, and a white man two hundred dollars and imprisoned, at the discretion of the court, the free Negro not exceeding ten days, and the white men not exceeding six months.

Any freedman, free Negro, or mulatto, committing riots, routs, affrays, trespasses, malicious mischief and cruel treatment to animals, seditious speeches, insulting gestures, language or acts, or assaults on any person, disturbance of the peace, exercising the

S̲aturday afternoon, Marcella Plantation, Mileston, Mississippi, 1939

functions of a minister of the gospel without a license from some
regularly organized church, vending spirituous or intoxicating
liquors, or committing any other misdemeanor, the punishment of
which is not specifically provided for by law, shall, upon conviction
thereof, in the county court, be fined not less than ten dollars, and
not more than one hundred dollars, and may be imprisoned, at the
discretion of the court, not exceeding thirty days.

All fines and forfeitures collected under the provisions of this
act shall be paid into the county treasury for general county purposes, and in case any freedman, free Negro or mulatto, shall fail
for five days after the imposition of any fine or forfeiture upon him
or her, for violation of any of the provisions of this act to pay the
same, that it shall be, and is hereby made, the duty of the Sheriff of
the proper county to hire out said freedmen, free Negro or mulatto,
to any person who will, for the shortest period of service, pay said
fine or forfeiture and all costs; Provided, a preference shall be given
to the employer, if there be one, in which case the employer shall be
entitled to deduct and retain the amount so paid from the wages of
such freedman, free Negro or mulatto, then due or to become due;
and in case such freedman, free Negro or mulatto cannot be hired
out, he or she may be dealt with as a pauper.

All freedmen, free Negroes and mulattoes may sue and be
sued, implead and be impleaded in all the courts of law and equity
of this State, and may acquire personal property and horses in action by descent or purchase, and may dispose of the same in the
same manner and to the same extent that white persons may: Provided, that the provisions of this section shall not be so construed
as to allow any freedman, free Negro or mulatto to rent or lease
any lands or tenements, except in incorporated towns or cities, in
which places the corporate authorities shall control the same.

No freedman, free Negro, or mulatto, not in the military service of the United States Government, and not licensed to do so by
the board of police of his or her county, shall keep or carry firearms
of any kind, or any ammunition, dirk, or bowie-knife; and on conviction thereof, in the county court, shall be punished by fine, not
exceeding ten dollars, and pay the costs of such proceedings, and
all such arms or ammunition shall be forfeited to the informer.

—BLACK CODES,
Mississippi, 1865

Evening, Belzoni, Mississippi, 1939

After Winter

He snuggles his fingers
In the blacker loam
The lean months are done with,
The fat to come.

    His eyes are set
    On a brushwood-fire
    But his heart is soaring
    Higher and higher.

Though he stands ragged
An old scarecrow,
This is the way
His swift thoughts go,

    "Butter beans fo' Clara
    Sugar corn fo' Grace
    An' fo' de little feller
    Runnin' space.

"Radishes and lettuce
Eggplants and beets
Turnips fo' de winter
An' candied sweets.

    "Homespun tobacco
    Apples in de bin
    Fo' smokin' an' fo' cider
    When de folks draps in."

He thinks with the winter
His troubles are gone;
Ten acres unplanted
To raise dreams on.

> The lean months are done with,
> The fat to come.
> His hopes, winter wanderers,
> Hasten home.

"Butterbeans fo' Clara
Sugar corn fo' Grace
An' fo' de little feller
Runnin' space. . . ."

—STERLING A. BROWN

When . . . you have succeeded in dehumanizing the Negro, when you have put him down to be but as the beasts of the field; when you have extinguished his soul in this world and placed him where the ray of hope is blown out as in the darkness of the damned, are you quite sure that the demon you have caused will not turn and rend you?

—ABRAHAM LINCOLN

Go Down Moses

Transcribed by the editor from
the singing of the Hampton students
led by Paige I. Lancaster

1 When Is-rael was in E-gypt's land, Let my peo-ple go;

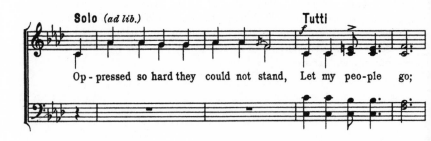

Op - pressed so hard they could not stand, Let my peo-ple go;

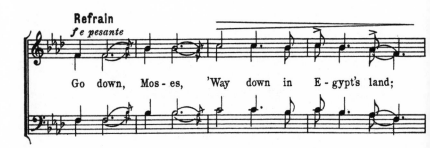

Go down, Mos - es, 'Way down in E - gypt's land;

Tell_ ole Pha - raoh_ Let my peo - ple go.

2

Thus saith the Lord, bold Moses said,
　Let my people go;
If not I'll smite your first-born dead,
　Let my people go.

3

No more shall they in bondage toil,
　Let my people go;
Let them come out with Egypt's spoil,
　Let my people go.

4

The Lord told Moses what to do,
　Let my people go;
To lead the children of Israel thro',
　Let my people go.

5

When they had reached the other shore,
　Let my people go;
They sang a song of triumph o'er.
　Let my people go.

.At Hampton Institute the first two measures of the last score are sung as here indicated, and
while this is undoubtedly a colloquialism it, nevertheless, is highly effective. — Editor

Tell_ ole Pha - raoh

The following story was often used by southerners to justify slavery. Hence, the appellation of blacks as "the children of Ham":

And the sons of Noah, that went forth of the ark, were Shem, and Ham, and Japheth: and Ham is the father of Canaan. These are the three sons of Noah: and of them was the earth overspread. And Noah began to be an husbandman, and he planted a vineyard: And he drank of the wine, and was drunken; and he was uncovered within his tent. And Ham, the father of Canaan, saw the nakedness of his father, and told his two brethren without. And Shem and Japheth took a garment, and laid it upon both their shoulders, and went backward, and covered the nakedness of their father; and their faces were backward, and they saw not their father's nakedness. And Noah awoke from his wine, and knew what his younger son had done unto him. And he said, Cursed be Canaan; a servant of servants shall he be unto his brethren. And he said, Blessed be the Lord God of Shem; and Canaan shall be his servant. God shall enlarge Japheth, and he shall dwell in the tents of Shem; and Canaan shall be his servant.

—GENESIS 9:18–21

These elected the Bilboes and voted indefatigably for the Vardamans, naming their sons after both; their origin was in bitter hatred and fear and economic rivalry of the Negroes who farmed little farms no larger than and adjacent to their own, because the Negro, remembering when he had not been free at all, was therefore capable of valuing what he had of it enough to struggle to retain even that little and had taught himself how to do more with less; to raise more cotton with less money to spend and food to eat and fewer or inferior tools to work with: this, until he, the Snopes, could escape from the land into the little grubby side street stores where he could live not beside the Negro but on him by marking up on the inferior meat and meal molasses the price of which he, the Negro, could not even always read.

In the beginning, the obsolescent, dispossessed tomorrow by the already obsolete: the wild Algonquian—the Chickasaw and Choctaw and Natchez and Pascagoula—looking down from the tall Mississippi bluffs at the Chippeway canoe containing three

Frenchmen—and barely had time to whirl and look behind him at a thousand Spaniards come overland from the Atlantic Ocean, and for a little while longer had the privilege of watching an ebb-flux-ebb-flux of alien nationalities as the magician's spill and evanishment of inconstant cards: the Frenchman for a second, then the Spaniard for perhaps two, then the Frenchman again for another two and then the Spaniard again and then the Frenchman again for the last half-breath before the Anglo-Saxon, who would come to say, to endure; the tall man roaring with Protestant scripture and boiled whiskey, Bible and jug in one hand and like as not an Indian tomahawk in the other, brawling, turbulent uxorious and polygamous: a married invincible bachelor without destination but only motion, advancement, dragging his gravid wife and most of his mother-in-law's kin behind him into the trackless wilderness, to spawn that child behind a log-crotched rifle and then get her with another one before they moved again, and at the same time scattering his inexhaustible other seed in three hundred miles of dusky bellies: without avarice or compassion or forethought either: felling a tree which took two hundred years to grow, to extract from it a bear or a capful of wild honey.

—WILLIAM FAULKNER

Even in Alabama—the repeated vowel sound of which seems to be a mimicking of "ma mama" or "ma mammy" and (because of all the songs) carries suggestions of banjos and black men and plantations—even in Alabama I found that Mississippi had a reputation for poverty and racial hardness.

—V. S. NAIPAUL

On the stage of Town Hall a few days before the 1964 Democratic
convention, a group from the Mississippi Freedom Democratic
Party talked of their experiences. To the facile eye, one of the men
who talked there might well have been mistaken for the Sambo
stereotype. He was southern, rural; his speech was heavily idio-
matic, his tempo slow. A number of his surface characteristics
seemed to support the stereotype. But had you accepted him as an
incarnation of Sambo, you would have missed a very courageous
man—a man who understood only too well that his activities in
aiding and protecting the young Northern students working in the
Freedom Movement placed his life in constant contact with death,
but continued to act. Now, I'm not going to reject that man because some misinformed person, some prejudiced person, sees him
as the embodiment of Uncle Tom or Sambo. What's inside you,
brother; what's your heart like? What are your real values? What
human qualities are hidden beneath your idiom?

—RALPH ELLISON

Sharecropper with cotton broker, Clarksdale, Mississippi, 1939

After the Egyptian and Indian, the Greek and Roman, the Teuton and Mongolian, the Negro is a sort of seventh son, born with a veil, and gifted with second sight in this American world,—a world which yields him no true self-consciousness, but only lets him see himself through the revelation of the other world. It is a peculiar sensation, this double consciousness, this sense of always looking at one's self through the eyes of others, of measuring one's soul by the tape of a world that looks on in an amused contempt and pity. One ever feels his twoness,—an American, a Negro, two souls, two thoughts, two unreconciled strivings; two warring ideals in one dark body, whose dogged strength alone keeps it from being torn asunder.

The history of the American Negro is the history of this strife,—this longing to attain self-conscious manhood, to merge his double self into a better and truer self. In this merging he wishes neither of the older selves to be lost. He would not Africanize America, for America has too much to teach the world and Africa. He would not bleach his Negro soul in a flood of white American-ism, for he knows that Negro blood has a message for the world. He simply wishes to make it possible for a man to be both a Negro and an American, without being cursed by his fellows, without having the doors of Opportunity closed roughly in his face.

—W. E. B. Du Bois

I could barely believe the destruction to these frail young bones. In my twenty-five years as a pathologist and medical examiner, I have never seen bones so severely shattered, except in tremendously high speed accidents or airplane crashes.

It was obvious to any first-year medical student that this boy had been beaten to a pulp.

—Dr. David Spain,
after the autopsy of James Chaney

Payday, Marcella Plantation, Mileston, Mississippi, 1939

Every lynching represents by just so much a loosening of the bonds
of civilization; that the spirit of lynching inevitably throws into
prominence in the community all the foul and evil creatures who
dwell therein. No man can take part in the torture of a human being without having his own moral nature permanently lowered.
Every lynching means just so much moral deterioration in all the
children who have any knowledge of it, and therefore just so much
additional trouble to the next generation of Americans. . . .

—THEODORE ROOSEVELT

Where all are guilty, no one is; confessions of collective guilt are
the best possible safeguard against the discovery of culprits, and
the very magnitude of the crime the best excuse for doing
nothing. . . . The real rift between black and white is not healed by
being translated into an even less reconcilable conflict between collective innocence and collective guilt. "All white men are guilty" is
not only dangerous nonsense but also racism in reverse, and it
serves quite effectively to give the very real grievances and rational
emotions of the Negro population an outlet into irrationality, an
escape from reality.

—HANNAH ARENDT

Juke joint near Clarksdale, Mississippi, 1939

I thought I heard them say
There were lions in the way
I don't expect to stay
    Much longer here.

Run to Jesus—shun the danger
I don't expect to stay
    Much longer here.

        —SLAVE SONG

We raise de wheat
De gib us de corn;
We bake de bread
De gib us de cruss;
We sif de meal
Dey gib us de huss;
We peal de meat
Dey gib us de skin
And dat's de way
De takes us in.

        —SLAVE SONG

I'd rather be a cockroach in New York than the emperor of Mississippi.

        —JOHN SAYLES

BLUES: Slow jazz song of lamentation, generally for an unhappy love affair. Usually in groups of 12 bars, instead of 8 or 16, each stanza being 3 lines covering 4 bars of music. Tonality predominantly major, but with the flatted 3rd and 7th of the key (the "blue notes"). Harmony tended toward the plagal or subdominant.

        —*Concise Oxford Dictionary of Music*

Gambling, Clarksdale, Mississippi, 1939

I'm tired of coffee and I'm tired of tea
I'm tired of you and you're tired of me

I'm tired of living and I don't want to die
I'm tired of working but I can't fly

I'm so tired of living I don't know what to do
You're tired of me and I'm tired of you

> —Mississippi plantation blues
> cited by DOROTHY SCARBOROUGH,
> *On the Trail of Negro Folksongs*

Sympathy

I know what the caged bird feels, alas!
When the sun is bright on the upland slopes;
When the wind stirs soft through the springing grass,
And the river flows like a stream of glass;

When the river flows like a stream of glass;
When the first bird sings and the first bud opens,
And the faint perfume from its chalice steals—
I know what the caged bird feels!

I know why the caged bird beat his wing
Till its blood is red on the cruel bars;
For he must fly back to his perch and cling
When he fain would be on the bough a-swing;
And they pulse again with a keener sting—
I know why he beats his wing!

I know why the caged bird sings, ah me,
When his wing is bruised and his bosom sore—
When he beats his bars and he would be free,
It is not a carol of joy or glee,
But a prayer that he sends from his heart's deep core,
But a plea, that upward to heaven he flings—
I know why the caged bird sings!

—PAUL LAURENCE DUNBAR

Jitterbugging, Clarksdale, Mississippi, 1939

A "blues" (or does one say a "blue")? What is the grammar of
the thing?

—DOROTHY SCARBOROUGH,
musicologist, circa 1920s

I woke up this mornin' feelin' round for my shoes
Know about that I got these old walkin' blues
I woke up this mornin' feelin' round for my shoes
I know about that, I got them old walkin' blues

Well, I'd leave the mornin' if I had to ride a blind
I feel mistreated and I don't mind dyin'
I leave this mornin', if I have to ride the blind
I feel mistreated and I don't mind dyin'

Well, some people tell me that the worried blues ain't bad
Worst old feelin' I most ever had
Well, some people say the worried blues ain't bad
It's the worst old feelin' I most ever had

—ROBERT JOHNSON,
"Walkin' Blues"

Sometimes I Feel Like a Motherless Child

To Miss Ruth Hale

home;_____ A long ways__ from home. True

be - liev - er, A long ways__ from home,_____ A

long ways__ from home. Some-times I feel like I'm

al - mos' gone, Some-times I feel like I'm al - mos' gone,

The blues is an impulse to keep the painful details and episodes of a brutal experience alive in one's aching consciousness, to finger the jagged grain, and to transcend it, not by the consolation of philosophy but by squeezing from it a near-tragic, near-comic lyricism. As a form the blues is an autobiographical chronicle of personal catastrophe expressed lyrically.

—RALPH ELLISON

Southern Road

Spring dat hammer—hunh—
Steady, bo';
Swing dat hammer—hunh—
Steady, bo';
Ain't no rush, bebby,
Long ways to go.

Burner tore his—hunh—
Black heart away;
Burner tore his—hunh—
Black heart away;
Got me life, bebby
An' a day.

Gal's on Fifth Street—hunh—
Son done gone;
Gal's on Fifth Street—hunh—
Son done gone;
Wife's in de ward, bebby,
Babe's not bo'n.

My ole man died—hunh—
Cussin' me;
My ole man died—hunh—
Cussin' me;
Ole lady rocks, bebby,
Huh misery.

Doubleshackled—hunh—
Guard behin';
Doubleshackled—hunh—
Guard behin';
Ball and chain, bebby,
On my min'.

White man tells me—hunh—
Damn yo' soul;
White man tells me—hunh—
Damn yo' soul;
Got no need, bebby,
To be tole.

Chain gang nevah—hunh—
Let me go;
Chain gang nevah—hunh—
Let me go;
Po' los' boy, bebby,
Evahmo'. . .

—STERLING A. BROWN

I woke up this mornin' with the blues all round my bed
Yes, woke up this morning with the blues all round my bed
Went to eat my breakfast, had the blues all round my bread

"Good mornin' blues, how do you do?"
"Good mornin' blues, how do you do?"
"I'm feelin pretty good, pal, how about you?"

If the blues was whiskey, I'd stay drunk all the time
If the blues was whiskey, I'd stay drunk all the time
Stay drunk, baby, just to wear you off my mind

If I feel tomorrow like I feel today
If I feel tomorrow like I feel today
I'll stand right here, look a thousand miles away

—TRADITIONAL

Surplus commodities, Natchez, Mississippi, 1940

Psalm 137

By the rivers of Babylon, there we sat down,
yea, we wept, when we remembered Zion.

    We hanged our harps upon the willows in the midst
  thereof.
For there they that carried us away captive required
of us a song; and they that wasted us required of us
mirth, saying, Sing us one of the songs of Zion.

    How shall we sing the Lord's song in a strange land?
If I forget thee, O Jerusalem, let my right hand forget her cunning.

    If I do not remember thee, let my tongue cleave
    to the roof of my mouth; if I prefer not
    Jerusalem above my chief joy.
Remember, O Lord, the children of Edom in the day of
Jerusalem; who said Rase it, rase it, even to the foundation
  thereof.

    O daughters of Babylon, who art to be destroyed;
    happy shall he be, that rewardeth thee as thou hast
    served us.
Happy shall he be, that taketh and dasheth the little one against
the stones.

       Been down so long,
       Being down don't bother me

            —TRADITIONAL

Maids, Gibson, Mississippi, 1940

FIVE

Walkin' Blues

BY THE TIME I went to homecoming at Ole Miss I had traversed Mississippi for several years, had renewed relationships with family and made new friends, had read volumes of books and documents, and had, through all of this, endured a steady darkening of my outlook. American history, and the future possibilities it implied, were becoming in my eyes a net of irony and sorrow from which I could not free myself. I was a young man, with a young person's taste for certainty and closure. But in sifting the complexities of Mississippi I found that each question I answered branched into three more, into infinitudes I could not grasp.

I couldn't believe how naive I had been about both history and its processes, and could not reconcile my growing knowledge with what I'd previously thought about my own life. On one level I felt privileged and lucky, the winner, as a black American, of a kind of lottery; but on a much deeper and darker level, I felt undeserving of my privilege. This feeling of unworthiness had grown from the initial impulse that led me to Mississippi, an impulse I'd thought my search would stay, and its increase had much to do, I realized, with my father.

From the things I'd learned I was beginning to see more fully than ever before just what my father had accomplished. He had created my privilege when he himself had none. My life was something he had dreamed and hoped and planned for, an extension of his own; and in order to see and understand myself I first would have to see him. My father's life was the Rubicon of my own imagination. Yet for years I had hardly considered him a part of my story; rural Mississippi had no clear ties to suburban Chicago. But I realized now that the one would not exist for me without the other.

What had happened to my father in Mississippi? How had he become the taciturn, often remote, yet unflaggingly resolute and loyal man he was? I needed to find out, and was scared to, concerned that I, in whom he had put so much faith, was not worthy.

WHEN MY FATHER boarded a Greyhound bus in Memphis, Tennessee, one warm Saturday evening in the summer of 1952, he had forty dollars and one suitcase, which contained everything he owned: two cotton suits, two pairs of pants and three shirts, underwear, socks, a toothbrush, baking soda, soap and a Bible, the only book he had ever owned. He was seventeen years old.

The suitcase was a step up. When Claude had arrived in Memphis from Mississippi two years earlier, he carried a shopping bag containing his work clothes, a denim shirt and a pair of blue jeans. Everything else he owned he'd worn: his "good jeans," a cotton T-shirt, his sturdy boots and a denim jacket. He had no money, having spent all his savings on the bus ticket from Holly Springs: he was dependent upon his cousin, Edgar, who had promised a couple of weeks' lodging and help in finding a job, and on the kindness of strangers.

In Memphis Claude had worked construction, retrofitting a building from an aircraft plant to a paper factory, then in an automotive repair shop rebuilding engines, carburetors and the like. He has said about leaving Memphis, "I felt that my time was up there. There didn't seem to be any interest in having black people employed on any kind of steady basis. Memphis was a permanent recession for black men." Claude had cousins in the North, and on trips home they flaunted evidence of the promising things he'd heard about

Chicago all his life. "Everybody in the North seemed to have a car, they had better clothes. I wanted to get in on that action. I wanted to try for some security. In Memphis they always treated you like a boy. I wanted to be a man. I was tired of the racism, the steady meanness."

So Claude set off on a journey, an odyssey even: in his search for a home he was leaving everything he knew and carrying only his memories. Those details, the specific slights, injuries, and humiliations he'd suffered as a black man in the South, things he would recount to his children about forty and fifty years later, would supply the fire he needed to endure lonely, barely literate years in Illinois, working in foundries and digging ditches, trying to figure out what to do next. He was one of millions of blacks who were willing, or forced, to leave Mississippi, headed for Chicago, Detroit, Milwaukee, Los Angeles. Robert Johnson sings, "I woke up this mornin' feelin' round for my shoes / I know about that, I got them old walkin' blues." Suddenly, strangely, I see my father as a young man, stuck in a dead-end job in Memphis, Tennessee, plotting, plotting, plotting his next move.

CLAUDE WAS BORN in 1935 in Marshall County, near the town of Holly Springs. In a story much like Richard Wright's, he started his life in poverty and degradation on a cotton plantation, born to uneducated and sometimes violent parents. His grandparents on both sides had been born into slavery and had become sharecroppers during Reconstruction. Some of Claude's uncles and cousins worked in construction, developing their own business years after he left. Claude, with only a grammar-school education, unknowingly traced Wright's path from Mississippi to Memphis, then Chicago, in search of liberty and something that could be called a better life.

On a humid summer afternoon we sat in the shade of a maple tree in a hill pasture southwest of Holly Springs—the site of Claude's grammar school, a wooden one-room building now nearly collapsed and faded from white to gray.

"Dad," I said, "tell me about what it was like when you were growing up down here."

"Ain't nothing to tell." Among black males of a certain age, reticence is a way of life, and I've never known whether my father truly dislikes talking about the past, or whether the habit of few words has simply become part of who he is. As he likes to say, "I did not get to be fifty and black by being stupid." By which he means silence is sometimes, especially in Mississippi, the easiest way for a black man to survive.

"What's the first thing you remember?"

"Bigotry." He said this quietly, as if there were nothing else to report and this single word explained it all.

"You were conscious of that as a little boy?"

He laughed. "Even when I was little, my mother would tell me about the things white people did, the things they wouldn't let black people do." This he said with an air of matter-of-factness. "They did not allow black men good jobs where they could make any money; I remember my mother telling me that, and that we couldn't drink out of the drinking fountains on the corners in town that the white people used. I remember her showing me the one in the courthouse that the colored could use. When we were in town we couldn't use the bathroom, we always had to go to some out-of-the-way place."

"White people did all this?"

"*Hell,* yes. They didn't want us to live as they lived, or have the means to."

"How old were you when you figured this out?"

"Three or four." He became, curiously, expressionless. "All I can say it did for me at the time was make me think that white people were awful mean."

"Do you think that now?"

"That was my thinking at the time. They had no right—I don't know that I could have figured it out it in those terms then, but in my heart that's what I felt, that they were unfair and unkind. I didn't think I could treat anyone like that. I knew there were rules black people had to follow, and I knew I was going to have to follow those rules as well, unless I found a way whereby white people wouldn't or couldn't lynch me like I'd heard they'd done to any number of black folks who wouldn't obey, or were considered to be unruly, or a threat. I didn't like it, but I can't say that as a child I knew what I was going to do about it."

Claude paused, then continued in a monotone. "It was a matter of getting old enough, then I was going to find someplace. I didn't know exactly where it would be, but that place was where I was going to move, someplace where I wouldn't be brutalized by men I didn't even know."

"What's the first bad thing you remember happening to you?"

He shrugged, then spoke as if the events he described had happened to someone else. "There were so many things that could happen and did. At school we would get our books and in the cover there would be this person's name; our schoolbooks were always used books. I remember this was like the second or third grade. There would be a person's name in there, and grade, and race, and it would always be 'white.' "

I expressed surprise. He chuckled, without smiling. "Sure. We always got the old books, the white kids got 'em first. And there'd always be pages missing, where if you read two chapters relative to something, you couldn't finish. If the third chapter completed the subject matter, then that chapter would be deliberately cut out, or the pages torn up, and you'd never know how it finished. I didn't understand it, why it was happening, but I talked to my parents and teachers and they said there was this school superintendent, a white woman, and she did this on purpose. She also never gave us enough books, or all the units in a particular subject. I think it was to keep us from doing enough work to get a high school diploma. She succeeded in my case.

"In those days black kids didn't ride the bus, we walked, sometimes miles. The white kids did get to ride, and the reason we knew it was because they'd ride past us on their buses and insult us, or yell something racist and laugh, and you'd be there out in the rain. This was 1941, '42, '43, in there. It was a little country school, one room, one teacher for nine or ten grades. The teacher handled all of them with the help of the older children. She had a lot of kids, as many as two hundred, and she had it organized so that some of them would be outside playing while others were getting their math class, then she'd switch. It was kind of amazing when I think about it. She did this all day, working her way up through the children. She'd use the older girls who could read and write well to fill in and help out."

"When did you decide to leave?"

"I had probably started to hear about Chicago, but I didn't know where it was or what it was like. I heard that black people lived there, that they seemed to live pretty good. They had things we didn't have. Cars, plumbing, electricity, money. So I knew I was going to go away to one of those cities where blacks could make it better. In Mississippi I was watching people work twelve hours a day for two dollars. This was like '46, '47, '48. You had to be on the truck or in the field at six o'clock and you didn't get off until six. And your travel time was on *you*. So sometimes, if the work was far enough away, it was really fourteen hours for two dollars. I figured if I had to work, why not go where I could make some money? I was only ten or eleven at that point, I wasn't old enough to leave, but I was planning on it by the time I was sixteen, eighteen at the oldest. If I worked and got paid, I figured I could get some of the things we didn't have." He stopped to think. "I couldn't see letting white people continually take advantage of me. I had to leave Mississippi because there was nothing I could do about that there, there was no way to confront them.

"Let me tell you a story. I worked for this man, his name was Smith. I think he was a Klansman, he had so much hatred in him. We were digging foundations to houses; he was paying fifty cents an hour. We dug five or six of these foundations, me and another guy, in two or three days. Smith wanted you to *get at it*. Ninety-, hundred-degree temperatures. This was July and August, after we'd laid by the crops. I remember we finished on a Wednesday, then it was time for the white men to come in and take over, pour the foundation, do the carpentry; they wouldn't let us do that. Anyway, Smith said he'd pay us on Friday, so I went over there about ten o'clock in the morning and asked him for my money. He got upset, said he would pay me when he paid everybody else, but I wanted to ride up to Memphis with my cousins and they were leaving. Besides, I wasn't one of his regulars. So he went inside, wrote the check, threw it out on the ground and told me I'd never work for him again, in fact, I was never to set foot on his property again. I figured, 'Why take this?' "

"Did you ever want to hurt white people?"

He flashed an ironic smile. "Most definitely. I hated white people, with a passion." Then the good Baptist in him reasserted itself. "Not all of them, of course. If I happened to know that the man was a good man and was straight and would treat me human, give me water if I was working for him, maybe even food, then I didn't have any problem with him. One man I worked with would even have his wife fix me something to eat. In those days that was important because a lot of the time black people only had food like greens and black-eyed peas and it's hard to carry that for lunch. A man like that, who treated you better, he might want you to stay in your place, but you didn't think about it much, at least he acknowledged that you were a person. I didn't think about him being white. But people that I knew were racists, that did not care for blacks—well, I didn't care for them. I hated them as much as they hated me. I often had visions of wiping out the entire white community."

As I listened I was stunned, because for so long I'd seen my father as a sincere Christian, virtually a pacifist, and now wondered if his dedication to nonviolence had been more a strategy than a belief. I asked why he and the other blacks had never lashed out.

"There was nobody to organize us. The people around me, my peer group, were as young and inexperienced as me. We weren't advanced enough, educated. We didn't know where to get the guns, the ammunition. We didn't know how to plan it so we could win. What was the use of starting something like that, getting caught and getting hung?"

"But you thought of it?"

"Hell, yes. There were times when somebody white did something to you that really hurt, really stung. You'd want to hurt them back. When I got older I understood that the reason white folks were so sure of themselves in their brutality to us was because the government, the politicians, the merchants and the rich people was all behind it. It came down from the top, from Washington, D.C., right on down: *Keep them niggers in their place.*"

WHEN WE were children, my brother and sister and I loved music. We still do, but not with the same fanatical purity that comes from not having much else on your mind. We'd wake up and put on records first thing in the morning: Aretha Franklin, B. B. King, Andrae Crouch and the Disciples or Al Green. We'd spend summer afternoons on the porch happily boogalooing to "Tighten Up," "Cold Sweat," "I Want You Back" and "Jimmy Mack." At night we'd lie awake in the dark and listen to the radio—WCFL, WGRT, WLS and WVON—until our parents yelled at us from the living room to knock it off. My father would sit in the yard with his friends sometimes, shaking his head and saying, "Them children *wake up* with the blues, sing the blues all day and then sleep with 'em." We'd just laugh and say, "Dad, what do you know about it?"

Memories of those days, and the irony of our arrogance, were in my thoughts as I drove down the rough and winding old Mississippi Highway 4 with Claude. My siblings and I actually thought our father knew nothing about "the blues," or the music we called by that name, which was really pop music. Whenever we'd impugn his understanding he'd only grunt or say something like "Everything in its place," or in a good mood he'd laugh and say, "I hope I never know as much about it as y'all." In a bad mood he'd say, "I have forgotten more about the blues than you will ever know." This last was, I now realize, closest to the truth.

What *did* I know about the blues? What could I? The landscape before me, Marshall County, five miles out of Holly Springs, couldn't have looked much different when Claude lived here in a tin-roofed log cabin tucked away in a bottom on Howard Jones's plantation. The land consists of rolling shallow hills covered with kudzu, hay fields, scrub fields, pine trees, oak trees and, in the bottoms, cleared fields bristling with endless cotton. The plants stood as small green shoots this May afternoon but were already in need of chopping. All of this was canopied by a huge blue sky, so bright the sunlight seemed to come from everywhere. In places, the kudzu—a weedy vine, *Pueraria lobata,* that can easily spread a foot a day—had overgrown everything, giving the landscape the feel of a science-fiction movie or a children's book, kudzu everywhere. The hilly vista was gentle and pretty—and full of rage; specifically, now, the dark undercurrent of my father's.

"Last time I was on this road, it was gravel," Claude said matter-of-factly. He had avoided Mississippi—excluding official occasions, mostly weddings and funerals—not enjoying the trip as my mother did and certainly not relishing his memories. *"I call it 'sippi 'cause I don't miss it,"* he'd often say. He had been back to Holly Springs, but never out here to the Jones farm. We stopped the car on a flat stretch of road, got out and walked down a muddy path. "We lived over there." Claude pointed down into the recesses of the bottom, where the ramshackle remains of a tenant cabin stood. Then he moved his left arm from noon to ten o'clock to indicate another run-down structure a short distance from the first. "Uncle Isaac lived down there." He pointed in a forty-five-degree angle away from the cabin at a small and faded, though still inhabited, white frame house on the top of a nearby hill. "And Big Mama"—his grandmother— "up there."

This was the place, the landscape, the image that had been in his mind, his memory, as he struck out from Mississippi for Chicago more than forty years earlier. He had been thinking about these hills and trees and fields spreading on either side of a winding gravel road that, aside from being paved, has not changed much since that time. My father's life had not immediately eased after he left Mississippi; he eventually went north, joined the air force, was honorably discharged and returned to Chicago, where he began working at a taxing factory job, a job he held for the next thirty-eight years, at which he still is working. I often wondered what could drive a man to work that hard that long, and here in Mississippi all around us were the roots of his ferocity and discontent.

Earlier that day we'd been up Highway 4 on the other side of Holly Springs, where the road swings northeast toward the town of Ashland and Benton County. The physical landscape is the same out there, rolling hills, hay fields and ever-thickening clumps of trees, all covered in kudzu. We chose to take that road because Claude had worked on the crew that put in the highway, his first job away from the farm. He was fourteen when he started in 1949, and the crew built the approximately forty-mile stretch that snakes through the Holly Springs National Forest to Ripley.

"Our job," Claude said, "was to plant the sod and grass along the side of the highway. The black men did all the heavy work, the dirty work, planting, tamping the sod into place. We had a machine, a big heavy tool that tamped the sod into place, and you had to be strong to lift it all day. The white guys drove the trucks. They were from the Delta, and they didn't believe in calling you by your name, they'd either call you 'boy' or 'nigger.' It didn't make them no difference." He half laughed, half winced at the memory. "They were a loud and rough bunch. It didn't seem to me like they did anything but booze and chase women and fight, and sit on the top of the truck and tell you what to do. When they got to the site, they felt they were on break and wouldn't do anything but wait for the blacks to unload. Some days the temperature would be as hot as one hundred one, one hundred two, one hundred three degrees, even one hundred four; you could bet that every single day it would be at least ninety-five degrees. We worked out here from April to September."

This sort of thing had fascinated and intimidated me about him even before I became fully aware of what he'd been through. When I was fourteen, my chief worry was not embarrassing myself on the freshman football team; Claude had been out in the world doing a man's job with men. "Dad," I said, "this may be a dumb question, but why were you out working?"

"We needed the money." His standard answer.

"Don't you think you were too young to be out on your own like that?"

"Yep."

"Then why'd you do it?"

He was calm. "I'm trying to tell you, I had no choice."

"But why not stay on the farm?"

"There wasn't any money on the farm. I could make thirty dollars a week for six days' work on the road, five dollars a day for ten hours. I'd worked jobs before, two dollars a day for a twelve-hour day. Living on Howard Jones's place was like being under a tyrant. He specialized in keeping black folks down. He took everything we earned. You had to buy everything from his store. He accounted for *everything*, kept the records. Some of the black folks couldn't read and write, some of them didn't think they needed to. Mr. Jones had gained their confidence. I used to think he was a hypnotist, that he could hypnotize black folks and make 'em think he was a good guy. Deep down inside you didn't believe that, but on the surface of your mind, maybe as a way of not facing reality, you'd want to believe whatever he'd told you. He had ways of making it seem like you were working together, you and him, like you were partners in the farm, and you'd accept less, even if you knew he was lying."

"How did *you* know he was lying?"

"I'd had other little jobs, working for white people in town. They were the ones that could pay to have work done in those days. I'd trim hedges, around the sidewalk, maybe somebody'd pay you a dollar and a half. They might cut their own grass but they might not like to trim, so I'd come along with my clippers and my hoe and I'd get that dollar and a half. Some of 'em would let me cut the grass. You'd have to hit as many as you could before noon, because if you waited much past one o'clock, somebody else'd be done cut that yard."

I laughed. "You and the other little black kids were in competition as businessmen?"

Claude didn't find this funny. "That happened all the time. If I could get to these places by the time I needed to be there, I could make six or seven dollars. This was when I was ten years old. I could make more cutting grass in half a day than I could working twelve hours for Howard Jones. I figured it out. I did not like it. I knew I could do better. You could make ten or twelve dollars a week off three, four yards. That was good money for a kid. The highway was the only job I could get that summer. I didn't think the man would hire me because I was skinny and didn't have no weight, but I went and asked him and he said, 'Get on the truck.'

"One day I pointed out to the foreman a place where a mistake had been made and needed fixing." Claude took a sharp breath. "One of his assistants said to him, 'This nigger knows everything.' All I recall from the rest of that is a cold chill going through me. Why was I a 'nigger' when all I was trying to do was work hard, do a good job? That day changed me. I just wanted to make a living and not depend on anybody, not be dependent on anybody else.

"To get to a day's job we had to ride on a flatbed truck with them hillbillies driving sixty, seventy miles an hour down them gravel roads like they were trying to knock us off. We could barely hang on, we'd be thinking we were going to be thrown off the truck. They had no respect for us at all, and any way they could think of to humiliate or embarrass us, they took it.

"When there was one around, he would be nice, but when there

were three or four, then all of 'em got filthy-mouthed and disrespect-
ful. Suddenly, anything that happened was 'the nigger's fault.' I
think they thought that we might jump on one of 'em, plus, when
they were all together, they wanted to impress each other and show
off. They liked to say to each other, 'You sure know how to handle
them niggers.' They were cowards. They knew they had the upper
hand. They were white trash who got treated like upper class and it
went to their heads. In them days any white man, whether he could
read or write, was above any black man, whether he had a college
diploma or a master's or a Ph.D. The black man would have to be
beneath the white man and address him as 'sir,' whether he could
read or write or anything else. But I learned something out there
working on that highway: I learned that I could do whatever they
could do; I learned that I could have put that road in if I had the
same equipment, the trucks and graders and bulldozers. It gave me
confidence. I wasn't as afraid as I had been. The work wasn't that
hard and they weren't that smart. And I was able to provide money
for my family at a time when we needed it."

BACK IN the fields and woods where he had grown up, Claude
waved his arm in a wide sweep across the horizon. "Black folks
owned this land! A black man named Good Nunnally, between
1880, '90, and 1920, managed to get all this land. He had eight or
nine families working for him and he was good to them, but his son
managed to mess it all up. White folks tricked him, they'd say, 'Virgil,' that was his name, 'Virgil, whatever you need, come and let us
know.' Virgil'd go to the bank to borrow a thousand dollars, and the
white folks would encourage him to take even more. He run up
twenty or thirty thousand at the bank like that. Then they called
his loan. A lot of people had been slaves here on this land and somehow his father had bought it from the owners, but white folks got
it back."

"What was an average day like on the farm?"

"From the time I was big enough to get the mules, we worked
from about four-thirty in the morning until nine at night, taking off
about an hour from twelve until one or one-thirty in the middle of
the day."

This was taking me back to the talks and riffs of my childhood, him telling me about how hard he'd had it in Mississippi, and how, by contrast, I "had it made." I asked, "What kind of work?"

"Well, I'd get up and get dressed and go out to look for the mules—they'd be out in the pasture—with a stick in my hands to make sure I didn't get bit by a snake." He laughed. "I had this long stick I'd bang through the weeds so anything in there would come out. Once I found the mules, I'd bring 'em back to the house and feed 'em, look 'em over and stuff. Then maybe I'd cut some wood so my mother could finish breakfast, or feed the hogs, whatever needed to be done. Then I'd go in and get something for breakfast, which usually wasn't much. We'd leave for the field by six-thirty, trying to be there by seven, and then we'd work until lunch."

"What was field work like?" This was an aspect of Mississippi black life I could not imagine, even beyond the racism. This inability indicates how privileged, relatively, my generation of blacks has been.

Claude walked a few steps down an incline into a stand of cotton. "Come here." I followed. "This was it. We'd plow, plant, chop cotton. You see this cotton here? Well, weeds start springing up and you have to keep 'em down, so the sunlight can get to the seedlings. That's chopping cotton, out there with a hoe all day."

I shook my head. "How long do you have to do that?"

"Chopping was usually the month of June, in there, until the plant was big enough. Sometimes there was other work, cutting trees and clearing land for more fields, but we'd usually done that in advance. We'd come home at noon to eat what we called dinner, and we'd rest until one o'clock. If it was really hot, over one hundred degrees, we'd wait a little bit longer. We'd have our sun hats on and we'd work until six or seven, sometimes dark, until we got done with whatever it was we had to do."

UNITED STATES Highway Number 61 is a black asphalt ribbon rolling straight through the quiet, squalid towns of the Mississippi Delta: Tunica, Clarksdale, Alligator and Shelby, Mound Bayou, Cleveland, Leland and Rolling Fork. Towns along the highway tend to consist of a train station across from a gas station and several stores—hardware, grocery, five-and-dime. Nearby towns off the highway usually contain a general store, a garage and several houses ranging in form from splendid to abandoned. Whatever its appearance, a Delta town is likely as not to have a cotton gin.

Highway 61 rides out of Memphis through DeSoto County, Mississippi, and hits the vast cotton, milo and soybean fields of the Delta in the next county, Tunica, fields stretching from there all the way to Vicksburg. The land is flat, the road is straight, the sky huge, a high, pale blue, and the horizon endless. For me and for many others, this is the hard-core Mississippi, home of Robert Johnson, *Cat on a Hot Tin Roof*, the poorest sixteen or seventeen counties in the country; the place where, as my father might say darkly, "you had to know the difference between 'come here,' and 'sic 'em.' " It's the place the writer Richard Ford calls "the South of the South."

But the Delta is also a place where ordinary, daily life goes on, amid millions of acres of farmland, some of the most fertile on the planet. This land was wrested from swamp and river bottom by men like Will Dockery, planters and railroaders and merchants of such ferocity they carved empires out of the wilderness where they reigned over thousands of men and women, black men and women, men and women like my parents and grandparents and their ancestors who drained the land, cleared it, built dikes and levees and then tilled it, raising the cotton that changed the world. Those men and women also invented the blues, which would likewise change the world, though they would never see that change, and wouldn't get paid for it either.

As I rode down Highway 61 with my father, thoughts on the confluence of the words "travel" and "travail," and on how those words were connected to the abstractions of black folks, cotton and the blues, played through my mind like some hallucinogenic, experimental film, images of black people traveling to and from the fields, the fields full of cotton, the white man's white gold, the work day after day, the constant dream of Chicago or Los Angeles, of getting away. In several places Highway 61 is paralleled by the tracks of the Illinois Central Railroad, another dream and road to freedom. Looking down the highway, over the fields and train tracks with Claude next to me in the car, I began to understand that his regular wisecrack, "It wasn't Lincoln who freed the slaves, it was the Illinois Central," was more than a joke. I also heard Robert Johnson's lines again:

> I woke up this mornin' feelin' round for my shoes
> I know about that, I got them old walkin' blues. . . .

CLARKSDALE IS the seat and largest town of Coahoma County. It's a "Saturday town," the center of commerce and social life for a twenty-mile radius, and has been home, at various times, to men as disparate and as influential in American culture as Tennessee Williams and McKinley "Muddy Waters" Morganfield. The town contains comfortable middle-class neighborhoods of brick-and-wood bungalows under mature oak and dogwoods, horribly decrepit blocks of shotgun houses, worn-looking housing projects, and, just west of downtown, a district of splendid mansions still kept with exacting care. As it passes through Clarksdale, Highway 61 is bordered by strip malls, gas stations and shopping plazas. The intersection of 61 and U.S. 49, rumored to be the legendary "crossroads" where Robert Johnson sold his soul to the devil, is now marked by a Kentucky Fried Chicken, a dilapidated gas station and several boarded-up storefronts.

Claude and I had driven to Clarksdale to visit the Delta Blues Museum, located downtown in a second-floor room in the older of the two buildings that make up the Carnegie Library. The museum holds bookshelves of blues literature and scholarship; glass display cases containing rare records, instruments and documents; and, lining its walls, paintings and photographs of blues greats. The museum collection also contains a bronze bust of Muddy Waters and a mockup of a statue of him that will be a feature of the planned future museum. In light of the fundamental role the blues, along with its stepchild jazz, has played in American culture, the museum appears oddly small and obscure, as if Charley Patton, Skip James, Kokomo Arnold, Robert Johnson, Muddy Waters, Howlin' Wolf et al. were destined to be neglected not only in life but even in monuments to their achievement.

When one listens to Jimi Hendrix, the Rolling Stones, Led Zeppelin, Bonnie Raitt, Prince or their legions of imitators, one is hearing permutations and echoes of the Delta bluesmen. Elvis Presley's first hit, "That's All Right, Mama," is a direct copy of an earlier record by Arthur "Big Boy" Crudup; Bob Dylan's pose of bemused resignation as cultural stance is at least partly traceable to the styles and, more important, the *attitudes* of blues musicians and their songs. Those attitudes gradually became a permanent way of being an American as young whites in the fifties, sixties and seventies became aware (as blacks always had been) of the treachery and duplicity inherent in American society. On a more superficial level, "I got the blues," "I'm a little blue" and scores of other folk sayings have become shorthand fixtures of our culture, and it all started or at least cohered here in the Delta, in the regions around Clarksdale and farther south, where the field hollers and work chants of slaves, sharecroppers, prisoners and heavy laborers evolved into the art form that would become rock and roll, the voice of young America and the world.

Standing there in that room dedicated to the blues, my father and I talked of how far these men and women had gone beyond Mississippi, and of how at the time no one could have predicted their reach. The blues had not been a large part of my father's life; I think he always regarded them like whiskey and voodoo, as a form of darkness, best avoided in a considered existence. He'd listen to a little B. B. King, but even this was tempered by my mother's taste, which came from the other side of the spiritual tracks in the black musical community. Over there were gospel and hymns, the patron saints being Thomas Dorsey and Mahalia Jackson, not Robert Johnson and Bessie Smith. This spiritual divide had been a source of mild conflict during my childhood and adolescence: Dorothy was constantly leading me and my siblings along the straight and narrow, backing this course with stiff doses of "Standing on the Promises," "Trust and Obey," "Just a Closer Walk with Thee" and "Amazing Grace"; we were *much* more interested in "Love and Happiness," "I Can't Quit You, Baby," "When a Man Loves a Woman" and "Ain't No Sunshine."

To be fair, my mother could, in certain moods, enjoy a good blues song, but she still felt that the blues were the Devil's Music, one step from perdition, a grave threat to the salvation of any soul. By contrast, I thought that the blues reflected what life was like *here*, on this plane of existence, and that the hereafter could take care of itself. This conflict, between the sinner begging forgiveness on Sunday morning and the sinner longing for another Saturday night— often one and the same person—is a commonplace of black life in America.

But as I've gotten older, I've seen that the conflict between sinner and would-be saint is highly nuanced, and the two states seem part of the same larger whole. To me, increasingly, the blues shadow everything, my own worldview and those of both my parents. When Dorothy was in church, wasn't she fighting, or running from, Robert Johnson's hellhound? When Claude was a boy on Howard Jones's plantation pining and plotting his escape, did he not have the walking blues *and* the dream of a kind of salvation?

EIGHTEENTH-CENTURY slave traders frequented an area of the West African coast known as Senegambia, which today is divided into the countries of Senegal and Gambia. Gradually, the areas now known as Sierra Leone, Liberia, Ivory Coast, Ghana, Togo, Benin, Nigeria, Cameroon and Angola, among others, were included in the regular traffic, and as these areas were quite varied in climate, topography and culture, they possessed widely varying musical styles—all of which were eventually incorporated into what we call the blues.

The blues. Everyone seems to know what the words mean, if only intuitively. If you understand "the blues," a definition like this from the *OED* will lead you to nod in recognition: "a melody of a mournful and haunting character, originating among the Negroes of the Southern U.S., frequently in a twelve-bar sequence, using many 'blue' notes." But that, in truth, is description, not definition, and defining the blues with precision is probably impossible. Is gospel master Thomas Dorsey's definition of the blues as "nothing but a good woman feeling bad" more accurate? Or the poet Michael S. Harper's distillation of folk wisdom, "The blues ain't nothin' but a poor man's heart disease"?

The term itself developed out of the traditional English usage of the phrase "blue devil," a baleful demon, to describe feelings of despondency and depression. (Interestingly, this term could also describe hypochondriacal melancholy.) The *OED* shows a usage of the term "the blues" as early as 1824, so it is likely that black slaves appropriated the phrase as accurate to their emotions.

The blues are the direct descendant of an earlier type of Afro-American "sorrow song," the spiritual. As slaves became Christianized, they took on the imagery and rituals of white religious practice, particularly Protestantism, and began learning the songs of that tradition, Africanizing some and developing others. These new hymns, ring shouts, chants, camp songs and funeral songs became a vastly popular American style that has influenced all North American church music; and this style mutated, along with the blues, into the contemporary style known as gospel. Spirituals have been and continue to be performed in venues far beyond the church, in concert halls, college auditoriums and television shows, by groups and individuals such as the Fisk Jubilee Singers, the Morehouse College Glee Club, Mahalia Jackson, Paul Robeson and Sister Rosetta Tharpe.

In spirituals one can hear strains of the same personality, the same voice that later became manifest in the blues:

> Sometimes I feel like a motherless child
> Sometimes I feel like a motherless child
> A long way from home, long way from home
> True believer, far from home

That voice, lonesome and suffering, spoke through a melody that was new in Western music. The traditional Western major scale was built on a whole-step/whole-step/half-step/whole-step/whole-step/whole-step/half-step climb, on the piano, in the key of C: C–D–E–F–G–A–B–C. To gain a more melancholy tonality from this scale, the third, E, is "lowered" a half step to E flat, and the seventh, B, is lowered as well, to B flat, creating a minor scale. This sort of alteration can be heard clearly in the tonally minor compositions of Chopin. Where the blues scale, and blues tonality, differ is in their use of the flat fifth (G flat in the key of C) for a diminished feel, and in its focus on a cluster involving the flat third, the fourth, and the flat fifth to produce the "true" blues dissonance or warmth (depending on the listener's ear). The blues scale can be thought of as a pentatonic (five-note) scale, utilizing the root, the flat third, the fourth, the flat fifth and the flat seventh. Focusing on those notes—and any others in or out of the tonic scale can be used, depending on the talent and ear of the musician—the vocalist or instrumentalist can begin to create the sound our culture calls the blues, and from there the wit and personality of the performer, whether spiritual or secular, become the defining elements of the music.

The area from which the largest number of slaves was gathered, Senegambia, contains very few trees, so its music was never primarily drum oriented; its people instead played string instruments of many types, with anywhere from one to twenty-odd strings. Senegambian culture features a category of singer-musicians called griots, keepers of the people's history. Griots play rhythms that accompany and aid workers in their tasks, and while alive are praised; interestingly, though, according to Robert Palmer, "When griots died they were not buried with the respectable people of the communities; instead their bodies were left to rot in hollow trees."

In this Senegambian tradition of the griot, one sees the outlines of the blues singer in American culture. The purpose of blues songs and singers often was to mark historical events ("John Brown's Body") or transient folk wisdom ("Frankie and Johnny"). The griot led a communal music that consisted of light percussion, hand clapping and call-and-response singing, all things that can be seen in any black church to this day, and their music was polyrhythmic and polyphonic, based on harmonies with intervals of a third, a fourth and a fifth, corresponding to the previously cited "blues cluster" of the pentatonic scale.

Another West African musical style antecedent to the blues, that of the Angolan Bantu, also has an extremely developed form of choral singing, utilizing call-and-response, solos, duets and trios with choral settings. Bantu singing further includes whooping and falsetto, two clear survivals into the blues. African singers slide, glide, growl, shriek, "dirty" and deliberately detune notes, all in order to heighten tension and add to the narrative drama within a song. This vocal mastery proved advantageous in America, as the playing of large drums by slaves was prohibited. Plantation masters feared that slaves would communicate with each other over long distances, as in Africa, via drum talk.

But the blues, or, more accurately, the Delta blues, transcend the sum of these various techniques. The Delta blues began to take shape during the rise of the sharecropping system. As noted by musicologist William Ferris, the instrument most identified with the blues, the guitar, is never seen in photos or drawings of black musicians prior to the Civil War. According to folklorist and poet Sterling A. Brown, another essential element of the style, the unique blues beat, came out of work songs used to time heavy labor, as members of the gang could work much more efficiently and keep track of each other's motions by tying their movements to song. As stated by Ferris, "The weight of [railroad] steel tracks makes it essential that every man work together. An individual's failure to do so places more strain on the rest of the crew or, even worse, may cause a fatal accident."

Cal Taylor, who worked in the Delta for fifty years, explains it like this: "When you're lining track you say,"

> Oh, up and down the road I go,
> skipping and diving for my forty-four
> Ha ha way over
> Ha ha way over
> Poor boys, pull together
> Track'll line much better
> Whoa!

These verses were alternated with others and improvised in countless ways, with only the beat remaining the same.

Mississippi blues are simple, built on modal one-, two- and three-chord harmonies, rhythmically intense and searingly emotional. Many see the blues as boozy, folk-existential wails, but as musician Vernon Reid notes, the blues are inevitably sociological. The style arose in part as a reflection of social unrest: the blues are the cries of souls under lock and key, a way of speaking when doomed to silence, a parallel language of human expressiveness. They are a way of analyzing, understanding and notating past experience and then distancing oneself from it with irony and humor that contain but do not deny the trauma. Bluesmen bewail "evil women," but such complaints are not a joke, as often relationships with women were the only wealth those men had; and muttering in a song about leaving for Chicago might have been their only means of criticizing the plantation boss.

THERE WERE great bluesmen before him—Charley Patton, Son House and Scrapper Blackwell; there have been great bluesmen since—Muddy Waters, Willie Dixon and B. B. King; but one bluesman remains, in the eyes of aficionados and, increasingly, America as a whole, king of them all: Robert Johnson. Several emergent images of Johnson exist in the popular imagination: musician extraordinaire, night-haunted blues poet, demonic fellow traveler, cocky young man who put the blues before everything else and, in the cosmology of African-American sacred tradition, paid for it. But who was he, this black man no one really knew who has come to personify the blues, this very young man who recorded only twenty-nine songs in his lifetime before dying, it is said, on his hands and knees, barking like a dog?

It is generally accepted that Robert Johnson was born between 1910 and 1912 (blues historian Peter Guralnick cites May 8, 1911) near Robinsonville, Mississippi, a tiny levee town in the north Delta. According to legend, Johnson's parents had been forced out of Hazlehurst, Mississippi, by the Ku Klux Klan, his "father" going to Memphis (some say his biological father was another man), while his mother moved throughout the Delta from plantation to plantation. In 1914, Johnson's legal father, Charles Dodds Spencer (who used several names to hide from his pursuers), took the toddler Robert to Memphis for several years before returning to the Commerce-Robinsonville area and the Abbay and Leatherman plantations. Whether Johnson received any formal education is not known, but by the age of sixteen he was playing harmonica and soon was playing guitar as well.

Johnson married a young local girl—perhaps the "Sweet Brown" of many of his songs?—who became pregnant and died in childbirth before he was twenty.

Son House relates a memory of Johnson from around this time: "When we'd leave at night to go play for the balls, he'd slip off and come over to where we were. . . . He'd get where Willie [Brown] and I were and sit right down on the floor and watch from one to the other. And when we'd get a break and want to rest some, we'd set the guitars up in the corner and go out into the cool. Robert would watch and see which way we'd gone, and he would pick one of them up. And such another racket you never heard! It'd make the people mad, you know. They'd come out and say, 'Why don't y'all go in and get that guitar away from the boy! He's running people crazy with it.' I'd come back in, and I'd scold him about it. 'Don't do that, Robert. You drive the people nuts. You can't play nothing. Why don't you blow the harmonica for 'em?' But he didn't want to blow that. Still, he didn't care how I'd get after him about it. He'd do it anyway."

Around this time Johnson left Robinsonville and went south to Hazlehurst. Unable or unwilling to work steadily, he ranged and foraged through the Delta, doing day labor but generally returning to Hazlehurst, where he married for the second time. He also learned how to play the blues. In the space of eighteen months, Johnson returned to Robinsonville, having, according to Son House, become a master. "I said, 'Well, boy, you still got a guitar, huh? What do you do with that thing? You can't do nothing with it.' He said, 'Well, I'll tell you what.' I said 'What?' He said, 'Let me have your seat a minute.' When he finished, all our mouths were standing open."

House and the others were convinced that there was only one way Johnson could have become so proficient so fast: he'd sold his soul to the devil. According to folklore, if you went to a crossroads at midnight and sat there playing a song, a black man would appear, grab your guitar and tune it. After playing a piece, the man would hand the guitar back to you, and, from then on, you'd be able to play anything you wanted. Johnson's crossroads was rumored to be just out of Clarksdale, at the junction of U.S. Highway 61 and Mississippi Highway 49.

If Johnson emerged as a master musician around 1931, he had only had seven more years (a folkloric number) to live. In those years he traveled incessantly, through Mississippi, Arkansas and Texas, Chicago, New York and Canada. In that time he created an oeuvre matched only by George Gershwin's in terms of its eventual impact on popular American music. He first recorded in November 1936,

laying down in that session the only song of his that would be widely
known in his lifetime, "Terraplane Blues." The song is a relative tri-
fle, using double entendres to equate the question "Who's been riding in my car?" (a Buick Terraplane) with "Who's been dating my
girl?" This early song already contains the Johnson verities of travel,
pleasure and loss in love:

> I said I flash your lights, mama,
> your horn won't even blow
> (somebody's been runnin' down
> the batteries on this machine)
> I said I flash my lights, mama
> the horn won't even blow
> Got a short in this connection
> hoo-well, babe, it's way down below

This sort of sly humor, enjoyable as it is, is commonplace in the
blues. What made Robert Johnson's work majestic was the way in
which he worked the trials of his own life into twelve-bar sequences,
trials faced not just as a black man in Mississippi but as a human in
the modern technological world.

On the surface, "Come On in My Kitchen" seems simply another tale of betrayal and seduction:

> The woman I love
> I took from my best friend
> Some joker got lucky
> Stole her back again
> You better come on in my kitchen
> It's gonna be raining outdoors

But there's something different about this song, something simultaneously more deliberate and more deranged. At first plodding and
mournful, the song develops from the opening to verses like:

> Winter time's comin'
> It's gonna be slow
> You can't make the winter, babe,
> That's dry long so
> You better come on in my kitchen
> It's gonna be raining outdoors

When paired with its musical accompaniment, solo slide guitar imitating a windstorm, the song expands to take on a broader meaning tied to the black experience of difficult winters, Johnson extending what seems at first to be merely sexual invitation into an invitation to shelter and safe harbor. This use of emotion and metaphor is much more complex than that commonly seen in blues songs of the period and is indicative of the unique quality of Johnson's work.

Johnson and his work must constantly be placed in the context of Mississippi in the twenties and thirties, the Mississippi of Vardaman, Bilbo and Will Dockery, in order to be understood fully. Johnson is more than a smart-alecky, sly black trickster with a fondness for whiskey, guns and other men's women. Listening to Johnson out of context, his classic "Love in Vain" (my personal favorite) can be heard as a lament by a Romeo more in love with love than anything else:

> I followed her to the station
> Her suitcase in my hand
> I said I followed her to the station
> With her suitcase in my hand
> It's hard to tell, hard to tell
> When all your love's in vain

The tune is gentle, swinging and sweet, showing an unexpected side of Johnson, the same man who in "Me and the Devil Blues" mumbles, "Gonna beat my woman until I'm satisfied."

> When the train rolled up to the station
> I looked her in the eye
> I said the train rolled up to the station
> And I looked her in the eye
> I felt so lonesome, felt so lonesome
> I could not help but cry
> All my love's in vain

When Johnson and the song are put into a demythologized human context, a very different portrait of the bluesman than is usual begins to emerge. The Illinois Central Railroad track is the spine of the Delta, running south from Memphis toward New Orleans through Clarksdale, Shelby, Cleveland, Shaw, Leland, a host of little cinder-block stations standing sentry alongside U.S. 61 for hundreds of miles. Aside from the small towns, nothing rests along these tracks but cotton and soybeans, and one can imagine the Depression-era Johnson walking into town behind the woman he loved, who to him would have represented the only worldly success and happiness attainable and who had decided to leave Poor Bob—Johnson's regular nickname for himself—and try her luck in Chicago. Suddenly, "I followed her to the station / Her suitcase in my hand" takes on a different, darker hue. Here's a lonely man, whose life is about to get much lonelier, walking the light of his life to the train that will carry her away. The third verse:

> When the train left the station
> It had two lights on behind
> When the train left the station
> I saw two lights on behind
> The blue light was my blues
> And the red light was my mind
> All my love's in vain

These metaphors marrying the technological world of lights and electricity to an emotional and psychological state had not to that point been heard in the blues, and the song in general locates blacks in the newer world of town and travel. And it is the fourth verse, a remarkable, almost wordless, short sequence, that makes the performance unforgettable:

> Ooooh, ooooh, Willie Mae
> Oh ohhh, Willie Mae
> Ah aaahhhh oh ee oh woe
> All my love's in vain

The verse's falsetto screams, punctuated by an easy shuffle beat reminiscent of a locomotive's chug-chug-chug, are the strongest evidence of Johnson's mastery, even supremacy, as a blues artist.

Purists can argue that "Love in Vain" is derivative of Leroy Carr's "When the Sun Goes Down," and it is; but for me, this only illustrates Johnson's true significance. He is the prism through which Leroy Carr, Charley Patton, Son House, Willie Brown, Lonnie Johnson, Tommy Johnson et al. fathered that most American of music, rock and roll. Those earlier musicians developed the rudiments of the blues from the spirituals, camp songs and field hollers of black folk life, but Johnson, more than any other single person, codified those techniques and attitudes, adding more of his own, into the style that would influence Muddy Waters, Howlin' Wolf, B. B. King and Chuck Berry. *That* music, the blues and rhythm and blues of the forties and fifties, would influence a certain white Mississippian, Elvis Presley, and many other young Americans and Britons who would extrapolate from it a new music that would forever change the world. When you hear Elvis's "Heartbreak Hotel" or "Hound Dog," Bruce Springsteen's "I'm on Fire," Michael Jackson's "Billie Jean," even the Police's "Every Breath You Take," you're hearing the style and attitude of Robert Johnson of Robinsonville, Mississippi. Elvis's "Since my baby left me . . . ," Springsteen's "Hey little girl is your daddy home . . . ," Jackson's "She's making plans and demands . . ." and Sting's "Oh can't you see, you belong to me" are distant and not-so-distant echoes of Robert Johnson's wail.

But, beyond his historical influence on pop music, there's something more to Robert Johnson than that wail—a pain and complexity, an insight and wisdom, that can't quite be accounted for. Johnson called the blues "a low-down achin' heart disease," and in his work we sense that the blues actually can be a physical feeling, an *illness*. Johnson's life—and, by extension, the lives of blacks in Mississippi—cost him, physically and psychologically. "I've been dogged and I've been driven ever since I left my mother's home," Johnson sings, and his every third song seems to begin with "I woke up this morning," reflecting the contingency and randomness of those lives, the sense that each day is a new challenge and a dangerous adventure, holding not much promise and certainly no guarantees.

In light of this, Johnson's "Cross Road Blues" becomes more than a "blues":

> I went to the crossroad
>   fell down on my knees

> I went to the crossroad
> >fell down on my knees
> Asked the Lord above "Have mercy, now
> >save poor Bob, if you please"
>
> Yeeo, standing at the crossroad
> >tried to flag a ride
> Oooo ooee eeee
> >I tried to flag a ride
> Didn't nobody seem to know me, babe
> >everybody pass me by

"Cross Road Blues," in the context of Mississippi between the wars, and of Robert Johnson's personal life as a black man of uncertain paternity, a widower at nineteen, a man who wanted to be, who *was*, an artist, but was expected only to get behind a mule and shut up, becomes an example of a soul in torment, dramatized in words and music. This song, like many other of his songs, is a great modernist poem of a losing battle for redemption. The image of being unable to thumb a ride in a Mississippi where a black man out after dark could be arrested for vagrancy and even killed is powerful enough; but this expands into a metaphor for a soul loose in a world without rest or love or comfort *except* for the road, which at the very least offers the possibility of something different, and maybe better.

> I got stones in my passway
> and my road seem dark as night
> I got stones in my passway
> and my road seem dark as night
> I have pains in my heart
> they have taken my appetite
> >("Stones in My Passway")

That man had a rocky road ahead, and the hellhounds on his trail. He didn't see even death as rest or escape, as in this image, perhaps the most stunning of all:

> You may bury my body down by
> the highway side
> You may bury my body down by

the highway side
So my old evil spirit can catch a
Greyhound bus and ride
          ("Me and the Devil Blues")

Robert Johnson saw, in Depression Mississippi, a world on which God had turned His back, in which an aware soul would know only pain that even the modern solaces of music, sex and altered consciousness could not transcend. Transient contingency, poor Bob might say, is the human condition, *the blues*.

CLAUDE LEFT Mississippi in 1950. The events of subsequent years in the state consisted of more of what he'd known, with one added complication. The invention of the mechanical cotton picker, first used in 1943, unsettled Mississippi's economy and demography with the same intensity as had the cotton gin. The cotton picker geometrically reduced the number of blacks needed for large farming operations, as a cotton harvest that once required hundreds of field hands could now be accomplished by three or four workers driving tractors.

Those "superfluous" blacks, most of them sharecroppers, were forced off farms and into nearby towns. Since there was little there for them to do, many continued on to Chicago, Milwaukee, Detroit or Los Angeles, cities where their fates would be complex and varied. Some would enter the mainstream middle class, others be consumed by the pathologies of the ghettos. But while millions of black Mississippians emigrated and scattered after the Second World War, to encounter the challenge of the industrial, "liberal," North, those who remained were to enter a crucible that would affect the course of American history like nothing since the Civil War.

THE CRUSHING BURDEN of poverty in Mississippi after World War II can best be understood by noting that while the rest of the nation went on an extended boom, and while in the years 1950 to 1960 the total personal income in the state rose 59 percent, from $1.5 million to almost $2.6 million, in 1960 Mississippi was, by far, the poorest state in the nation. The most economically successful decade in the state's history had finished with the state even farther behind. Given the pyramidal structure of its economy, clearly those on the bottom were living in near peonage; and, tragically, white Mississippi, both as an institution and in the form of its individual citizens, would waste vast amounts of money and time in the ensuing thirty years trying to hold back the tide of black aspirations, and to check as well the protection of that rising tide by the state's traditional enemy, the federal government.

The early fifties were relatively quiet in Mississippi, national notoriety largely limited to the Willie McGee case, in which a young black man was condemned to death and executed for raping a white woman in Laurel. Several circumstances combined to make that case a cause célèbre: the lack of solid evidence against McGee (that which existed pointed to a frame-up), the fact that no white had ever in the history of Mississippi been executed for rape, and the likelihood that McGee and the alleged victim, Willametta Hawkins, had been secret lovers for almost four years, from 1942 to 1945, and that she'd charged him with rape in a jealous rage after he ended the relationship. The NAACP, *The New York Times*, *Time*, *Life* and the *Daily Worker* all focused on the case, to no avail, and McGee went to the electric chair after five years of legal wrangling and his third trial (with a jury including three blacks, a rarity designed to preempt any federal intervention), on May 8, 1951.

The McGee case illustrated how far white Mississippians were willing to go in order to preserve the color line. But an event that would push them further still, and would finally ignite the years of smoldering racial resentment into open conflict, came three years later almost to the day. On May 17, 1954, the United States Supreme Court handed down perhaps its most fateful decision since *Marbury v. Madison*, the 1803 case which established its jurisdiction as the court of last resort: *Brown v. Board of Education of Topeka*. As read by Chief Justice Earl Warren in the court's unanimous decision, the court concluded that "segregated schools are not 'equal' and cannot be made 'equal,' and that hence [blacks] are deprived of the equal protection of the laws."

The legal abstractions "equality" and "equal protection under the laws" were embedded in the U.S. Constitution at its framing, but had never quite been made to include blacks. In the South in particular, the legal structure of racial segregation and, as a consequence, white superiority was built on the doctrine of "separate but equal," which held that blacks, in the terms of the Fourteenth Amendment, were entitled to the same rights and opportunities as whites, but that these guarantees were valid only in an all-black world parallel to that of whites. In the 1896 *Plessy v. Ferguson*, the Court had legally endorsed this practice, ruling that while the Fourteenth Amendment intended "undoubtedly to enforce the absolute equality of the law . . . in the nature of things, it could not have been intended to abolish distinctions based upon color, or to enforce social as distinguished from political equality. . . ."

This particular case turned on an incident of June 7, 1892, involving Homer Plessy, a black man who had purchased a first-class ticket on the East Louisiana Railway. When he tried to take his seat, he was ordered to the colored section and, when he refused to comply, was jailed. Plessy, a light-skinned Negro, argued that his civil rights had been violated, but the Court held that "if he [Plessy] be a colored man and be so assigned, he has been deprived of no property, since he is not lawfully entitled to the reputation of being a white man. . . ." Later in the opinion, the majority argued "we consider the underlying fallacy of the plaintiff's argument to consist in the assumption that the enforced separation of the two races stamps the colored race with a badge of inferiority. If this be so, it is not by reason of anything found in the act, but solely because the colored race chooses to put that construction upon it." Logically consistent or not, the die was cast; and, coupled with the rampages of late Reconstruction, *Plessy* stifled the hopes of blacks for another sixty years.

The lawyers who litigated *Brown*, led by Thurgood Marshall, understood the crucial social aspect of racial segregation: the inferiority it engendered in the minds of its victims and the way in which it falsely authenticated a perverse status quo. Marshall and his fellow lawyers chose to attack segregated schools because they believed those schools imposed a racial burden upon black children from the moment they entered public and social life, wounding many irreparably. And such segregation, they felt, with harsh ramifications for society, kept black and white children psychologically apart, kept them from knowing large parts of each other and so of themselves, and set the table for adulthoods of mutual fear, mistrust and manipulation.

Thurgood Marshall had been working toward the *Brown* decision since 1940, when he took over as NAACP chief counsel from his mentor Charles Hamilton Houston. Houston had begun in 1935, after serving as dean of Howard Law School, where Marshall and other key civil rights lawyers were trained, to try a series of constitutional cases designed to weaken the legal basis for segregation. Continuing this work, Marshall crisscrossed the South, filing a lawsuit each time a black student was rejected from a white graduate school in states without such schools for blacks. In 1950 the United States Supreme Court decided favorably on two of those cases for Marshall and the NAACP, and as a result more than one thousand black students gained admittance to graduate and professional schools.

But the battle to desegregate elementary, secondary and undergraduate education, in which schools were less vulnerable to charges of general unavailability to blacks, would prove more difficult. Though Mississippi, for instance, in 1952 spent $117 for each white child in public schools and $45 for each black child, still there *were* schools for blacks, and the society fulfilled its proclaimed mandate. Marshall and his fellow NAACP lawyers decided that rather than employ the patient tacking maneuvers they'd used against the graduate schools, they would have to attack unequivocally the general principle of school segregation with a direct assault on *Plessy v. Ferguson*. The NAACP chose to argue that there could be no such thing as "separate but equal," that the very fact that something as fundamental as schooling was separate made it inherently unequal. As Marshall said: "Millions of blacks could not feel themselves clothed in the minimum dignity of men as long as they suffered under certain legal disabilities."

After a nationwide search, the first appropriate case was found in Clarendon County, South Carolina. The *Briggs* lawsuit grew out of statistics that the 75 percent of the county's students who were black received less than 40 percent of the county's educational funding. A new technique was utilized by the plaintiff, involving the development of a "Brandeis brief," named after the lawyer who first presented in court this compilation of economic, sociological and psychological evidence.

Included in the brief was the following report by Dr. Kenneth Clark, a psychologist. Clark went to South Carolina and tested sixteen black children, who were shown a white doll and a black doll and were given these instructions:

1. "Give me the doll you like best."
2. "Give me the doll that is the nice doll."
3. "Give me the doll that looks bad."
4. "Give me the doll that is a nice color."
5. "Give me the doll that is most like you."

According to Dr. Clark, "some of the children reacted with such intense emotion to the 'dolls test' that they were unable to continue. One little girl who had shown a clear preference for the white doll and who described the brown doll as 'ugly' and 'dirty' broke into a torrent of tears when she was asked to identify herself with one of the dolls." Clark added, "These children saw themselves as inferior, and they accepted the inferiority as part of reality. . . . Segregation is the way in which a society tells a group of human beings that they are inferior to other groups of human beings in the society. It really is internalized in children. . . . It influences the child's view of himself."

The *Briggs* case was lost in federal district court, with two of the three judges refusing to accept the Brandeis brief, entitled "The Effects of Segregation and the Consequences of Desegregation: A Social Science Statement." The dissenting judge, J. Waties Waring, gave the NAACP lawyers hope, and while appealing *Briggs* they took on a new case, *Brown v. Board of Education of Topeka.* Linda Brown was a seven-year-old black girl who lived in a white neighborhood in the Kansas town. Brown had to endure a dangerous journey through a rail yard to embark on a long ride to the black school on the other side of Topeka. Her father, the Reverend Oliver Brown, wanted Linda to attend the white school several blocks from their home. Though dismissed in district court, the *Brown* suit was appealed and combined with two others, *Briggs* and *Davis v. Prince Edward (Va.) County*.

On December 9, 1952, backed by a 235-page brief, Thurgood Marshall and Robert Carver delivered their final argument in the cases, with Marshall stating in clear, simple English:

> I got the feeling (from what has been said here) that when you put a white child in a school with a whole lot of colored children, the child would fall apart or something. Everybody knows that is not true. Those same kids in Virginia and South Carolina—and I have seen them do it—they play in the streets together, they play on their farms together, they go down the road together, they separate to go to school, they come out of school and play ball together. They have to be separated in school. . . . Why, of all the multitudinous groups of people in this country [do] you have to single out the Negroes and give them this separate treatment? It cannot be because of slavery in the past, because there are very few groups in this country that haven't had slavery some place in the history of their groups. It cannot be color, because there are Negroes as white as drifted snow, with blue eyes, and they are just as segregated as the colored men. The only thing it can be is an inherent determination that the people who were formerly in slavery, regardless of anything else, shall be kept as near that stage as possible. And now is the time, we submit, that this court should make it clear that that is not what our Constitution stands for.

The Court concurred on Monday, May 17, 1954, a date known throughout the South as Black Monday (which is also the title of an anti-*Brown* book by Mississippi judge Tom Brady). Chief Justice Earl Warren read the decision:

> Does segregation of children in public schools solely on the basis of race, even though the physical facilities and other tangible factors may be equal, deprive children of the minority group of equal educational opportunities? We believe it does. . . . To separate them . . . generates a feeling of inferiority as to their status in the community that may affect their hearts and minds in a way very unlikely ever to be undone. We conclude, unanimously, that in the field of public education the doctrine of "separate but equal" has no place.

The white reaction in Mississippi was at once both frenzied and deliberate. Senator James O. Eastland stated publicly to his white constituency, "You are not obliged to obey the decisions of any court which are plainly fraudulent." Six months after the decision, in December, the state legislature passed an amendment permitting the abolishment of public schools, in order to keep *Brown* from being enforced. As the year turned, whites in Mississippi launched a two-pronged attack against desegregation: random violence and the revival of the Ku Klux Klan were intended to instill fear in the black community, and a new group, the White Citizens Council, "the white-collar Klan," placed economic pressure on blacks and whites alike to toe the racial line, making it impossible for any person who advocated desegregation to find or maintain employment in Mississippi, make any purchases on credit, receive a bank loan or get a mortgage.

There were many racial killings that year, including one that seemed symbolically to represent the state's reply to *Brown*, triggering, in turn, national revulsion and focusing worldwide attention on Mississippi for the first time since the Civil War: Emmett Till. On a dare, Till, a Chicago teenager visiting relatives in the Delta, allegedly whistled at and made sexually suggestive comments—said to consist of a leering "Hey, Baby" and a comic wolf whistle—to a young white woman minding a store in Money, Mississippi. The incident appeared to blow over, child's play, until the woman's husband, Roy Bryant, returned from out of town and, with his brother-in-law J. W. Milam, seized the fourteen-year-old Till from his grandfather's cabin in the middle of the night. The grandfather, Mose Wright, attempted to apologize, explaining that the boy was from Chicago and unaware of southern customs, but Bryant and Milam threatened to kill Wright and then drove off into the dark with Emmett.

Till's body was found three days later, floating in the Tallahatchie River with a cotton-gin fan tied to its neck. One of Till's eyes had been gouged out, he'd been beaten so severely that one temple had collapsed, and he had been shot in the head. Later it was discovered that the bloodied and traumatized boy, refusing to apologize, had been forced to carry the heavy gin fan down to the riverbank before he was shot. He had sealed his fate by showing Bryant and

Milam a photograph of a young white girl he claimed was his girl-friend back in Chicago.

Such violence was not uncommon in Mississippi; but this killing was to become more widely known than most. Black newspapers like the *Chicago Defender* and New York's *Amsterdam News* gave blanket coverage, and when photos of the corpse were printed in the black magazine *Jet* the case exploded into the white media, prompting an unprecedented show of support from whites for the NAACP. Emmett Till was buried on September 3, 1955, after a funeral attended by thousands, and after thousands more had filed through the funeral home to view the body during a four-day wake his mother had insisted upon, so that the nation and the world could "see what they did to my boy."

White Mississippians were shocked by the opprobrium heaped upon them and promptly closed ranks. Bryant and Milam were tried on September 19, and after five days were acquitted by an all-white jury, despite testimony from local blacks and the direct identification of the accused by Mose Wright—the first occurrence in the state of a black man testifying against a white in open court. The nation had seen southern justice in action, and the Till murder, coming so soon after *Brown*, placed racial issues at the forefront of national concerns.

Three months later, as if in a preordained third act, Rosa Parks, a young black seamstress in Alabama, refused to give her seat to a white man on a Montgomery city bus.

IN THE EARLY 1940s, Swedish sociologist Gunnar Myrdal coined the phrase "the American dilemma," describing it in his book of the same name as the tension generated by the contradiction between the stated ideals of American society—justice, liberty, equality—and the intentional, organized and ongoing mistreatment of the country's largest minority. The reality and consequences of this conflict in the hearts and minds of white Americans were nowhere more visible in the twentieth century than in the Mississippi of the sixties. The nature of this conflict was articulated by the leader of the state's White Citizens Council, William J. Simmons:

I was born in Mississippi and the United States and I'm the product of my heredity and education and the society in which I was raised, and I have a vested interest in that society, and I along with a million other white Mississippians will do everything in our power to protect that vested interest. It's just as simple as that. . . . It's primarily a struggle for power and I think we would be stupid indeed if we failed to see where the consequences of a supine surrender on our part would lead.

Here, as elsewhere, the struggle for racial justice would largely come down to the struggle for the right to vote. Black Mississippians would have no hope of transforming their situation until they had a say in choosing who governed them. In the late fifties and early sixties, at the behest of Simmons and his Citizens Council, the rhetoric of statewide political contests became increasingly racist and segregationist, as candidates had to prove that they were "right" on the Negro question. Hugh White had won two terms as governor (1948 to 1956) by stressing the need for modernization and business development, but in the 1955 gubernatorial campaign J. P. Coleman, previously considered something of a moderate on race, reverted to Vardamanism and won the election by pledging to defend segregation at all costs. As governor, Coleman signed the notorious "Interposition" bill, which—illegally and in violation of the United States Constitution—placed the authority of the state over that of the federal government and called for the establishment of the State Sovereignty Commission, intended "to resist usurpation of the rights and powers reserved to this state." This commission in effect became a racist shadow government.

In the fall of 1959, Ross Barnett was elected governor. Barnett was the man who later would stand on the steps of the Lyceum at Ole Miss to "defend the honor" of Mississippi, promising to go to jail or even close the university to prevent black enrollment. The Ole Miss confrontation was only the most visible battle of Barnett's tenure, as blacks throughout the state, perhaps emboldened by the election of explicitly pro–civil rights John F. Kennedy, pressed harder and harder for change.

After the Freedom Rides of 1961, activists in southern Mississippi were led by C. C. Bryant, a local railroad worker, and Bob

Moses, a schoolteacher from New York who worked for the Student Nonviolent Coordinating Committee. Moses had been invited by Amzie Moore, leader of the NAACP in the Cleveland area, to bring SNCC members to Mississippi to help with voter registration. Registration had been a prominent national issue since 1960, and in April 1961 Justice Department lawyers John Doar and Bob Owen made a secret tour through Mississippi with Medgar Evers, gathering information and informal affidavits. Their resulting analysis led to the federal government to conclude that the easiest breaking point of the South in terms of registration would be Dallas County, Alabama. Civil rights groups began working in Selma, but Moses, impressed with the local NAACP chapter, chose to work in Pike County, Mississippi. In the Pike County seat of McComb, 250 blacks were already registered. McComb was ahead of other Mississippi towns in part because its status as a railroad center meant that many local blacks were actually paid in Chicago and so were impervious to the surplus-food cutoffs, firings, sharecropper evictions and other economic pressures used by whites.

In the summer of 1961, the black citizens of Pike and the surrounding counties of Amite and Walthall staged a civil rights campaign unprecedented in a rural area, starting voter schools, holding sit-ins and organizing blacks into circles of support and strength. Local whites reacted violently, beating those, including Moses, who attempted to register to vote; arresting, indicting and convicting protestors on trumped-up charges, then jailing them; and, at the end of the summer, on September 25, assassinating NAACP volunteer Herbert Lee, a farmer and father of nine who had been chauffeuring Bob Moses. When Moses and fellow SNCC activist Charles McDew started a school for teenagers who had been expelled from public school for their involvement in the movement, the two were arrested and sent to jail for four months for "contributing to the delinquency of minors."

Their jailing effectively ended the McComb/Pike County campaign; but a fire had been lit in the state. Increasing black activism throughout Mississippi met with increasing resistance from whites, setting the snarls of race relations in sharper relief. The next year brought the Meredith showdown at Ole Miss, legal action in Jackson and in Leake County, and the vicious beating of two black soldiers, one of whom later died, for breaching Jim Crow laws. After his success at Ole Miss, Medgar Evers prepared with optimistic determination for the events of 1963: the Jackson boycotts, his television speech and John Kennedy's television speech on civil rights, which aired the night of Evers's death. Also in 1963, the Council of Federated Organizations (COFO)—consisting of the major civil rights groups, including SNCC, the NAACP, the Congress of Racial Equality (CORE) and the SCLC—conducted its Freedom Vote, a mock election designed to demonstrate and promote black interest in voting and to educate black Mississippians in voting procedures. Students from Yale and Stanford, recruited by Bob Moses and Allard Lowenstein, assisted in organizing and campaigning for the election. This project proved extremely useful, since, as Lowenstein said, "we have discovered . . . the people who run Mississippi today can only do so by force. They cannot allow free elections in Mississippi, because if they did, they wouldn't run Mississippi." Moses, commenting on the fact that black candidates were slated in the Freedom Vote, concurred: "Eventually, black people were going to be electing people to office—black people to office. But it wasn't a thought in their mind at that time. So what you had to do was . . . use the voter registration drive as a way of preparing them [blacks] for what was coming next."

What came next was Freedom Summer, a series of events that would come to mark the dividing line between the past and the future in Mississippi. Following up on the initiative of the previous fall, in the summer of 1964 more than a thousand college students, most of them white, traveled to Mississippi to serve as foot soldiers in a massive SNCC/COFO campaign to register voters, run Freedom Schools—"an educational experience for students which will make it possible for them to challenge the myths of our society, to perceive more clearly its realities, and to find alternatives"—and found community centers where blacks could meet and associate privately.

White Mississippians interpreted this activity as a full-scale invasion and responded with harassment and violence. The Jackson *Clarion Ledger* stated in an editorial, "This newspaper a long time ago pointed out that it is a deliberate attempt by Communist forces in the United States to stir up racial strife in this nation. The ultimate aim is, we believe, a black revolution. . . . The naive inexperience of these youngsters has been preyed on and they have been stirred up by tales of horror and violence that simply don't exist in Mississippi." This editorial ran on July 30, more than a month after the disappearance of Michael Schwerner, Andrew Goodman and James Chaney, Freedom Summer workers, from a jail in Philadelphia, Mississippi.

Schwerner, twenty-four, and Goodman, twenty, were white men from New York, while Chaney, twenty-one, was a black native of Meridian. Their abduction and subsequent murder three days into the project was likely calculated to terrorize and discourage the other volunteers; if anything, however, it energized them. The bodies, shot in the head execution-style (Chaney was brutally beaten as well), were not found until August 4, after a massive manhunt involving the FBI and hundreds of sailors. But throughout that summer civil rights activities proceeded as planned, resulting in the growth of Mississippi Freedom Democratic Party membership. Two weeks after the discovery of the bodies, the MFDP, led by Bob Moses, Aaron Henry, Fannie Lou Hamer, Victoria Gray, Annie Devine and Ed King, went to the Democratic National Convention in Atlantic City and spoke before the credentials committee.

As a result of the Schwerner, Chaney and Goodman lynchings, the MFDP's speeches received wide coverage. Fannie Lou Hamer's testimony in particular struck a chord in the national television audience as she related, weeping, her punishment for organizing: "They beat my arms 'til I had no feeling in them."

After two days of negotiations, Senator Hubert Humphrey, speaking for President Johnson, offered the MFDP the compromise of two at-large delegates in the current convention and, in the future, integrated southern delegations. The Mississippi regulars refused to be integrated with even token MFDP delegates and left the convention in protest; the MFDP also refused anything but complete victory. Fannie Lou Hamer led MFDP representatives onto the convention floor, where they sat in the Mississippi chairs until forcibly removed, repeating the maneuver again the next night as Hamer led the convention in freedom songs. No Mississippi delegation was ever officially seated, but the MFDP's point was made, and, as Hamer later said, "Negro people in the Delta began moving. People who never before tried, though they had always been anxious to do something, began moving . . . even Negroes who live on the plantations slip off the plantations and go to civil rights meetings. 'We wanted to do this for so long,' they'd say. . . . To see kids, to see these people—to see how far they've come since 1964! To me it's one of the greatest things that ever happened in Mississippi. And it's a direct result of the Summer Project in 1964."

The next summer, on August 6, in the same room where Abraham Lincoln signed the Emancipation Proclamation, President Lyndon Johnson signed the Voting Rights Act, saying, "Ninety-five years ago our Constitution was amended to require that no American be denied the right to vote because of race or color. Almost a century later, many Americans are kept from voting simply because they are Negroes. . . . It is wrong—deadly wrong—to deny any of your fellow Americans a right to vote in this country. . . . History and fate meet at a single time in a single place to shape a turning point in man's unending search for freedom."

The Voting Rights Act outlawed literacy tests for voter registration and provided for federal registrars throughout the South. When coupled with the Twenty-fourth Amendment of the previous year, which prohibited the use of poll taxes in federal elections (state poll taxes were later eliminated by the Supreme Court), this act created the legal structure needed to safeguard the sea changes occurring in Mississippi society.

THE WHITE POWER STRUCTURE, in response to the Voting Rights Act, adopted a new strategy to maintain the status quo, a largely nonviolent but legalistic series of stalling and flanking maneuvers known as Massive Resistance. By 1967, 59.8 percent of eligible blacks in Mississippi were registered to vote, but only twenty-nine black officials were elected, less than 1 percent of all state officials. In 1972 there were 129 black officials; in 1976, 210; and in 1980, 387, or 7.3 percent of the state's total—though Mississippi had remained at all times 35 to 50 percent black.

This slowing of black progress was engineered by the white majority in several ways. Voting districts were gerrymandered to deny blacks a majority in any one district; multimember legislative districts were designed to force at-large elections of state representatives, and so to circumvent all-black districts that would guarantee black victories; at-large, countywide elections were held for the same reasons for school board and all-powerful county supervisor positions, though these had previously been "neighborhood" posts; increased filing requirements were mandated for political candidates; "open primary" and runoff statutes were instituted; large cities and towns switched to at-large city council elections; and cities and towns annexed large all-white tracts into their municipalities while bypassing and hopscotching black settlements in order to increase the white vote.

The blueprint for much of this activity was drawn in the regular and special sessions of the 1966 Mississippi state legislature. House Resolution 911 gerrymandered congressional districts to weaken black voting power in the Delta, House Resolution 223 changed the county supervisor system, House Resolutions 275 and 1074 switched school board elections to at-large and House Resolution 183 changed school superintendents from elected to appointed. House Concurrent Resolution 35 allowed the legislature to combine counties (to preserve white majorities). House Resolution 68 increased qualifying requirements for electoral candidates. House Resolutions 436 and 793 provided for open primaries and prevented electoral victory with only a plurality. Senate Resolution 1504 broke up the old legislative districts and implemented multimember, at-large districts that diluted black majorities.

There was slang for this policy: cracking, stacking, and packing. Cracking was the splitting of heavy black concentrations, stacking was putting a large number of blacks in a district with even more whites, and packing involved, in the rare instances where blacks could not otherwise be silenced, drawing the district so that it was totally black, thus ensuring that neighboring areas would provide safe white seats.

The overthrow of Massive Resistance began with a 1969 case known as *Allen v. State Board of Elections*. In this case, the black plaintiffs argued that, pursuant to Section 5 of the Voting Rights Act, the 1966 legislation should have been submitted to the federal government for clearance prior to its enactment. The plaintiffs' indirect method of attacking the legislation worked, as the Supreme Court ruled that the Voting Rights Act was to be broadly construed and that the state had been in error. In the future, state officials throughout the South would not be able to make any such political changes without first consulting the Justice Department.

Allen was no magic wand, but it struck white resistance a tremendous blow. Still, a full ten years would pass before the state gained a significant number of black legislators, from one in 1968 to seventeen in 1980. These black legislators in 1980 made up only 14 percent of the state's lawmakers and so were largely ineffective. But in 1992, forty-two blacks were elected to the legislature, which meant that a black coalition would have the power to influence finance and revenue bills. And in 1986, the Second Congressional District sent a young black lawyer, Michael Espy, to Congress, the first time a black had represented Mississippi in Washington since Reconstruction.

During Reconstruction, the second-district seat had been held by a black man, John Roy Lynch, who won three races (and lost one, in 1877) between 1873 and 1883 before being forced out violently as whites regained political control. Whites had held the seat, though blacks had a majority in that district, until Espy's victory. Black state representative Robert Clark of Ebenezer set the table for Espy, running strongly against incumbent Webb Franklin in 1982 and 1984, losing both times by less than 2 percent.

Espy was born in 1953 in Yazoo City, the child of undertakers. After attending local black schools, he studied at Howard University in Washington, D.C., and then at the law school at the University of Santa Clara in California. Before running for Congress, he served as the director of a legal services office, as an assistant attorney general in Mississippi and as assistant secretary of state.

Through careful strategic planning, organized registration and get-out-the-vote efforts, Espy won 51.7 percent of the votes cast, 95 percent of his supporters black. In 1988, he raised his white percentage to 40, won easily and was virtually unopposed in 1990 and

1992, becoming a star in the national Democratic Party. After Espy's elevation to the cabinet as secretary of agriculture in the Clinton administration (a job from which he would resign under a cloud of scandal in late 1994), he was replaced by black activist Bennie Thompson following a divisive and hotly contested primary in which blacks argued vociferously about who should inherit the mantle. Blacks were, however, able to unite behind Thompson after the Democratic primary and to prevail over white Republican Hayes Dent—who openly campaigned on a divide-and-conquer strategy, hoping to lure whites and middle-class blacks away from the outspoken Thompson, an activist presence in the state since the sixties.

Black electoral successes notwithstanding, a cursory look at the Second District in the Delta today reveals that equity is socially, culturally and economically a long way off, and that hopes for progress must be measured and realistic. The shacks of Ruleville and Indianola and the crumbling buildings of Mound Bayou testify to conditions that seem beyond political remedy. One of Michael Espy's chief claims to success has been the spread throughout the Delta of catfish farms, agricultural processing centers where fish are raised in large, artificial ponds, then are harvested, rendered and packaged for sale throughout the world in large factories by armies of poor black women paid minimum wage. Mississippi is the world's largest provider of farm-raised catfish, producing more than 150 million pounds per year. The factory women stand ankle deep in water all day and are surrounded by fish guts and scales as they cut and gut and slice, cut and gut and slice. Workers complain of carpal tunnel syndrome and are allowed only two bathroom breaks per eight- to ten-hour shift. One of the leaders of this billion-dollar business, Delta Pride, has been fined by OSHA. Espy and local businessmen point with pride to the thousands of new jobs created by the industry, but to an informed observer the fish factories look like nothing more than a new kind of plantation.

A trip through any number of Mississippi towns—Clarksdale, Friars Point, Indianola, Tunica, Metcalfe—reveals the distance the state would have to travel in order to make society work for all its citizens. Indianola, known mainly as the birthplace of B. B. King, sits hard by U.S. Highway 82 between Greenville and Greenwood and contains scenes of suffering that would not be out of place in a documentary on the Depression. Many of its inhabitants still live in tin or tar-paper shacks without plumbing or running water. In 1967, Robert Kennedy looked upon these shacks and said, "My God, I did not know this kind of thing existed. How can a country like this allow it?" The same statement could be made today; and that this kind of poverty sits in plain view in 1995 is an indictment of the priorities of both state and federal government, and of the millions of Americans who profess concern over the sharp racial and economic divisions in faraway Haiti, El Salvador and South Africa while failing to redress such divides in their own country.

There is no reason to expect this situation to change; eloquent pleas were made on behalf of these Mississippians in times more receptive to idealistic mass action than today. Contemporary Mississippi exists, beyond its poverty, in a state of low-intensity racial war, where in Amite and Grenada Counties conflicts over school integration and funding have become violent, and where on Frat Row at Ole Miss the black fraternity house has burned, mysteriously, to the ground. It is, tragically, the way things are, the logical harvest of past events and practices.

In towns like Tunica, home of the infamous Sugar Ditch, a neighborhood where poor blacks used a sewer drainage ditch as a water supply until the federal government finally moved them into improved housing in 1990, race conflict takes even more diabolical turns. Large numbers of federal dollars have been given to Tunica County for water and sewer projects in the past, but that money has been used to build white middle- and upper-middle-class subdivisions. This sublimated racial conflict—in many ways the story of the United States as a whole—is indicative of the new Mississippi, and even in today's Tunica, a growing gambling mecca with riverboats and casinos, arguments over whether tax money should be spent on schools or roads, on housing or business incentives, and whether the hundreds of new jobs should go to locals or outsiders, rage on and on, often assuming racial form. For such conflicts not to take this form in Mississippi seems impossible.

———

O N E   O F the reverberations of the civil rights movement still sound-
ing in the state is a direct consequence of the *Brown* decision. It, too,
is a court case involving education, known in the U.S. Supreme
Court as *United States v. Fordice*, and is revelatory of contemporary
challenges and conflicts in the South. After working its way through
the federal courts, the case was argued on November 13, 1991.
The Court's final decision—against the state—was handed down on
June 26, 1992, and its ramifications, however they are resolved, will
shake the foundations of Mississippi culture, politics and society.

The *Fordice* case (so named after the present governor) was filed
in federal district court in 1975 by black community organizations
claiming that the state had failed, after twenty years, to live up to the
dictates of the *Brown* decision. The suit alleged that the university
system was designed and maintained in the following ways to foster
separation of the races: the majors offered by the black schools were
situated so as to direct white students away from them; the funding
of the various campuses of the system was determined by race; and
the admissions process, based on standardized test scores, was inten-
tionally implemented to steer black students away from such traditional white strongholds as Ole Miss, Mississippi State and Southern
Mississippi.

The public university system in Mississippi consists of eight colleges, organized into comprehensive, regional and urban divisions,
each having a different "mission" as determined by a 1981 statement
of the board of trustees. All eight campuses were strictly segregated
in 1954. Only after more than two decades of ignoring, then stalling,
federal directives did the state attempt a "voluntary" dismantling of
the system.

After 1981, the schools which had been white schools prior to
1954—Ole Miss, Mississippi State, Delta State, Southern Mississippi
and Mississippi University for Women—had as the sole admission
standard an ACT score of 15 or better. (MUW's standard of 18 is
perhaps illustrative of how far Mississippi will go to insulate white
females.) The three pre-1954 all-black schools—Jackson State, Alcorn State and Mississippi Valley State—required a score of only
13, even though formerly white schools that shared the same mission
as regional schools had higher standards. The beauty of the plan,

from a segregationist's standpoint, lies in this fact: in 1985, 72 percent of white students scored 15 or better on the ACT, while less than 30 percent of blacks did so. Mississippi, by considering *only* the ACT score (against the advice and counsel of the company that supplies the test), had discovered a systematic way of funneling the vast majority of white and black students to specific campuses, maintaining the basic separation of the races. This was found by the Supreme Court, along with duplication of programs and unequal facilities and funding for the black campuses, to be intentional and unconstitutional; and in a decision written by Justice Byron White, Mississippi was ordered to meet "its affirmative obligation to dismantle its prior dual [university] system."

ACCORDING TO sociologist William Julius Wilson, racial conflict in the United States has moved from the economic into the social sphere—meaning that the battles of tribe and caste are no longer fought in the fields and mills but in our public rituals and places. The *Fordice* case is a clear example of this, and there will be no easy resolution to such statewide or national racial strife. Caught redhanded forty years after *Brown*, the segregationist elements of Mississippi can be expected to retreat and flank in some other manner to maintain the status quo; blacks, however, face a more painful and ultimately tragic path. The price of implementing the *Fordice* improvements will be the closure of at least one black campus, if not all of them, which will come as a serious blow to black life in Mississippi. The state, though, strapped for funds, will have to shut down white campuses as well, and it's foreseeable that only the "comprehensives"—Ole Miss, Mississippi State and Southern Mississippi— and perhaps Jackson State will remain. The black university system has been a backbone of the black community for much of this century, training its leaders and professionals, providing a network through which accomplished blacks can locate one another and work together, forming a center for social and community life. Black Mississippi, for example, would be diminished without the Jackson State–Alcorn game, a combination sporting event, family reunion, church picnic, professional convention and tribal affirmation.

It's strange, and sad, how snakebitten things can seem in Mississippi; the past cannot be transcended. In 1954, the Supreme Court ordered desegregation: forty years later, the schools, through various deliberate maneuvers, are still segregated. In March 1995, the federal district judge who ruled in favor of the plaintiffs in *Fordice* also ordered the state to provide more funding for its historically black institutions and to find ways to encourage white students to attend the black schools. The judge did not, however, rule out closing black schools, particularly Mississippi Valley State, to free money for other uses. The state did, of course, appeal the decision for several years before giving up in 1994, clearing the way for the funding decision. After *Fordice*, progress could require demolishing one of the bulwarks of black life in Mississippi, and any inclination to regard such progress as the bringing of light is overshadowed by the looming failure of *Brown*.

ONE EVENING in New Orleans, sitting on the balcony of a house in the French Quarter, I had a long conversation with a white man from the Delta town of Cleveland. We talked about poetry, his son's electric guitar and drum lessons, college basketball and, as usually was the case during my talks with Mississippians, race. This time the topic evolved from our discussion of several Habitat for Humanity projects in Cleveland that for the first time had pulled together white and black churches to build houses for the town's poor and homeless. "There was a black man in town, the black plumber," the man told me, "who was helping us get the various materials and figure out how to hook it all up. I had driven past this man just about every day for twenty years, him in his truck, me in mine, and I had never spoken to him or even waved. I knew who he was and he knew who I was, but there was just never any occasion or reason for us to talk. But in the course of his working with us and lending his expertise, I got to know him and I started liking him. And as we worked together and came a little closer to each other, I started to realize that I liked how he worked. I respected him. In fact, he was one of the best men I'd ever known in Mississippi. I realized that I had missed knowing, missed being friends with, someone I would have benefited from and enjoyed knowing. That made me feel bad, and stupid."

He lapsed into silence and looked off the porch into the distance.

"Things are gonna change," he said quietly. "They have to. They already have."

I asked him what he meant.

"When you know a man, when you've worked with him, you just can't do him like that. You cannot mistreat him. You just can't."

"I DON'T quite feel at home," my father said as we sat one afternoon in the town square of Holly Springs. "I don't quite feel a part of the surroundings." He looked around, taking in the dingy stone buildings, then stared into the distance. "It has something to do with the way things went when I was here, being treated in such a way that I never felt like it was my home. I was never proud to be from Mississippi. Things were never comfortable, they never quite fit. When I was young I felt like I'd been cheated by my parents or something by being black—you know, racism and so forth.

"Leaving was the best thing that ever happened to me. Literally the single most important thing in my life. More important than meeting your mother, joining the service, whatever. Forty years ago there was nothing here for black folks but oppression. Leaving brought our whole family out of darkness and deprivation. Living in a shack as sharecroppers, existing on the meager things that were available to us. Always the minimum. It never allowed us to be totally free to do what we desired to do or go where we wanted to go, have what we wanted to have. It was just existence, that's all it was. We existed—and we, my brothers and sisters, seemed to have been trapped by the fact that our parents did not seem to think they could do anything else. By me getting out I think it led to them thinking *they* could get out. They saw one doing better and it encouraged them."

Claude went north in 1950 and in 1955 settled into the job he has held ever since. I had always wondered what sort of memories could drive a man to stand in one place, so to speak, that long.

"Now there's some other circumstances," he continued, "that I think, had they existed in Mississippi at that time, could've made everything different. If we had our own land, our own tractor, our own home and independence and had been able to determine our own destiny, then I would've had a different set of values; and not only that, it would have made me proud that I grew up here. I love being outside and I love farming, but I didn't like how black folks had to farm down here—working from four o'clock and four-thirty in the morning until nine o'clock at night all year long and when September, October, November or Christmas come, we still had no money. I'd have to wear one pair of shoes and one pair of pants and some kind of cheap little coat all winter to school. I was told to wait until next year, and when next year come, all I would see was a repeat of the year before. I felt that I should be rewarded or compensated for what I did. I felt that white people were getting too much from me for nothing. I thought that if I went somewhere where I'd be treated more as an equal, I would have a better chance of earning more money and therefore better my existence. I wanted to get as much out of life as I could. I knew someday if I had kids, I didn't want them to come up in the same deprivation. I saw other people and when I looked and compared their situation to ours in my own mind and imagination, I figured that they had the guts to do it, and we did not. That was the difference. My daddy was afraid of something."

We had never much discussed Claude's father, James. They had not gotten along as adults, and to me their relationship was something of a blank page. James, known as Chunky, had been extraordinarily bright and full of stories, tales and imaginings and had been extremely personable as a young man, but was rumored to have fallen into voodoo and the occult, an unforgivable sin to the hard-shell Baptist Claude. I asked what he thought James had been afraid of.

"I think it was just fear of fear. I think it was darkness in the sense that he saw everything as being impossible, he didn't see things in the right light."

"Given the history of Mississippi and when he grew up, could it have been any different?"

"People around us, black people, were doing better."

"Maybe he was too gifted to be a black man in the time he had to live."

"That was on the back burner, part of it. I think he had it in him to be a leader, but couldn't do anything with it. That helped bring him down, helped break his spirit."

"But didn't his society have something to do with it?"

"It had a lot to do with it." He paused. "Slavery itself, and just being black, played a big role. When you're born in a racist society, you're automatically handicapped, being of a different persuasion. You're thirty to forty percent handicapped by the mere fact that you are born black, and black is not popular. That had something to do with Chunky's failure, but I think that every man has to look to try to overcome his circumstances, say to himself, 'Other men are not going to hold me down.' And if they can legally do it in Mississippi and Alabama, but they can't do it in Illinois, why not go to Illinois? There was a seed of freedom planted in me and my generation that simply was not going to put up with the bull these white folks are putting down. I'm not going to let them run me over."

In Illinois, Claude had achieved significant economic success, using his factory job and hard-nosed financial acumen to accumulate a comfortable home in an upper-middle-class neighborhood, several cars and rental property. Of those millions of blacks who migrated north, his story had to be counted a success, one of many such. As we sat there in downtown Holly Springs, which appeared so still and ordinary that summer afternoon, life around us and our place within it seemed stable, calm. Yet right there in front of us, fifty years ago, Claude had witnessed something he would never not remember, the murder of his friend, and that seemed to me to describe Mississippi as a whole for black folks. There was too much that was unforgettable, unforgivable, for it ever to be a comfortable, "normal" place. A friend of ours had, in all seriousness, warned us about our trip together: "There's a lot of grief down there." Sitting in the square thinking about the murdered James Crump, I began to wonder if this grief had been, perhaps, the fundamental force shaping my father's life.

He looked far off into the distance, as if past Holly Springs and into another life. "I was hurt when James died, very deeply hurt. I felt like the white people were just tyrants. I remember Holbrooks, the man who shot James, he walked up to him and took his foot and pushed him over and saw that he was dead. Then he put his revolver back in his holster and walked on down the street like a big shot. All the white people applauded him. They made him head sheriff of the town.

"That scared me. The way I've come to understand it is that I think they've killed so many Indians and other people that they began to enjoy killing. That became a part of white people, got in their blood. But there's no reason for it, in my mind, I don't see why everything that was done, accomplished, couldn't have been done without the innocent blood. I think whites became afraid of what they had done, and they singled out the black folks, the weakest links in the chain, to prove their power to themselves. They knew they couldn't be punished. These people are the descendants of the people who killed off the Indians, and when you kill that many people and still prosper, do you think killing is going to mean anything to you? Not likely. The only thing you worry about is that nobody kills you. You have the same power that you had twenty years ago or fifty years ago or that your forefathers had. You're still in charge, and you want to see the same patterns and the same reflections in things as time goes by."

We walked back to the car and drove out of town, passing a weather-beaten and shuttered old weigh station at the junction of Highways 7 and 4. That sight stirred more memories for Claude, and he pointed out the window. "We used to make money at the weigh scales there," he said. "We would hang out waiting for an overnight truck to come through, because many times the driver would pay us a dollar apiece to help them unload thirty pieces of lumber or fifty pieces or whatever they were overweight. Sometimes we could make three or four dollars in an afternoon." He shook his head, as if startled by the recollection. "We used to wait in the same place for the truck to the sawmill. That work was so hard I could only work three days and then I'd give out. I'd work Monday, take Tuesday off, work Wednesday, skip Thursday, work Friday. But I'd have made twelve dollars. I was light for that work, but the old man liked me and I could come in and work. All I had to do was be on that corner when he came by in his truck and he'd say 'Get in.' "

We saw more cotton fields, not the endless expanse of the Delta, but smaller individual fields amid houses, barns, hills and stands of trees. This was Claude's home landscape, but he did not claim it. Did he feel at home anywhere?

"I feel more 'at home' in Illinois," he said. "Nothing good ever happened to me in Mississippi. Do I feel roots here? I never had what I wanted. I never got any respect. I got worked like a grown man at twelve years old and I hadn't done anything except be born black."

"Were you scared when you went north?"

"No. Apprehensive."

"What did you think about on the bus?"

"Getting some sleep."

When Claude woke up he was in Chicago, amazed at the vast busyness of the city. He shortly thereafter abandoned Chicago for Aurora, a move that he regularly credited, after leaving Mississippi, as the best of his life.

"The South Side," he said, "reminded me too much of Mississippi."

"The blacks?"

"The tension. The same meanness and arrogance. I didn't like black men being hostile to one another for no reason. There was enough of that down south. One day I bumped into somebody by accident and he cursed me out, just for that. I didn't like that, being threatened just for making a mistake. He was so angry—and that's how a lot of people were, that's how things were, like a jungle even then. I didn't leave Mississippi to be killed in Chicago by a black man I did not even know."

We swung back toward town, circling around the square and past the courthouse, then went back to our motel. Before turning off the ignition I asked Claude how it felt, after everything, to be staying in the best place in Holly Springs with a pocket full of money, only a few miles from the plantation on which he was raised.

"It feels good, but I deserved it long before I got it, before I was able to do it. I don't have any apprehension or afterthoughts about taking advantage of it either. I think it's built into each one of us to like nice things, to enjoy nice things. I think there's a demon or something that comes along and gets inside of a lot of us and causes us to settle for less than God intended us to have. I think this ends up getting built into people, and it keeps us from thinking that we should have the best. That happened to a lot of black people around here. I feel like I'm entitled to ride around in a big Cadillac, just like Howard Jones. I'm a black man in America, and I've worked almost fifty years, and for twenty of those fifty years I didn't really get paid for it. I worked in Memphis and they didn't pay us for what we did. So I left, looking for better wages, better conditions. I don't know what that was, but something in me made me want you all to go to good schools, have good clothes to wear. I did not want you to be ashamed. What people don't understand is that most black folks spend so much time worrying about survival that they can't think about triumph. I thought that maybe if I could worry about survival, then maybe you all could triumph. When I got north, I don't think any of the jobs I had ever provided enough, but they provided more than I'd ever had.

"Life is a gamble. If you read the twenty-fourth or the twenty-fifth chapter of Matthew, about the master who gave out talents, well, the guy who got ten talents went out and invested his and got ten more when the master came back, and the guy who got five went out and invested his and got five more. The guy who only got one buried his, and when the master came back he was angry and called him a slothful and ungrateful servant, and said that he should be cast into damnation. A man should take a chance. Even Jesus said that to us, he was the one quoting the parable. If we're afraid, we're never going to do anything. I had to do something. That's why I left Mississippi. I couldn't see the big picture, I could only work with my hands and I knew that wasn't good enough, wasn't fast enough, but I had to do something. I had to be more than I was."

Robert Kennedy in Mississippi

He did things that I wouldn't do. He went into the dirtiest, filthiest, poor black homes . . . and he would sit with a baby who had open sores and whose belly was bloated from malnutrition, and he'd sit and touch and hold those babies. . . .

—MARIAN WRIGHT EDELMAN

I was born in darkness after my brother
died, death shred the veil before my eyes.

Privilege. I had thought the Delta
down at the bottom, near the ocean,

but they brought me to this flat land
below the river, dusty fields and gravel

roads going nowhere, godforsaken, flat,
only cotton and shanties and something they call

milo, I couldn't help being startled that the Klan
would kill for it. Say what you will, that it was

politics, or pity, but when I saw that child
I had no choice but to embrace darkness, black

children, black people. I knew at that moment
that America had grown beyond me, that I was lost,

another white man with a compass that did not
work. I fondled his stomach—the hungry belly

bloats dreaming of food—and I knew I could not
help him, and it came to me that people cannot help

who they are: why should they be held accountable?
Who was I? Neither Joe's son nor Jack's brother,

just a white man trying to jump the canyon
of my loneliness, wishing I could wear the shame

and pain of my countrymen like my fate.
I wanted to pray in the name of God, then

I thought of all we've accomplished in His name,
Harlem, Dakota, Kentucky, Mississippi,

and I could no longer take His name
in vain. I chose instead to embrace

my furies, love, justice, compassion,
and to flee with Lot the burning cities. . . .

Walking with My Father Through the Fields of His Youth

Muddy red fallow this year,
    he stares as though these acres
were bristling green, demanding
    his hoe, plow and back.

The sweat of fifty years
    ago wells from the cloud
of his brow as he says
    a white man name of Howard

Jones owned all this,
    his gesture sweeping across
the sky. We used to do it
    by hand, Howard Jones

wanted you to work, boy,
    I'm talking hands full
of cotton, bags full
    of cotton, cotton as far

as you could see, cotton
    in your sleep. Wiping his face
with his sleeve, he takes
    a long moment and breathes

a smile. By the time I turned
    thirteen I couldn't dream
any more cotton, that plow
    dragged me clear to Chicago.

The Lovesong of Emmett Till

More than likely she was Irish
or Italian, a sweet child who knew him
only as a shy clown.
Colleen, Jenny or Marie, she
probably didn't even know
he had her picture,
that he had traded her cousin
for baseball cards or a pocketknife,
that her routine visage
sat smoldering in his wallet
beyond any price.
He carried his love
like a burden, and devotion
always has to tell.
Hell, he was just flirting
with that lady in the store,
he already had his white
woman back up in Chicago.
He wasn't greedy, just showing
off, showing the rustics
how it was done. He had an eye,
all right, and he was free
with it, he knew they loved it.
Hey baby, was all he said,
and he meant it as a compliment,
when he said it in Chicago
the white girls laughed.
So when they came to get
him, he thought it was
a joke, he proclaimed himself guilty
of love, he showed them
the picture and paid the price of
not innocence, but affection, affection
for a little black-haired, blue-eyed
girl who must by now be an older
woman in Chicago, a woman
who will never know
she was to die for, that he died
refusing to take back her name,
his right to claim he loved her.

Schwerner, Chaney and Goodman

Still green silence of the piney hills,
Blood red earth, redder still.

The World Before the Blues

What was the world like
before the blues,
when there was only a clean whir
into infinity,
when there was only round and round
on a faultless geometer?

How did the blues bleed into the flawless
works, seeping and sludging
and slowing the heretofore silent
gears, the ticking click
of history that had not yet worked itself
into a wail?

Blues

Wind blow the screen down
Black cat through the door
Trees make a rattlesnake sound
Shotgun on the floor

Trees whisper like a woman
Hours past midnight
Blind man on the highway
Runs for daylight

Epilogue

... it's impossible to escape the mortal sin of our time: the
desire not to come to grips with oneself...

—CHRISTA WOLF

I REMEMBER walking home in Oxford late one summer
evening, warm in the glow of streetlights and the heavy humid
Mississippi air. Everything took on a kind of fuzzy seductive-
ness, and, as I was the only person on the street, I began thinking, This isn't such a terrible place. I could like it here. . . . Then I
stepped off the curb into an alley and was jarred from my reverie.
Could this, I wondered, have been the alley out of which cars roared
pursuing the soon-to-be-lynched Will Mayes in Faulkner's "Dry September"? Had I just left the square that, in the same story, blacks
had avoided for days? Conjecture, yes, but it reminded me that I was
in Mississippi, not Connecticut, not California, and reminded me of
why that word—"Mississippi"—is perhaps the most loaded proper
noun in American English. I would always be uneasy there, no matter what I did or how long I stayed. I knew too much, saw too many
shadows and bad memories everywhere I turned.

When I went to Mississippi I was in pursuit of clarity and understanding because I had begun, inevitably, to know things about
America, about racism and, as it turns out, about life, that I did not
want to know. In the months before my travels I was slowly becoming aware, through direct experience, of the intractable nature of
racism in this country, the ugliness of its manifestations and the im-

plications of its presence for my family and my life. After years of sleepwalking I was waking up, and I thought that entering Mississippi—both the actual, physical place and the abstract, psychic construct of history, memory and folklore—would give me a clear means of interpreting the realities I was facing, and a strategy for moving forward into the future with the same hope and sense of purpose that had always characterized African-Americans. In short, I was discouraged in that time, but chalked my sadness and unease up to inexperience and thought that learning the past and mastering the historical tradition of my people would equip me for what I needed to do as a black man, for seizing and enjoying the opportunities purchased at such great cost.

I was wrong. What I discovered in Mississippi was not truth or enlightenment, but the painful knowledge that my nascent understanding of the costs and casualties of American history was naive, glib, even superficial. I found myself in a sort of spiritual quicksand, and each new fact I learned only plunged me deeper into confusion. I had become accustomed to thinking of history as being progressive, as having a purpose. Learning the extent of what had happened there, in Mississippi, learning how so much suffering had been inflicted and endured to so little profit, the plain low-down meanness of it, was profoundly dispiriting. I had known, of course, that America's history was tragic and sordid, but had not understood how pervasive was its darkness. I had long known William Carlos Williams's statement, "History begins for us with murder and enslavement, not with discovery," but had not quite believed it.

Going to Mississippi was, for me, eating the fruit of the Tree of Knowledge, bitter fruit that changed my life as I became aware of things I could never again not know. What disturbed me most was realizing that Mississippi cast a large shadow over not only our history, but also our present. The straight-lined distinctions I'd always kept between past, present and future collapsed as I saw how those three strands of time crossed and snagged to form the dark weave of this country. To me, American amnesia about the past was perhaps worse than the many crimes that had been committed, because that willful refusal to confront history made impossible any meaningful action now.

Those whites who lined the streets of Bensonhurst, so proud in their rage and disdain for blacks even after the senseless murder of Yusuf Hawkins, might have acted differently had they acknowledged the history of Mississippi. White Americans might understand and show more compassion toward the problems of blacks in New York, Chicago, Miami and Los Angeles were they to admit that many of those situations are best understood as continuations of the tragedy of the South. Black Americans, in turn, might reassess the true nature of their predicament, and reassess their goals and possibilities. As I linked, in my mind, the savagery of Mississippi's past with the apathy and aggression shaping antiblack sentiment in the post-Reagan era, I began to lose the simple optimism that had always colored my outlook on the future. Much of the current discussion surrounding matters of race in the United States involves apportioning and rejecting blame and guilt, but this bickering misses the larger point of responsibility. The furies of our national tragedy are still at large, but no place is being made for them; they are not seen, or even sought. If we, as Americans, are not responsible for Mississippi and everything following from it, who is? And if we Americans did not commit and suffer the crimes perpetrated there, who did?

Those sorts of questions, the questions of a young man, plagued me for months because I was under the illusion that what I had come to know could be made to mean something. Surely America was involved in a millennial transcendentalism and all the lost souls had been sacrificed for the sake of something, for the sake of the more perfect Union. But it seems to me now that this moment of possibility has passed. I think of all the commonplace, even banal, small towns and cities and fields in Mississippi where so much has happened both so long ago and so recently, of how the wind blows through them indifferently, just as it did before the first drop of blood was shed. Maybe these things don't mean anything. Maybe they only prove William Golding right, that "Man produces evil as bees produce honey." Maybe these matters are better left to Darwin and Saint Paul.

What I am left with are the people: those I know as well as I know my parents; the great heroes of the battles from the Civil War to civil rights; the anonymous millions who struggled and suffered and died in the human drama of trial by existence. I see how Mississippi fostered two profound worldviews, my mother's:

> Amazing grace, how sweet the sound
> that saved a wretch like me
> I once was lost, but now am found
> Was blind but now I see.

And my father's:

> When a woman get the blues
> She hang her head and cry
> When a man get the blues
> He catch a freight and ride.

In the end, what is most intriguing about Claude and Dorothy, Aunt Pernie and Uncle Floyd, Medgar Evers and Fannie Lou Hamer and thousands of others is not that they suffered but that they stayed intact, human, and did not push their suffering down into another generation. This was true emancipation. I am left amazed at how many people did not let Mississippi destroy them or their spirits and amazed at how resilient humans can be and at how they—as in the spiritual—can make a way out of no way. I am also ashamed of how far, at times, I had gone over to the other side, being contemptuous of poor blacks, thinking of them as losers unwilling to deal with the future; and I was particularly ashamed of how little I had known about my parents' lives—especially my father's—and of how that had caused me to misunderstand them. How *had* they held it together? After Mississippi, I also was better able to understand why others did not, or could not, do so.

When I went to Mississippi, I was an American innocent, innocent of history, happily suffering the historical amnesia that leads Americans to think that because they "won"—their values prevailed, their goals were achieved—what had transpired was nothing to be overly concerned with or troubled about. We Americans love to think ourselves innocent of the tragedies—personal and public—that the past and our compulsions have visited upon us, all of us. Most of all, we want to be innocent of how much the ghosts and bones of our beautiful landscape have shaped and twisted virtually everything that has happened here; and we want to remain ignorant of how costly our innocence is to our government, our communities and our hearts. In Mississippi I wandered among some of those ghosts and bones, and it is my great lesson to have learned to stop trying to evade and forget what I have seen and heard and understood and now must know, but rather to embrace the ghosts and cradle the bones and call them my own.